The Beginning Guide to
# Microsoft Word 2010
Microsoft Office Specialist Exam 77-881 Study Guide

**another
Computer
Mama
Guide**

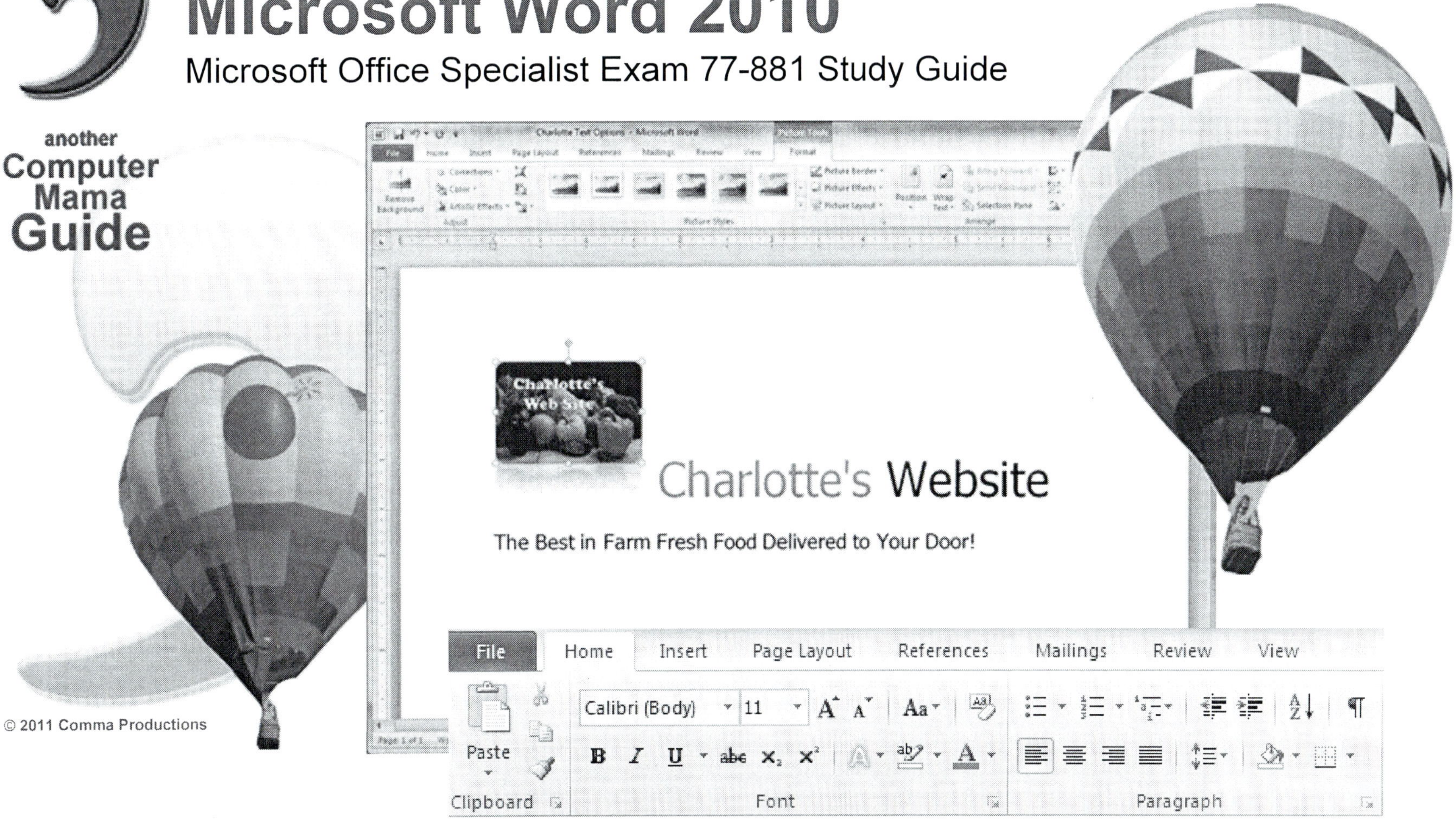

Charlotte's Website

The Best in Farm Fresh Food Delivered to Your Door!

© 2011 Comma Productions

# Beginning Guide to Microsoft Word 2010

© 2011 Comma Productions
9090 Chilson Road
Brighton, MI 48116
978-0-9838917-0-3

**another**
**Computer**
**Mama**
**Guide**

## Trademark and Copyright

## Limit of Liability/Disclaimer of Warranty:

# Table of Contents

# ☺ The Benefits of Certification

**For More Information:**
www.certiport.com
www.microsoft.com

## Why Get Certified?

For employers, the certification provides skill-verification tools that not only help assess a person's skills in using Microsoft Office programs but also the ability to quickly complete on-the-job tasks across multiple programs in the Microsoft Office system. (http://www.microsoft.com/learning/en/us/certification/mos.aspx). Certification proves a certain level of advanced competency with the programs in question. Employers don't have to wonder if the skills stated on the resume are honest and without exaggeration. This can lead to further employment opportunities and increased pay.

A person holding Microsoft Office Certification shows not just a level of skill, but an ability to quickly complete tasks, due to familiarity with the program and it's many time-saving features. The hard work that goes into learning Microsoft Office programs to the level of proficiency necessary for successful completion of the Certification Exams also indicates a desire on behalf of the student to learn and succeed.

## The Benefits: Earn More, Find Jobs Quicker

Research indicates that employees with Microsoft Certification earn more and find jobs quicker than those employees without certification. Furthermore, employees with certification report a greater feeling of confidence. These things translate into greater job satisfaction. (http://www.microsoft.com/learning/en/us/certification/mos.aspx)

Research also shows that individuals with certification make up to 12% more than those without certification. In addition, 82% of Microsoft Office Specialists report a salary increase after receiving certification. Managers like the skills proven and the ability demonstrated by those with Microsoft Office Certifications.
http://www.certiport.com/Portal/desktopdefault.aspx?page=common/pagelibrary/mos2003.html

# Microsoft Office Specialist Certification

## What is the Microsoft Office Specialist Certification?

The Microsoft Office Specialist certification validates through the use of exams that you have obtained specific skill sets within the applicable Microsoft Office programs and other Microsoft programs included in the Microsoft Office Specialist Program. The candidate can choose which exam(s) they want to take according to which skills they want to validate.

**CertiPort** is the premier provider for validating technology skills.

The **Microsoft Office Specialist** tests are offered at authorized testing centers.

For more information on the MOS exam topics or to find a testing center near you please contact: **www.certiport.com**

## What is the Microsoft Office Specialist Certification Program?

The **Microsoft Office Specialist (MOS) Certification Program** enables candidates to show that they have something exceptional to offer – proven expertise in Microsoft Office programs. Recognized by businesses and schools around the world, millions of certifications have been obtained in over 100 different countries. The **Microsoft Office Specialist (MOS) Certification Program** is the only Microsoft-approved certification program of its kind.

## The Microsoft Office Specialist Certification Series

Core Certification: Pass any 1 test:
Word 2010 Core: Exam 77-881
Excel® 2010 Core: Exam 77-882
PowerPoint® 2010: Exam 77-883
Access® 2010: Exam 77-885
Outlook® 2010: Exam 77-884

Expert Certification: Pass either test:
Word 2010 Expert: Exam 77-887
Excel® 2010 Expert: Exam 77-888

Master: Pass 3 required and 1 elective test:
Required
Word 2010 Expert: Exam 77-887
Excel® 2010 Expert: Exam 77-888
PowerPoint® 2010: Exam 77-883

Elective
Access® 2010: Exam 77-885 or
Outlook® 2010: Exam 77-884

# About Our Certification Program

**Books in this Series:**
Beginning Guide to
Microsoft® Word 2010

Intermediate Guide to
Microsoft® Word 2010

Advanced Guide to
Microsoft® Word 2010

## Microsoft Office Specialist (MOS) Certification for Word 2010

**Overview**: Our Microsoft Office Specialist certification program for Word 2010 has three levels of mastery: Beginning, Intermediate and Advanced. In general, the CORE exam topics are demonstrated in the Beginning and Intermediate Guides. EXPERT concepts are included where relevant, with the Advanced Guide only covering EXPERT concepts

**Our Approach:** In designing these Guides, we found that it made more sense to write the lessons based on the Ribbons and Tasks. For example, the Beginning Guide to Microsoft Word 2010 shows all of the Picture Tools: CORE and EXPERT. The beginning of each lesson provides an overview of the Ribbons and Tasks covered.

**The Beginning Guide to Microsoft Word 2010** demonstrates the following Ribbons: **Home, Insert, Picture Tools, Drawing Tools, and SmartArt Tools:** Design. The lesson activities focus on basic text and mouse commands, as well as inserting and formatting graphics.

**The Intermediate Guide to Microsoft Word 2010** demonstrates the following Ribbons: **Page Layout, Mailings, Insert, and Table Tools**. The lesson activities focus on managing page layout, working with tables and creating Mail Merges in practical applications such as newsletters and other workplace documents.

**The Advanced Guide to Microsoft Word 2010** demonstrates the following Ribbons: **Table Tools, Home, Header and Footer Tools**, References, **Developer.** The lesson activities further work with tables in addition to other document work, such as for report writing and creation of forms.

**Course Prerequisites:** Students who enroll in Microsoft Office Specialist (MOS) program should have basic computer skills including how to turn on the computer, how to use an Internet browser and how to select commands from a menu. Students should know how to save files and send attachments by email as well.

# Microsoft Word 2010 Study Guide: Beginning Word

**Microsoft Office Specialist (MOS):** Exam 77-881 for Word 2010

## 1. Sharing and Maintaining Documents
### 1.1 Apply Different Views to a Document

### 1.2. Apply Protection to a Document
### 1.4. Share Documents

### 1.5. Save a Document

## 2. Formatting Content
### 2.1. Apply Font and Paragraph Attributes

### 3.3. Construct Content with Quick Parts

### 3-5. Create and Modify Headers/Footers

## 4. Including Illustrations and Graphics
### 4.1. Insert and Format Pictures

### 4.2. Insert and Format Shapes, WordArt, and SmartArt

### 4.3. Insert and Format Clip Art

### 4.4. Apply and Edit Text Boxes

## 5. Proofreading Documents,
### 5-1. Validate content With Spelling and Grammar Checking,
### 5-2. Configure AutoCorrect Settings,

Keep going. There's more...

# Microsoft Word 2010 Study Guide: Beginning Word
**Microsoft Office Specialist (MOS):** Exam 77-887 for Word 2010

**From the Word 2010 Expert Exam 77-887**
**1. Sharing and Maintaining Documents**

**2. Formatting Content**

# About the Authors

**Elizabeth Ann Nofs**

*Elizabeth is the Computer Mama. She developed the teaching methodology in the Complete Computer Guide series using breakthrough research in gender balanced training. Elizabeth has taught several thousand men and women from government, manufacturing, small business, and education in both online and hands-on classrooms.*

*She is the author of the Complete Computer Guides as well as a Microsoft Certified Office Specialist. She earned a BA in Biology from the University of Michigan.*

**Alex Sergay, Senior Instructional Designer**

*For more than 20 years, Alex has made complex technology easy to understand. Alex has developed instructional multimedia software for educational websites including the Sounds of English, a linguistics-training tool that earned a ComputerWorld/Smithsonian Laureate.*

*Alex earned his Masters of Educational Technology from the University of Michigan, Ann Arbor.*

**Clair Dickson, Student Services**

*Clair works with adult learners in online, face-to-face and hybrid classroom settings. She is considered "highly qualified" to teach introductory computers, including Microsoft Office.*

*Clair has a Graduate Certificate in Educational Media and Technology, an program that explored ways to infuse technology into the learning experience so that learning is interactive. She has earned Microsoft Office 2007 Master Certification. She also holds a BS in Secondary English Education from Eastern Michigan University.*

**Leo Michael Nofs, Technical Writing and Quality Control**

*Leo is a Microsoft Certified Professional and an Access database designer. He uses his exemplary attention to detail for copy editing the computer instructions for accuracy and clarity.*

**Traci DeRosiers Nofs, Photography and Photo Editing**

*Traci has been photographing children and nature since 2000. She works freelance out of her home, including weddings, engagements, and particularly children's photography. She has further enhanced her photos by use of image manipulation, focusing on light and color.*

**M. Jeanette McCrickard, Office Manager**

*Jeanette has years of experience as an office manager, including the increasing use of computer-related tasks. Her excellent attention to detail has lead her to work as an Access database administrator and a copy editor.*

*All of my books*

*are dedicated to*

*Fr. Paul Cummings*

*who taught me*

*computers.*

*Love, eBeth*

# How To Use This Guide
## Microsoft Office Specialist Certification Training

### The Comma Method
*Observation* is a perceptual strategy that asks: why am I doing this and which tools would be most effective? Each lesson begins with a discussion of the purpose and the objectives.

*Orientation* helps students start at the right place. The screen shots in the *Complete Compute Guides* show the entire window as well as a close up of the particular button or command.

*Notation* There are "breadcrumbs" above each screen image. Like Hansel and Gretel, the breadcrumbs show the pathway to a button or option. Our notation uses the following convention:
**Ribbon->Group->Button->Options**

### Menu Maps
The Comma Method recognizes that there is a difference in how men and women navigate the menus. Men typically have the ability to see the map first. This method of acquiring knowledge is called *Breadth-first*. [1] Women tend to work with the details first. They learn several commands, such as copy, cut, and paste, then they put those concepts under the label, "edit." This method of learning is called *Depth-first*.

The Comma Method uses menu mapping to assist men and women to see both the Breadth and the Depth. An example of the menu map is can be seen here.

[1] Ford, Nigel, Sherry Chen, Matching/mismatching revisited: An Empirical Study of Learning and Teaching Styles. British Journal of Educational Technology v.32 no1 (Jan. 2001)

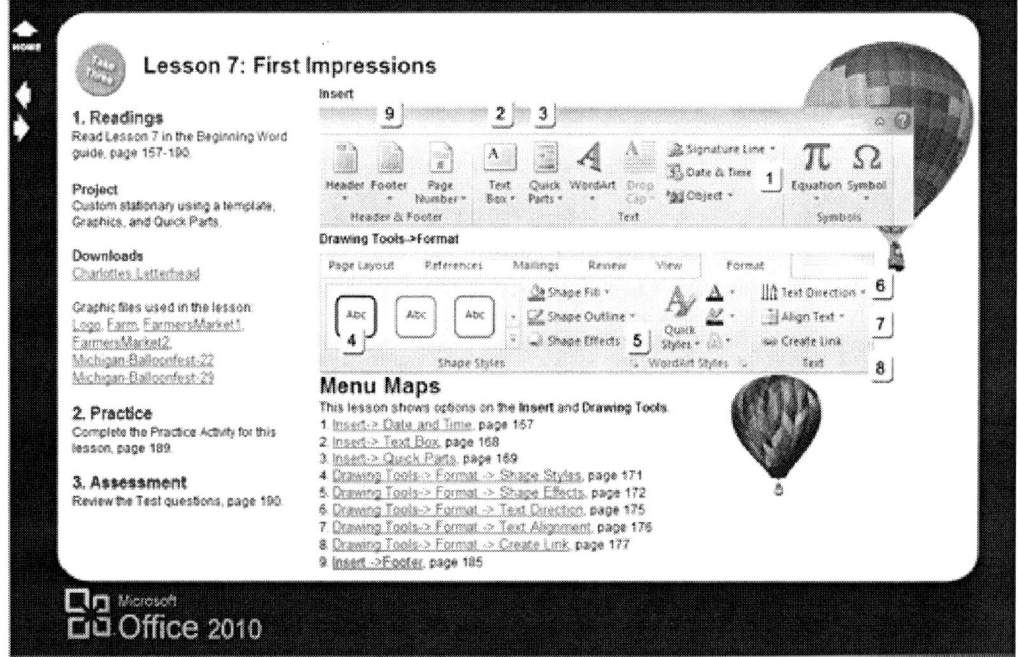

**Data-> Data Tools**

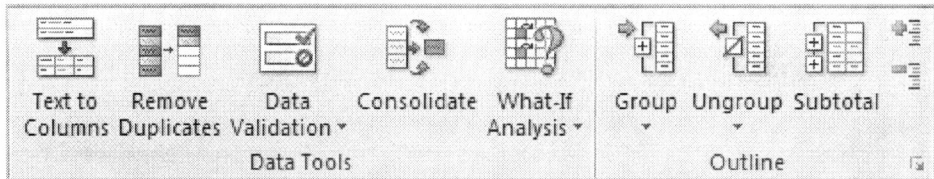

**Word 2010: Getting Started**

# Welcome!

**Course Objectives**

Students will be able to:

1. Log in to the online course

2. Navigate the outline and lessons

3. Take quizzes online

4. Submit assignments online

5. Participate in the forums and chat

# Welcome

This course presents a practical, hands-on approach to computers. The lessons are based on what you see on the screen, what you can do with the options, and what works on the job. The goal is to enable you to use Microsoft Windows and Office 2010 effectively, even creatively.

Use this *Guide* as part of your professional development plan to prepare for the Microsoft Business Certification tests, Microsoft Office Specialist (MOS), or as a reference book to solve problems as they come up.

This introduction provides information on:
• Navigation
• Practice
• Sample Documents
• Assessments

## Log into the course

This online course requires a User Name and Password. You probably received an email with your username and password when you enrolled.

**Try This: Login**
1. Go to the website for your course.
2. Click on the (Login) link.
3. You will be prompted for your Username and Password.

**What If This Doesn't Work?**
First, look at the keyboard and make sure the Caps Lock is off (no light.) Passwords may include both upper and lower case letters.

Second, check the spelling. Your user name may not be exactly the same as your email address.

Third, you can click on the Live Chat and get immediate assistance.

**Memo to Self:** It's OK if your computer does not match exactly. The logon screen may show a logo or it may be a different color.

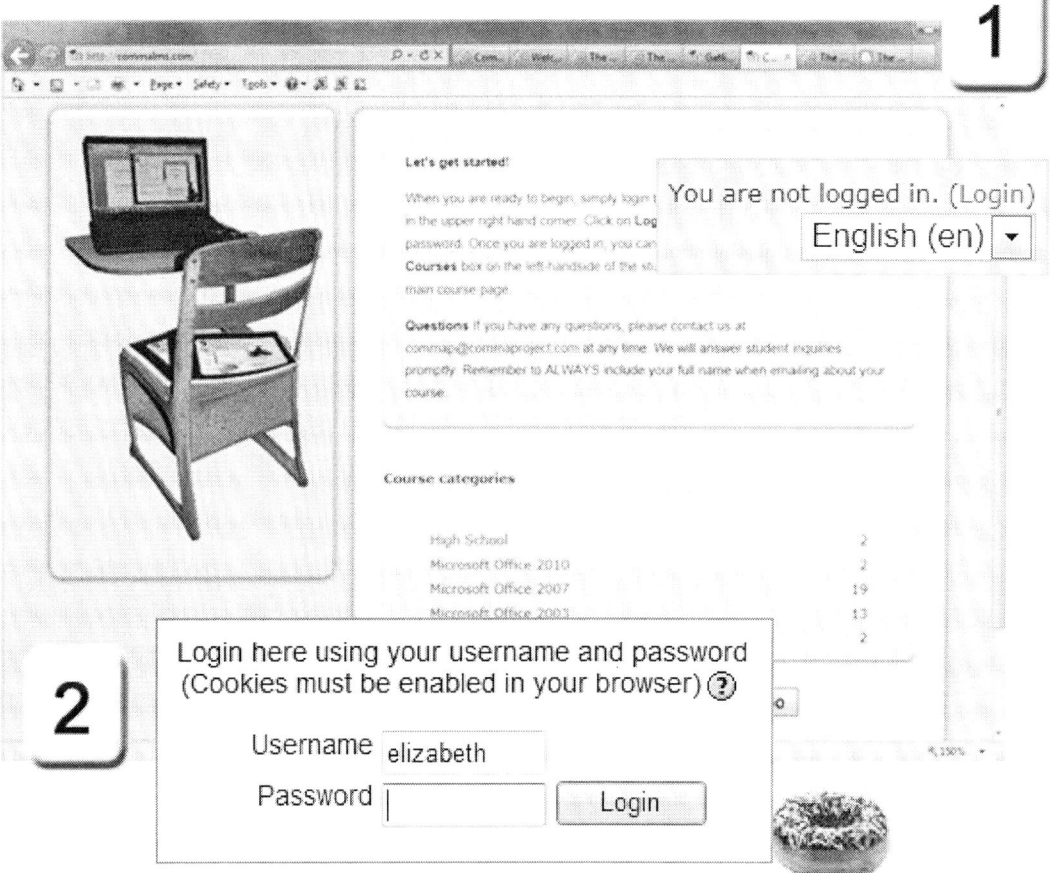

## The Topic Outline

When you log into your course, you should see the **Topic Outline**. The Topic Outline is a course syllabus: it lists your lessons, practice and quizzes.

Each Level has Lessons and Assessments. The lesson links are short discussions that demonstrate the options on a particular Ribbon. The lessons links may also list the page number where these pages can be found in the print version of the computer guides.

Many students prefer to read the lessons on a second monitor or in print, rather than switch from the lesson screens to Microsoft Office to practice the options

**Memo to Self:** It's OK if your computer does not match exactly. The important part is learning the steps. Please contact your facilitator if you have any questions

**My Course ->Topic Outline**

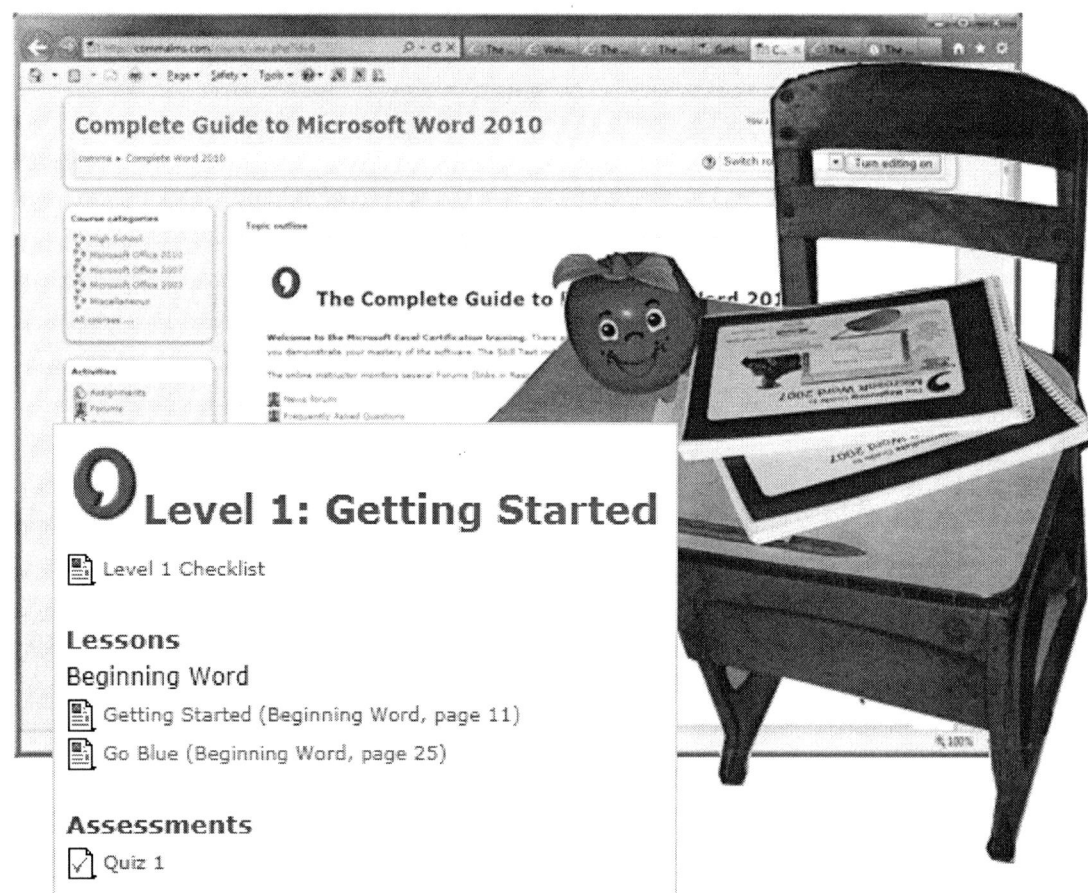

## Lesson Links

When you click on a hyperlink to read a lesson, a new window will open.

**What Do You See?** On the left side of each screen you should see the white navigation arrows: Next, Previous, and Home

**What Else Do You See?** When you are done with a lesson, you can close the browser window. Go to the upper right corner of the lesson window and click on the X to Exit.

The Topic Outline should be there, the window was left open behind the lesson screen.

My Course ->Topic Outline ->Lesson

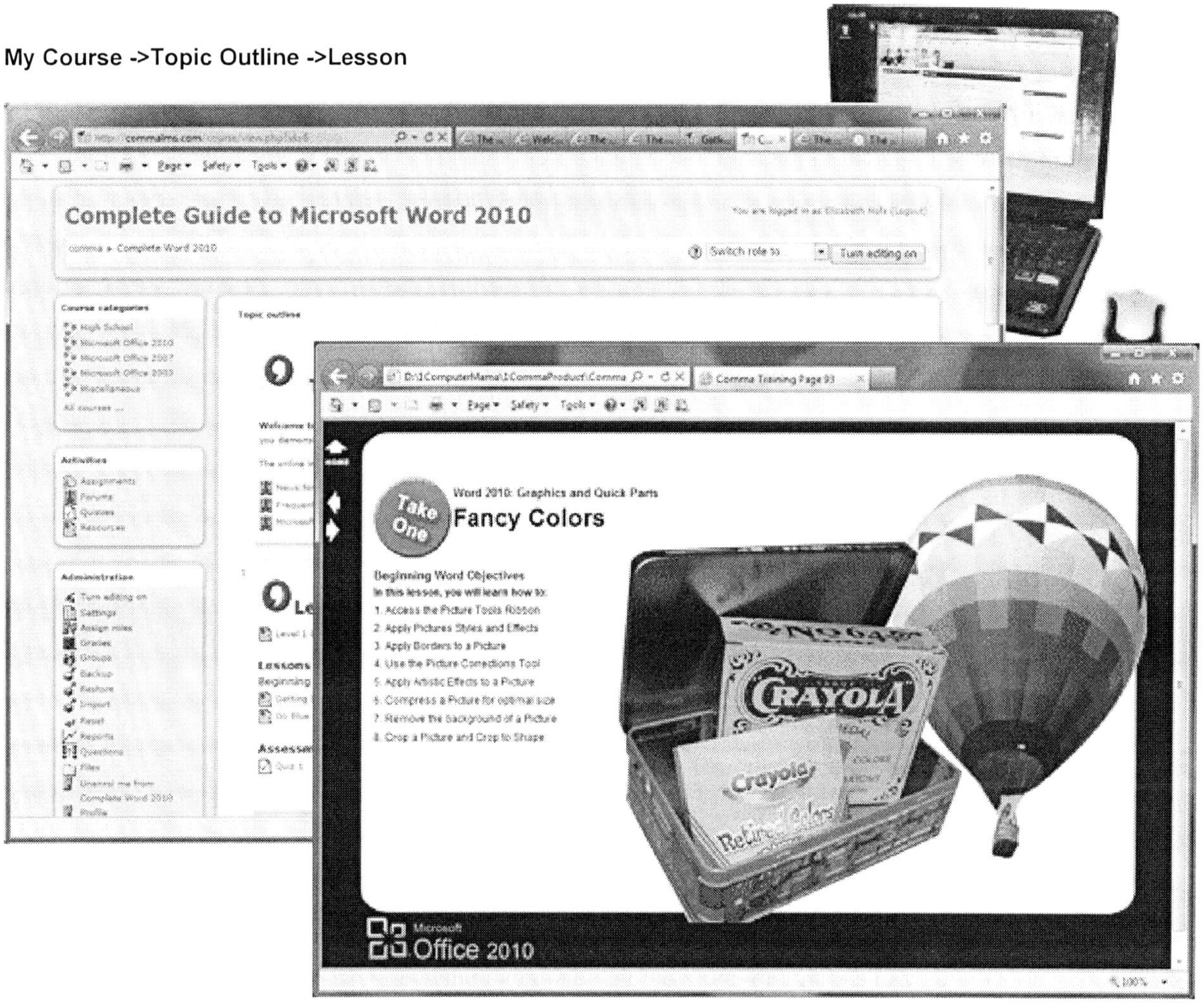

## Level Checklists

Each Level has many lessons, sample files and practice sheets, depending on which course you are in. The **Level Checklists** offer a complete list of the lessons, download, practice and quizzes.

**Downloads**

When you click on a link to a Download, you will be prompted to **Open** or **Save** this file.

Click on **Save.**

**Browse** to your Documents folder. This will save a copy of the file on your computer.

**Memo to Self:** It's OK if your Checklist does not match exactly. Please contact your facilitator if you have any questions

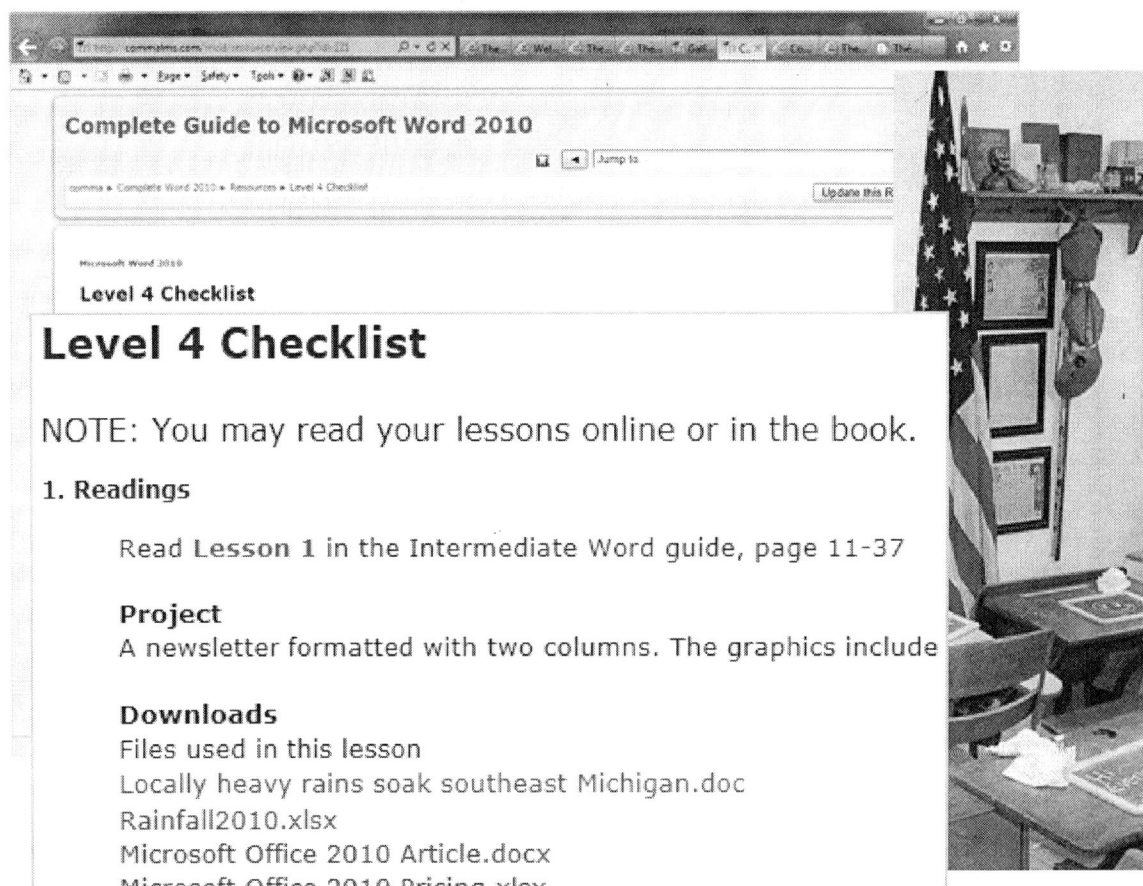

Complete Guide to Microsoft Word 2010

Level 4 Checklist

# Level 4 Checklist

NOTE: You may read your lessons online or in the book.

### 1. Readings

Read **Lesson 1** in the Intermediate Word guide, page 11-37

### Project
A newsletter formatted with two columns. The graphics include

### Downloads
Files used in this lesson
Locally heavy rains soak southeast Michigan.doc
Rainfall2010.xlsx
Microsoft Office 2010 Article.docx
Microsoft Office 2010 Pricing.xlsx

## Take a Quiz Online

After you review the materials online or with the *Guides*, you can log into the course online and take a **Quiz**. This is an open book quiz. You are allowed to look up the answers in your notes, online, or in the computer *Guides*.

**Review the Quiz Buttons**
**Submit:** This button posts your answer for the current question.

**Save without submitting:** This button saves your answers. You can leave the quiz and finish it later.

> Save without submitting

**Submit page:** This button sends your answers to all questions on the page.

**Submit all and finish**: Use this button to finish the quiz and submit your quiz online. When you Submit all and finish, you cannot go back and print your answers. So, print first!

> Submit all and finish

## Submit Your Work

Most of our online courses ask you to upload a document or a spreadsheet. Here are the steps you can take when you are ready to submit your work.

**Review This: Upload a file**
1. Go to the **Topic Outline**.
Click on **Beginning Word Skill Test.**

**What Do You See?** You will be taken to the Upload screen. The instructions should be available.

2. Click on **Browse** to select the file you want to upload. Navigate to your file, then click **Open**. The path and file name will appear in the upload box.

3. Click **Upload this file** to submit your Skill Test online. Your instructor will be notified automatically

My Course -> Topic Outline -> Upload a file

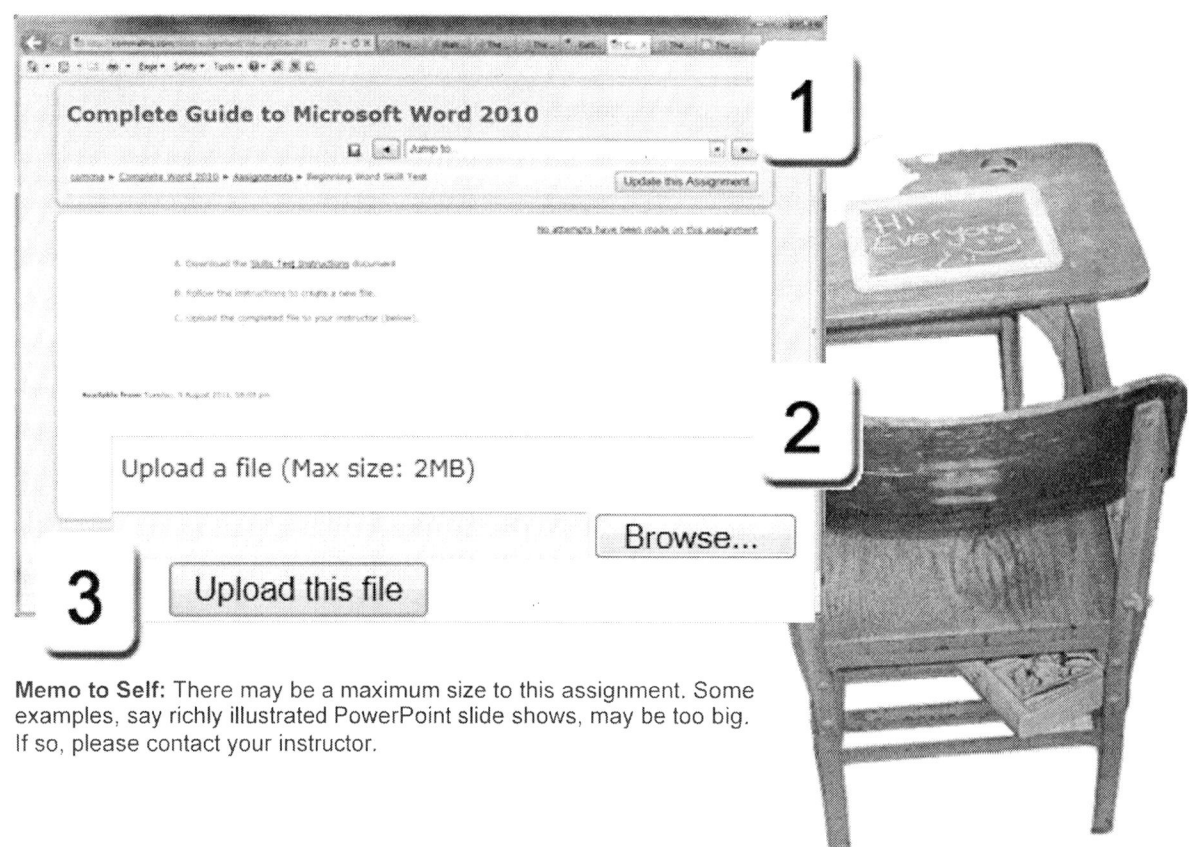

**Memo to Self:** There may be a maximum size to this assignment. Some examples, say richly illustrated PowerPoint slide shows, may be too big. If so, please contact your instructor.

## Use the Forums

In an online class, a **Forum** is similar to raising your hand and asking a question. When you post a question to a Forum anyone can reply with a suggestion or comment. Some of the answers are very creative and useful.

Your instructor may also post an explanation or offer additional links.

Edit | Delete | Reply

## Live Chats

Many instructors keep Office Hours. Chat allows you to type questions online and get an answer immediately from your instructor when your instructor is in the office.

**Don't Explain and Don't Complain:** Please keep your posts professional and on topic!

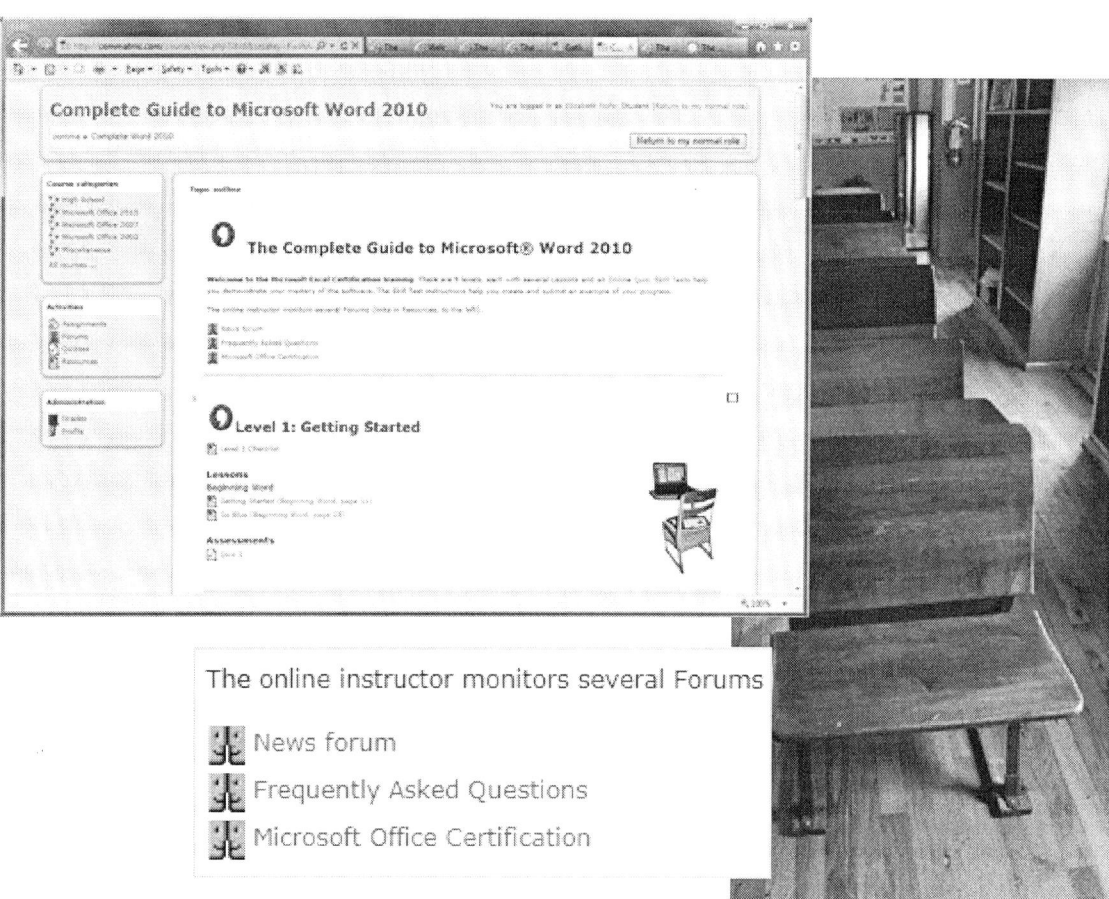

The online instructor monitors several Forums

News forum

Frequently Asked Questions

Microsoft Office Certification

## Practice

This *Guide* offers additional reference materials and practice certification tests. You can use the multiple choice quizzes and skill tests to practice if you wish. When you are ready, please log into the course and do the assessments online.

The Microsoft certification tests are timed: you have to perform the process steps very quickly and efficiently in order to pass.
**That takes practice!**

## More practice

If you have a question about a document or file you are working on you are always welcome to email a copy of your work to your instructor as an attachment.

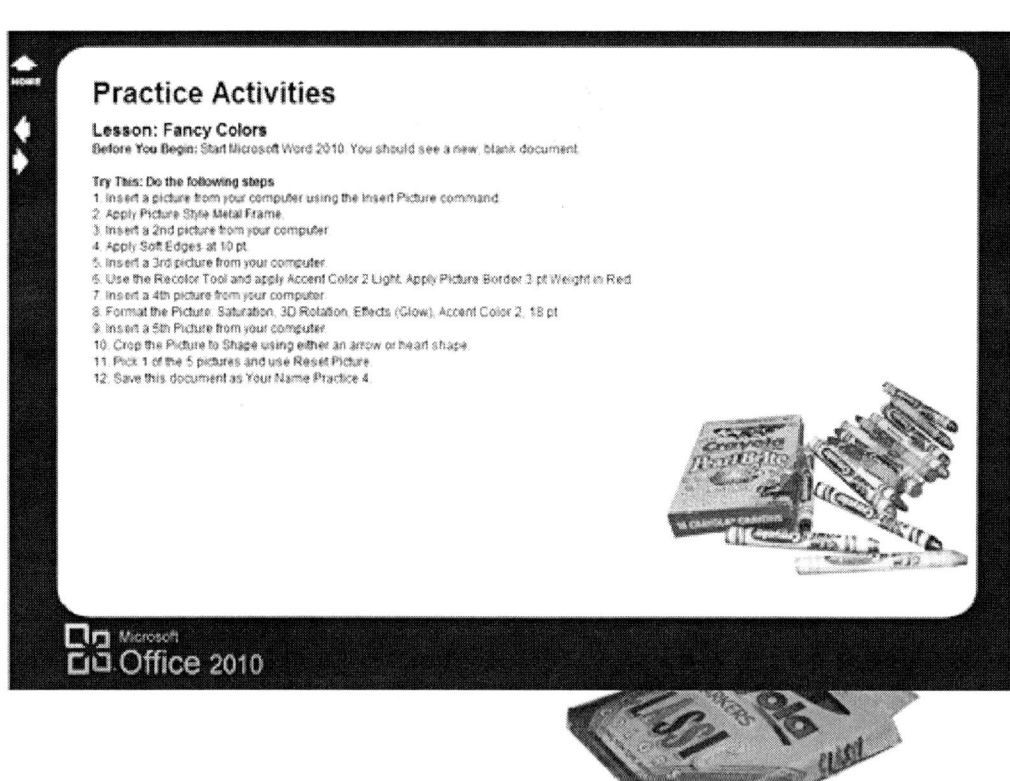

### Practice Activities

**Lesson: Fancy Colors**
**Before You Begin:** Start Microsoft Word 2010. You should see a new, blank document.

**Try This: Do the following steps**
1. Insert a picture from your computer using the Insert Picture command.
2. Apply Picture Style Metal Frame.
3. Insert a 2nd picture from your computer.
4. Apply Soft Edges at 10 pt.
5. Insert a 3rd picture from your computer.
6. Use the Recolor Tool and apply Accent Color 2 Light. Apply Picture Border 3 pt Weight in Red.
7. Insert a 4th picture from your computer.
8. Format the Picture: Saturation, 3D Rotation, Effects (Glow), Accent Color 2, 18 pt.
9. Insert a 5th Picture from your computer.
10. Crop the Picture to Shape using either an arrow or heart shape.
11. Pick 1 of the 5 pictures and use Reset Picture.
12. Save this document as Your Name Practice 4.

Microsoft
Office 2010

# Microsoft Business Certification

The course prepares you to pass the **Microsoft Office Specialist (MOS)** exams. This credential recognizes the business skills needed to get the most out of Microsoft Office 2010.

Microsoft Certification Exams are available through authorized testing centers. They are not included as part of the certification training program in the same way that taking the Bar Exam is not included with getting a degree in Law from a college or university.

**More Information Online.**
**Certiport** provides the official Microsoft certification tests.
You can download the Microsoft certification topics and study guides.
Here is their address: www.certiport.com

*Please Note: Comma Productions, LLC. is independent from Microsoft Corporation, and not affiliated with Microsoft in any manner. While the Complete Computer Guides may be used in assisting individuals to prepare for a Microsoft Business Certification exam, Microsoft, its designated program administrator, and Comma Productions, LLC. do not warrant that use of these Complete Computer Guides will ensure passing a Microsoft Business Certification exam.*

## Can Microsoft Office 2010 Starter be used for Microsoft Office certification training?

Yes and No. The Microsoft Excel 2010 Starter software has all of the features required to practice and prepare for the Microsoft Excel 2010 CORE certification test. The Microsoft Word 2010 Starter software is missing several key features that are part of the Microsoft Office 2010 CORE certification requirements.

**Compare the MOS CORE certification topics**
**The Microsoft Word 2010 Starter:**
Word 2010 MOS CORE certification topics (PDF)

**The Microsoft Excel 2010 Starter:**
EXCEL 2010 MOS CORE certification topics (PDF)

**With the Office 2010 Starter evaluation:**
Office 2010 Starter evaluation (PDF)

**More information on Office Starter software:**
View an image of Word 2010 Starter
View an image of Excel 2010 Starter

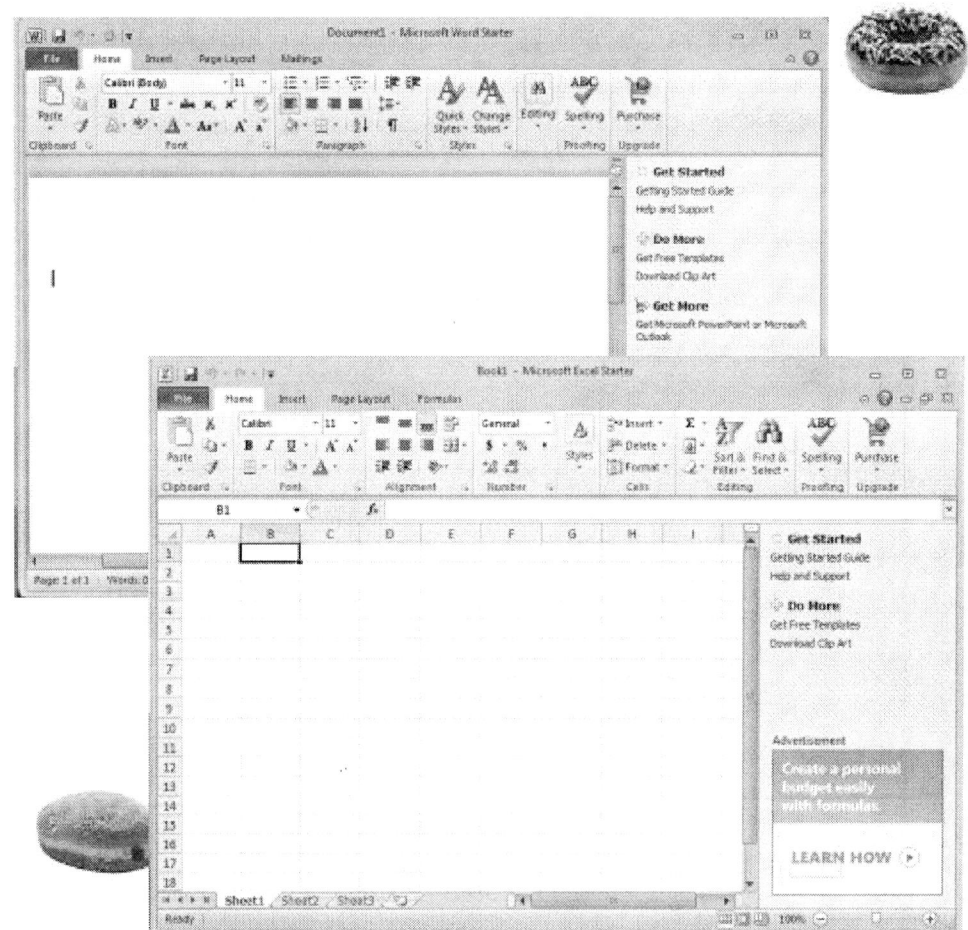

# Self-Assessment

| Skill Level-Beginning | Mastered | Needs Work | Required for my job |
|---|---|---|---|
| Create a new document | | | |
| Select, copy and paste text | | | |
| Format text | | | |
| Format columns | | | |
| Format borders and shading | | | |
| Spell and Grammar Check | | | |
| Insert a picture from ClipArt or a file | | | |

**Beginning Word is recommended if you selected "needs work" on three or more skills**

| Skill Level-Intermediate | Mastered | Needs Work | Required for my job |
|---|---|---|---|
| Create a watermark | | | |
| Use Headers and Footers | | | |
| Create a template | | | |
| Create a table | | | |
| Add, delete and modify rows, column and cells | | | |
| Create a Mail Merge | | | |
| Insert a bookmark or a hyperlink | | | |
| Create an on-line (Web) page | | | |

**Intermediate Word is recommended if you selected "needs work" on three or more skills**

| Skill Level-Advanced | Mastered | Needs Work | Required for my job |
|---|---|---|---|
| Format text with Styles | | | |
| Navigate with the Document Map | | | |
| Insert captions, footnotes or endnotes | | | |
| Create a Table of Contents | | | |
| Track Changes | | | |
| Create an on-line form | | | |
| Create a Master Document | | | |

**Advanced Word is recommended if you selected "needs work" on three or more skills.**

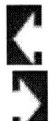

# Memo to Self:

## My Login Information
User Name:

Password:

Website:

## My Instructor
Name:

Email:

Office Hours:

### Word 2010: Getting Started
# Go Blue!

## Beginning Word Objectives
**In this lesson, you will learn how to:**

1. Open Microsoft Word

2. Align Text center, left, right, and justified

3. Format Font color, size, face, and case

4. Identify the Home Ribbon, Font Group & Paragraph Group

5. Identify and apply Line Spacing options

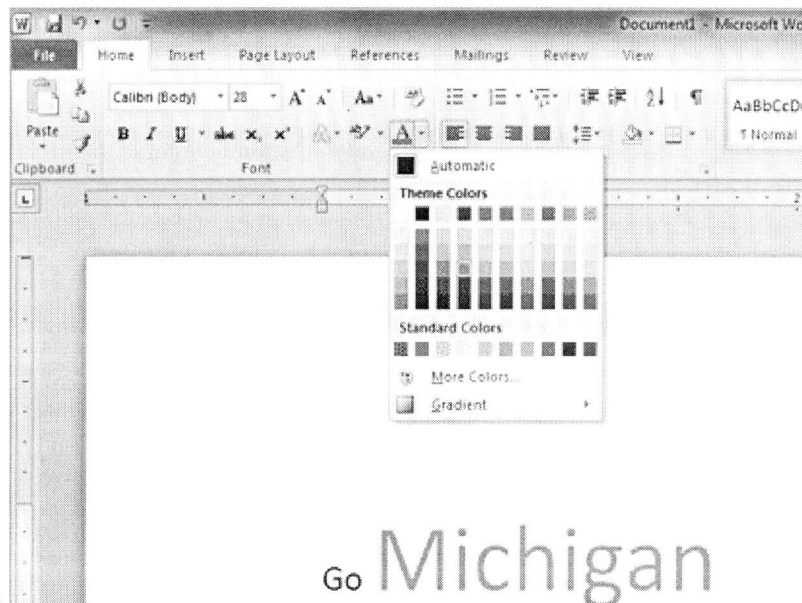

 # Lesson 2: Go Blue

## 1. Readings

Read Lesson 2 in your Beginning Word Guide, page 25-38.

## Project

A sample document that you do not need to save.

## Downloads

There are NO downloads for this lesson.

## 2. Practice

Complete the Practice Activity on page 39.

## 3. Assessment

Review the Test Yourself questions on page 40.

**Home**

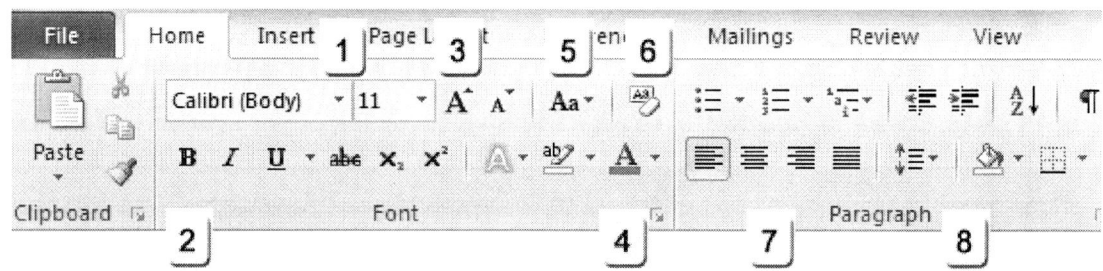

## Menu Maps

This lesson introduces the **Home** Ribbon.

1. Home ->Font, page 33
2. Home->Font->Bold, page 32
3. Home ->Font-> Size, page 32
4. Home->Font->Color, page 32
5. Home->Font->Change Case, page 34
6. Home->Font->Clear Formatting, page 35
7. Home->Paragraph->Alignment, page 36
8. Home->Paragraph->Line Spacing, page 37

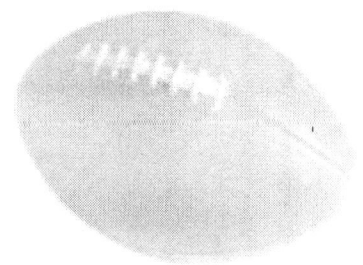

**Start -> All Programs -> Microsoft Office -> Microsoft Word 2010**

# Hello Microsoft Word!

Say, "Hello" to Microsoft Word. The *Complete Computer Guide* introduces Microsoft Word at the Newbie level, for folks who are new to computers. If you are farther along, that's OK. You can still pick up some tricks and nomenclature.

Look at the label in **BOLD** above the picture of the Start menu on this page. This label is a method for writing out the path that your mouse travels. You will see this map at the top of every picture in our course.

**Try it: Start Microsoft Word**
Go to **Start**
Click on **All Programs**
Go to **Microsoft Office**
Click on **Microsoft Word 2010.**

**Start -> All Programs -> Microsoft Office -> Microsoft Word 2010**

What do you see from the top of the screen? Is there a **Title Bar** that says Microsoft Word? Yes.

Is there a **Home Ribbon** with the Clipboard, Font and Paragraph Groups? Yes.

If your screen looks similar to the example on this page, then you are ready to get started.

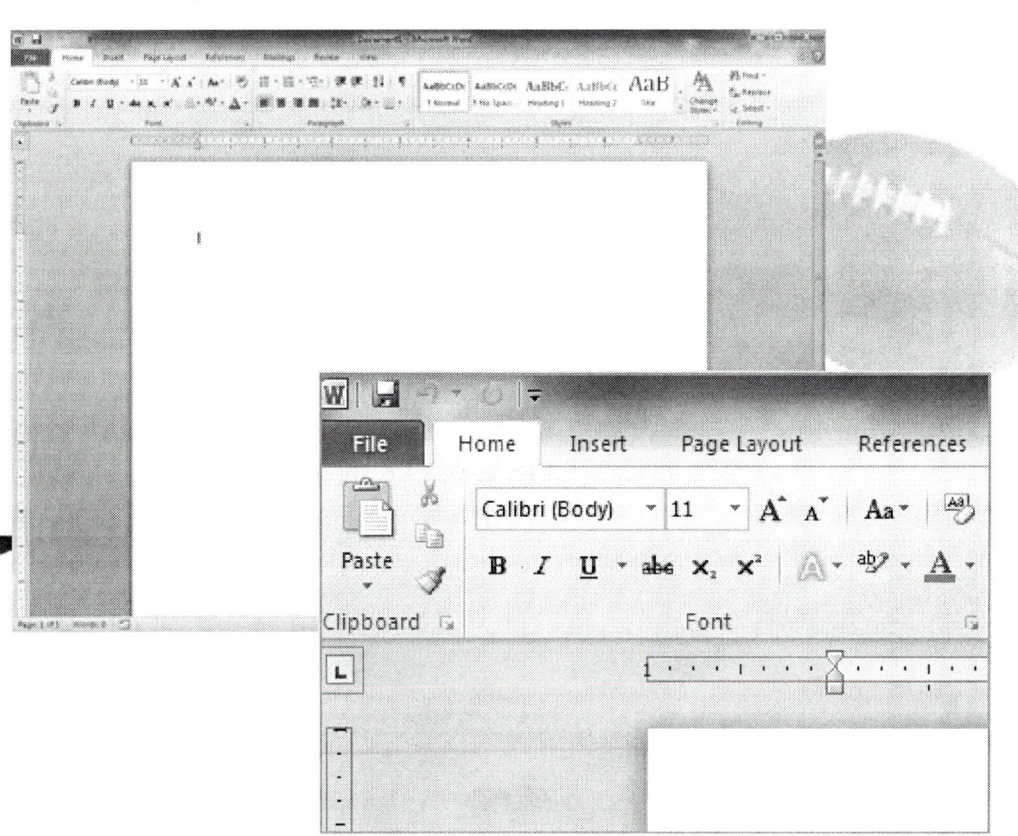

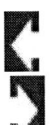

## Getting Started

Microsoft Word, Microsoft Works, and Word Perfect are all word processors. The original purpose of a word processor was to work with text. Many of the steps for entering text mimic an old typewriter: word processors competed with typewriters in the early days. This lesson is basic: can you type in text? Can you select the text and format it?

**Try it: Enter Type**
**Type** the words: Go Blue.
Press the **Enter** key on the keyboard.

Using Enter is like hitting the return key on an old typewriter. It gives you a new line.

Move your mouse around the page. The mouse looks like an I-beam. Click your mouse at the end of the word "Blue." Do you see a flashing vertical line? That's the **cursor**, insertion point. Whatever you type next will start from that point.

**Delete Type**
Click your cursor at the end of the word "Blue."
Use the **backspace** key on your keyboard.
The word is removed one letter at a time.

**Microsoft Word 2010**

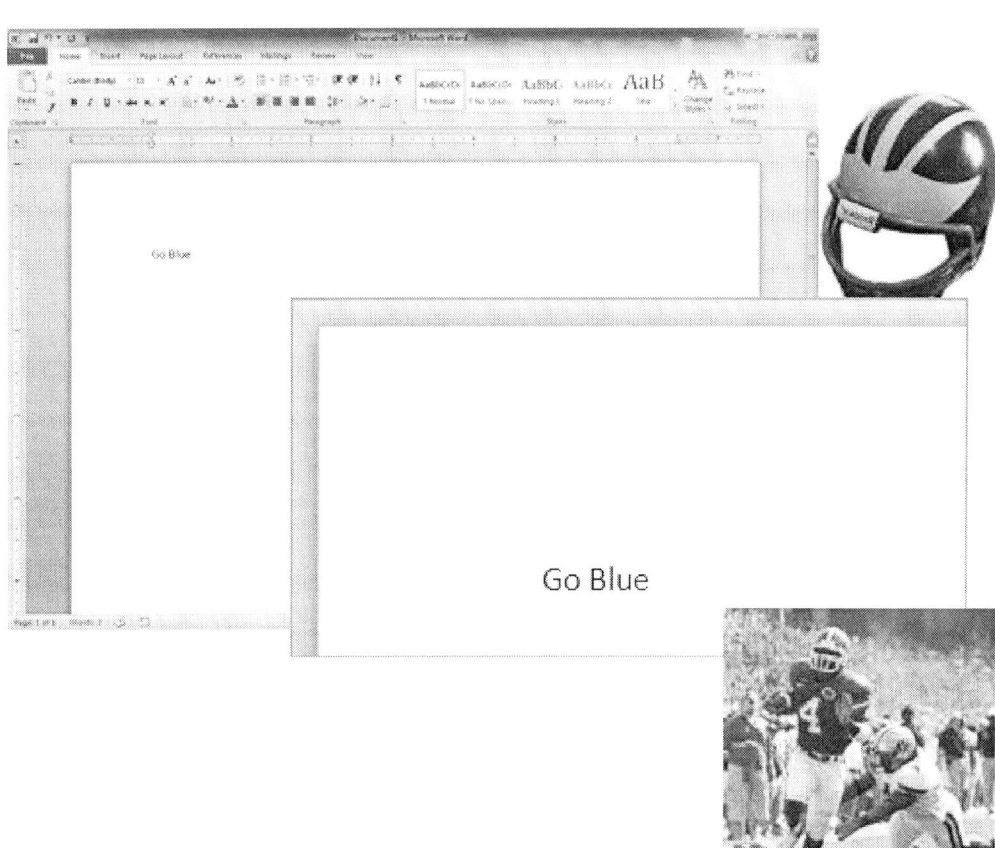

## Text Editing

Microsoft Word includes a 20,000 word dictionary. The word processor compares your typing to the words listed in the dictionary. If Word cannot find a match, you will see a red, wavy line.

**Try it: Correct a spelling mistake**
Type in the word: Miichigan
Place your cursor between the two "i's" and backspace or delete the extra letter.

After you correct the spelling, the red wavy line for the Spell Checker will disappear.

Not bad for a start. But we live in the age of color, graphics, and videos. What can you do to make this more exciting? What tools are available for formatting the text?

**Microsoft Word**

## Select the Text

**Nothing happens on a computer until you select it.** Double click on the word, "Michigan." to select it. You should see a blue box around the text when it is selected.

**Single click** just places your cursor.

**Double click** on a word to select it.

**Triple click** to select a paragraph.

**Old tricks:** To select a line of type, place your cursor between the edge of the paper and the first letter of type for the sentences you want to highlight. The cursor changes from an I-beam to a white arrow. Click and hold your left mouse button to drag and select the type you want.

**Microsoft Word**

Go Michigan

Exam 77-881: Microsoft Word 2010 Core
2. Formatting Content
2-1. Apply font and paragraph attributes: select and format text

# Format the Text

### 1. Change the Size
Use the **Font** group on the **Home** Ribbon to make the word "Michigan" big, bold and blue. The default Font size is 11 pts. Look for the small down arrow by the number 11 and select 28 from the list.

### 2. Make It Bold
Go to the **Home** Ribbon
Click on "B" for **Bold** on the Font Toolbar.

### 3. Make It Blue
Now, make it blue by going to the button on the far right: it's a letter "A" with a color bar underneath. See the little arrow to the right ? Click on it to bring up the color palette.

The **Live Preview** in Office 2010 lets you see your changes as you sweep the color palette with your mouse.

**WYSIWYG**: What you see is what you get.

**Home -> Font**

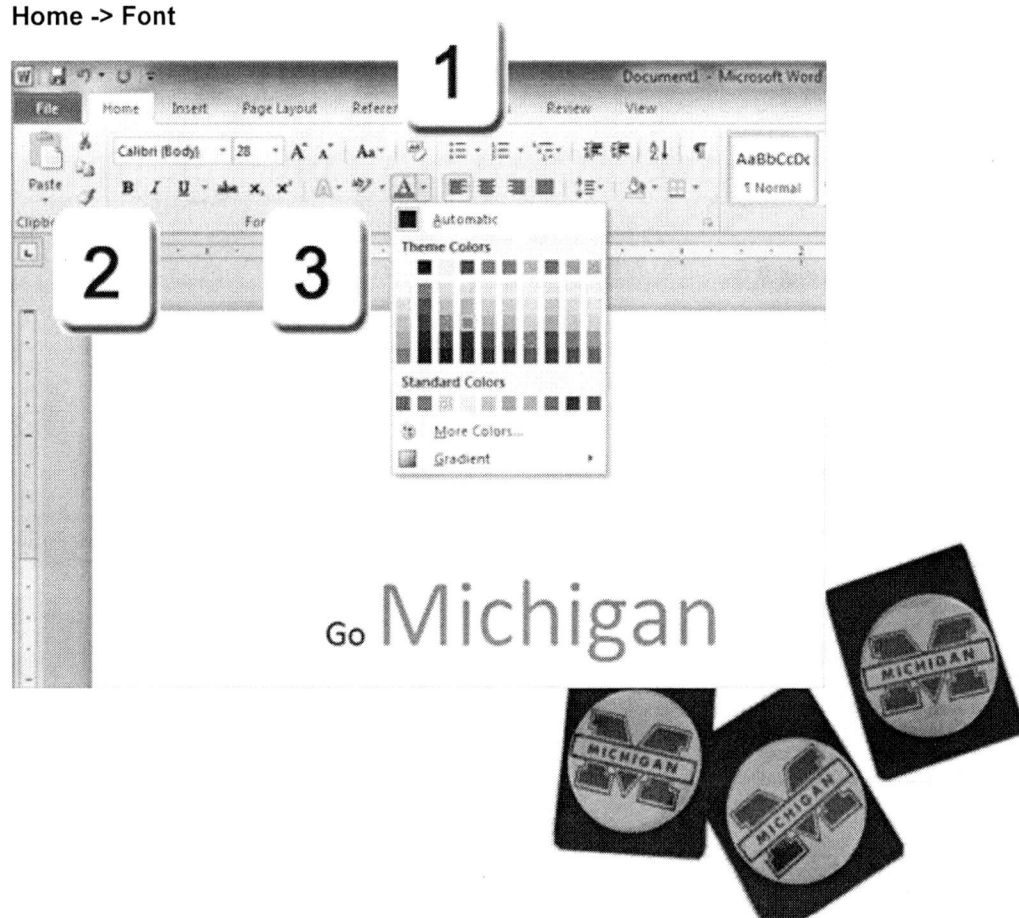

Exam 77-881: Microsoft Word 2010 Core
2. Formatting Content
2-1. Apply font and paragraph attributes: select and format text

## Format the Fonts

A **FONT** is a type face. Formatting the text with a bold or decorative Font distinguishes your document.

For example, a business letter should have a simple font that is easy to read. A wedding invitation has a different audience and a different purpose. Your invitation might have a handwritten font that looks as elegant as calligraphy.

**Try This: Change the Font**
**Double click** the word Michigan. This will highlight the text and **select** it.

Go to **Home ->Font**.
The default font in Microsoft Word 2007 and Word 2010 is called Calibri. Click on the down arrow on the left and select a different font from the list.

**Home -> Font**

Exam 77-881: Microsoft Word 2010 Core
2. Formatting Content
2-1. Apply font and paragraph attributes: select and format text

## More Format Options

You can change whether the text is Upper or Lower case with the Home Ribbon, too.

**Try This, Too: Change the Font Case**
1. **Select** the text: Michigan.

**2. Go to Home->Font ->Change Case.**
The **Change Case** button looks like a Capital "A" and a small "a."

**3. What Do You See?** The options include:
**Sentence Case**: Make the first letter in the sentence big, upper case.

**Lowercase**: All small, lower letters.

**Uppercase**: All big, upper letters.

**Capitalize**: Make the first letter of each word big, upper case.

**Toggle**: Change Upper to Lower and vice versa. You would use this to change the text if you kept the Caps Lock on while typing.

Home -> Font ->Change Case

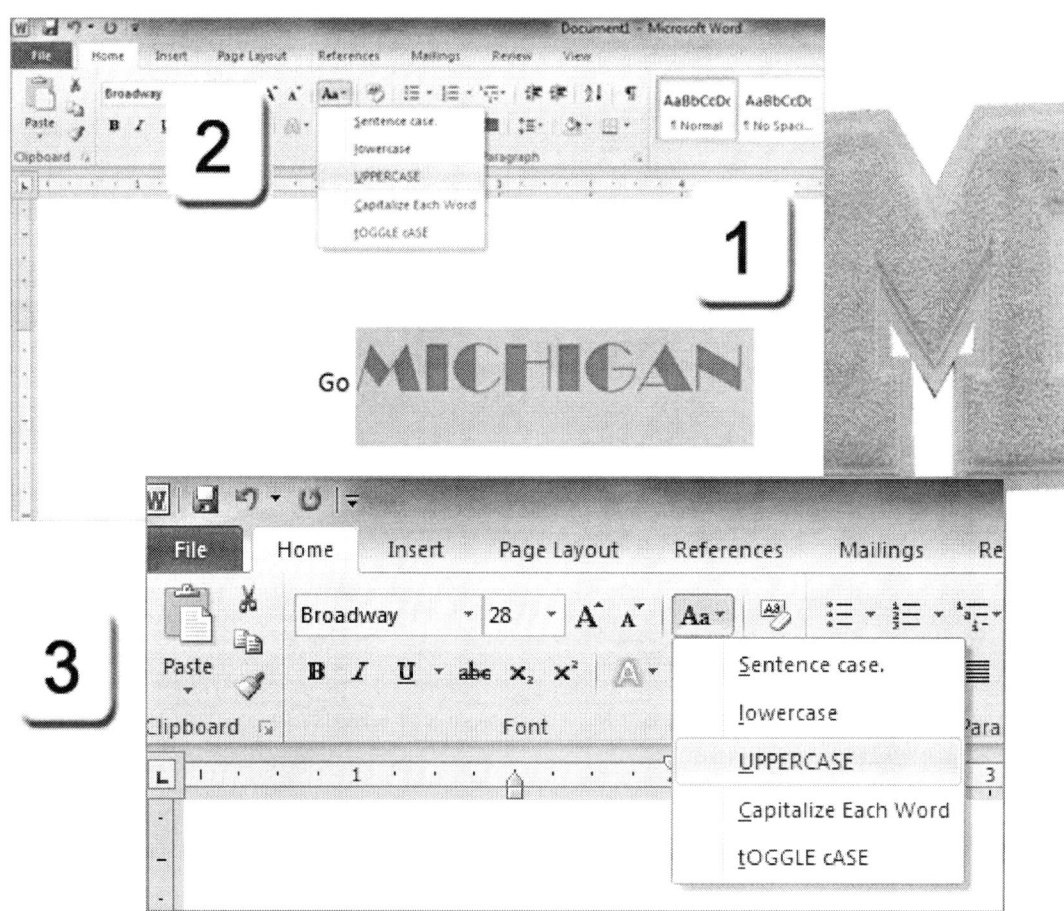

Exam 77-881: Microsoft Word 2010 Core
2. Formatting Content
2-1. Apply font and paragraph attributes: Change Case

## Clear the Formatting

Say you wanted to remove all of the formatting that you added to the text. This option can be useful when you copy and paste information from a web page.

**Try This: Clear the Formatting**
**1. Select** the text: Michigan

**2. Go to Home ->Font ->Clear Formatting.**
The Clear Formatting button is in the upper right corner of the Font group.

**3. What Do You See?** The text will return to the default Font (Calibri) and size (11 pt.)

**Memo to Self:** You do NOT need to match the formatting on this page. The goal of this lesson is to find and practice the options in the Font group.

Home -> Font ->Clear Formatting

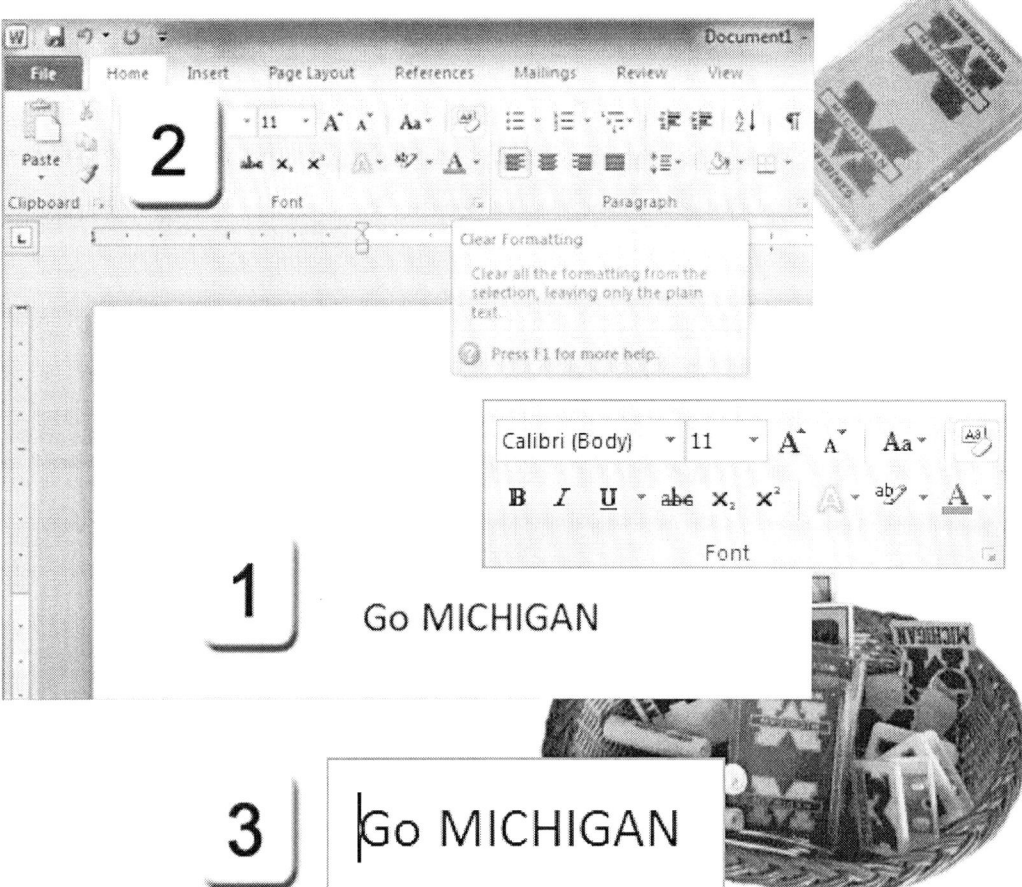

Exam 77-881: Microsoft Word 2010 Core
2. Formatting Content
2-1. Apply font and paragraph attributes: Clear formatting

## Format the Paragraph

**Try This: Change the Alignment**

**1. Triple click** the word Michigan. Triple click selects a paragraph.

**2. Go to Home -> Paragraph.** You can use the **Paragraph** group on the **Home** Ribbon to align the words "Go Michigan" to the **center** of the first line.

**3. What Do you See?**
**Left, Center** and **Right** are kind of obvious alignments. **Justified** looks like the columns in a printed newspaper. Justified text is distributed evenly within the column.

The default alignment for letters, books and reports is Left with a "ragged right" edge.

**Home -> Paragraph ->Alignment**

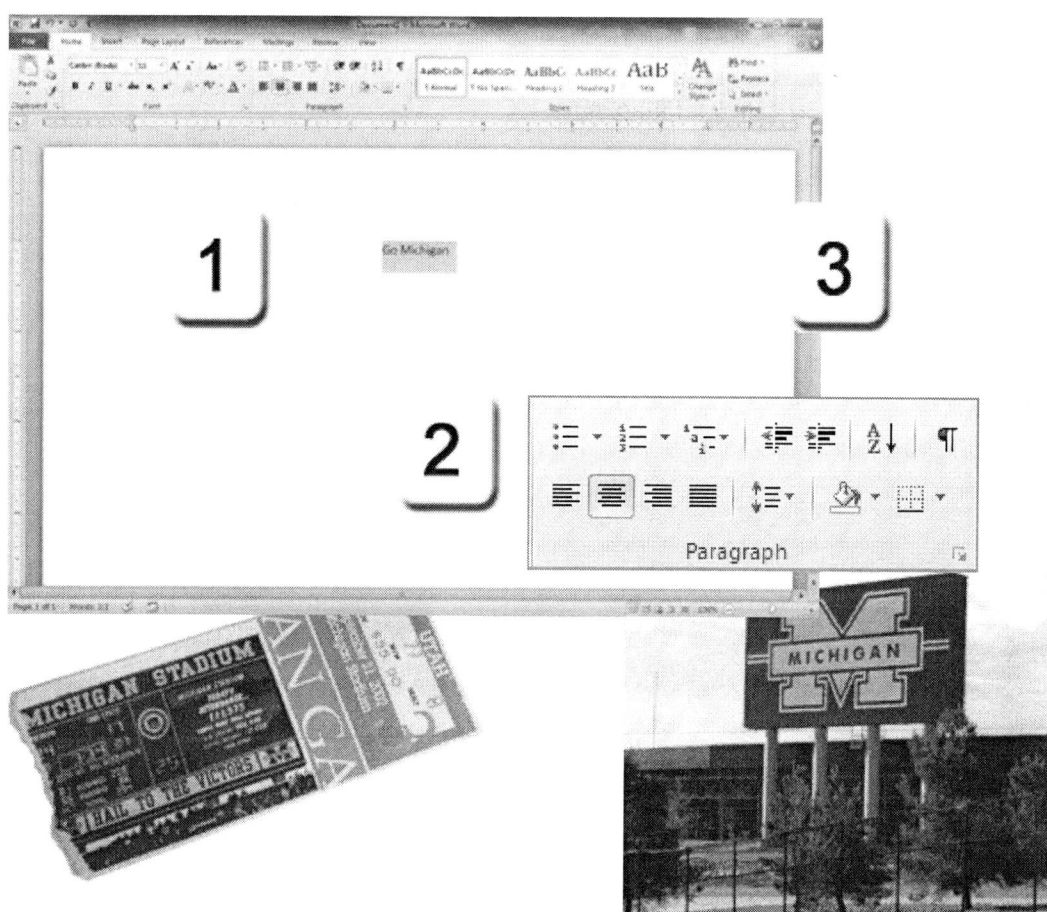

Exam 77-881: Microsoft Word 2010 Core
2. Formatting Content
2-1. Apply font and paragraph attributes: Change alignment

## Format the Paragraph

The amount of space between the lines of text is technically called **leading** in the print business. For several hundred years each letter of type was made from wood or metal and placed into a key frame. The rows of type were separated by strips of thin, lead bar: the leading. In Microsoft Word the leading is called **Line Spacing.**

**Before You Begin**
Place your cursor before the M of Michigan Click ENTER on the keyboard to force a new line. Now you have two lines of type.

**Try This: Increase the Line Spacing**
**1. Select both lines of type** by dragging the mouse over the text.

**2. Go to Home ->Paragraph ->Line and Paragraph Spacing.**

**3. What Do You See?** There are several default sizes. The number 1.0 means that there will be one blank line between and that the space, or leading will be the same height a one row of type. 2.0 means 2 rows of type.

Home -> Paragraph ->Line and Paragraph Spacing

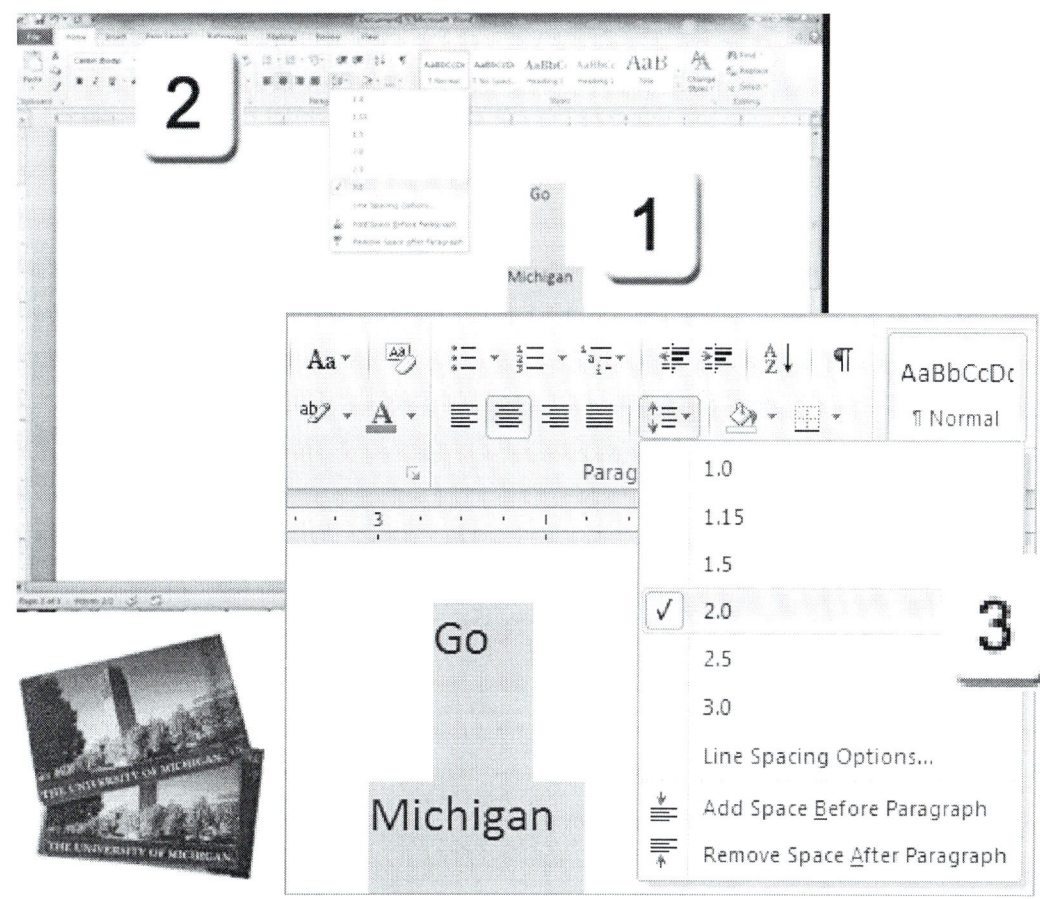

Exam 77-881: Microsoft Word 2010 Core
2. Formatting Content
2-1. Apply font and paragraph attributes: Change the line spacing

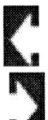

## Rich Text Formatting

And that's all there is to it.

What you have been doing is called **Rich Text**. It's good for getting attention in your letters or email. "Mama, send money!"

It's also a fun way to get to know text editing in Microsoft Word.

Well, you done good. You get the cookie. <grin>

# Practice Activities

## Lesson: Go Blue

**Before You Begin:** Start Microsoft Word 2010. You should see a new, blank document.

**Try This: Do the following steps**

1. Type your name. Click ENTER on the keyboard to create a new line.

2. Type your favorite color. Click ENTER on the keyboard to create a new line.

3. Type the name of your favorite movie. Click ENTER on the keyboard to create a new line.

4. Type the words Microsoft Office. Click ENTER on the keyboard to create a new line.

5. Format your name to be 36pt font size. Set the Alignment as Right.

6. Format the name of your color to be that color text. Set the Alignment as Left.

7. Format the name of your favorite movie to a font style other than Calibri (such as Comic Sans or Times New Roman.)

8. Set the line spacing for all of your text to be 1.5

9. Select the words Microsoft Office and apply Toggle Case

10. Close Microsoft Word. When you are prompted, click Don't Save.

This is a practice document that you do not have to submit.

# Test Yourself

1. Which of the following is in the Font group? (Give all correct answers.)
a. Size
b. Bold
c. Italic
d. Color

Tip: Beginning Word, page 32

2. Text cannot be formatted unless it is selected first.
a. True
b. False

Tip: Beginning Word, page 31

3. What Ribbon is the Font group on?
a. Home
b. Insert
c. Format

Tip: Beginning Word, page 28

4. Which of the following is true about the Paragraph Group?
(Give all correct answers.)
a. It includes Alignment
b. It includes Line Spacing
c. It is on the Home Ribbon

Tip: Beginning Word, page 36

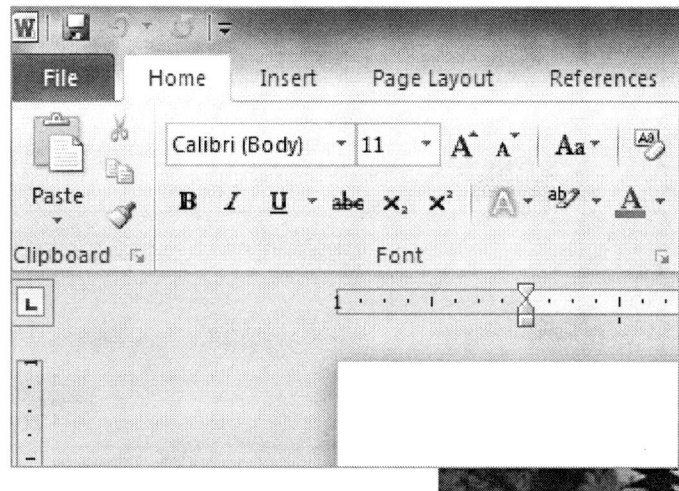

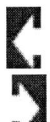

Word 2010: Working with Text

# Horses and Zebras

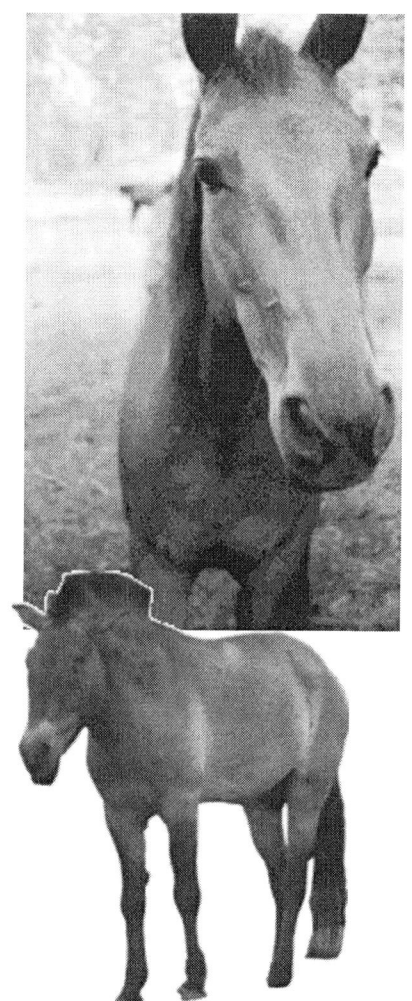

## Beginning Word Objectives

**In this lesson, you will learn how to:**

1. Use Copy and Paste commands on text & pictures

2. Use Drag and Drop editing on text & pictures

3. Insert Pictures from Clip Art

4. Apply position formatting to a Picture

5. Access the Picture Tools Ribbon

6. Resize and move a Picture

# Lesson 3: Horses and Zebras

## 1. Readings
Read Lesson 3 in the Beginning Word guide, page 41-60.

## Project
A sample document that you do not need to save.

## Downloads
There are NO downloads for this lesson.

## 2. Practice
Complete the Practice Activity on page 61.

## 3. Assessment
Review the Test questions on page 62.

Home

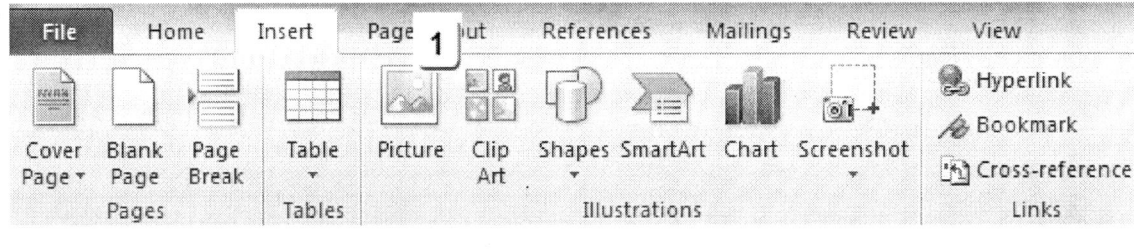

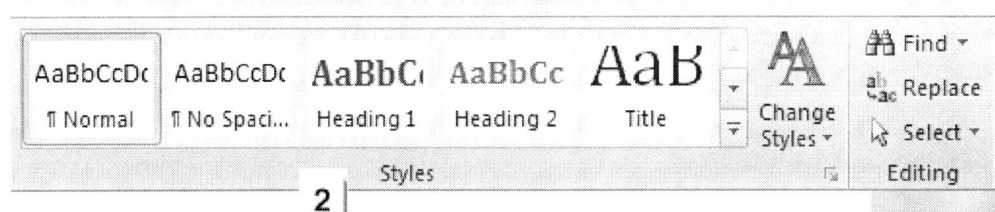

# Menu Maps
This lesson introduces options on the **Insert** Ribbon.
1. Insert->ClipArt, page 50

This lesson introduces options on the **Home** Ribbon.
2. Home->Styles, page 56

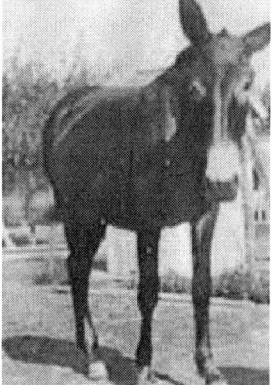

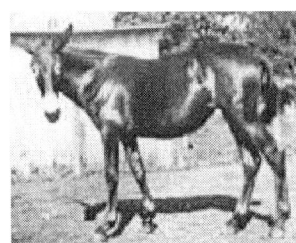

# Start Microsoft Word

The purpose of this lesson is to learn how to use the basic edit commands: **Copy**, **Paste** and the Computer Mama's favorite: **Undo**. If you were familiar with Microsoft Word in a previous version, this is a good place to get reacquainted with the new toolbars. So, **Start** the **Program** Microsoft Word.

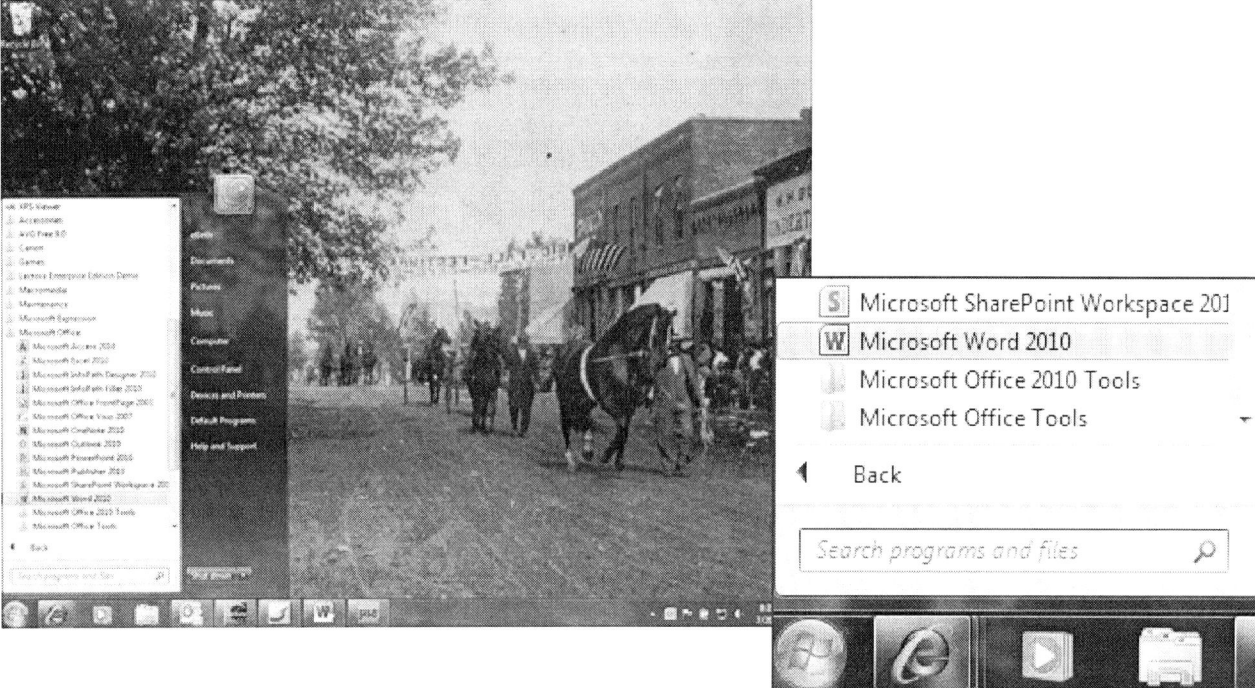

Take One

**Start -> All Programs ->Microsoft Word 2010**

## Where Are You?
What do you see from the top of the screen? Is there a **Title Bar** that says Microsoft Word? Yes.

Is there a **Home** Ribbon with the Clipboard, Font and Paragraph Groups? Yes.

If your screen looks similar to the example on this page, then you are ready to get started.

## Where Are You Going?

Microsoft Office 2007 was redesigned based on user experiences. The design teams determined the tools that people used the most and placed them "up front." The menus were replaced with Ribbons. Ribbons are **Tabs** of functions that work together.

For example, all of the options for making a Mail Merge have been gathered on the **Mailings** tab.

Some tool bars are activated when you need them. When you click on a picture, the **Picture Tools** are displayed. When you click back on text, the Picture Tools are turned off.

Each **Ribbon** may have many **Groups**, and **Commands**. In the example on this page, the **Font** group includes Bold, Italic, Underline, etc.

**Office 2010 builds on that rich Ribbon experience.**

**Microsoft Word 2010 -> Home**

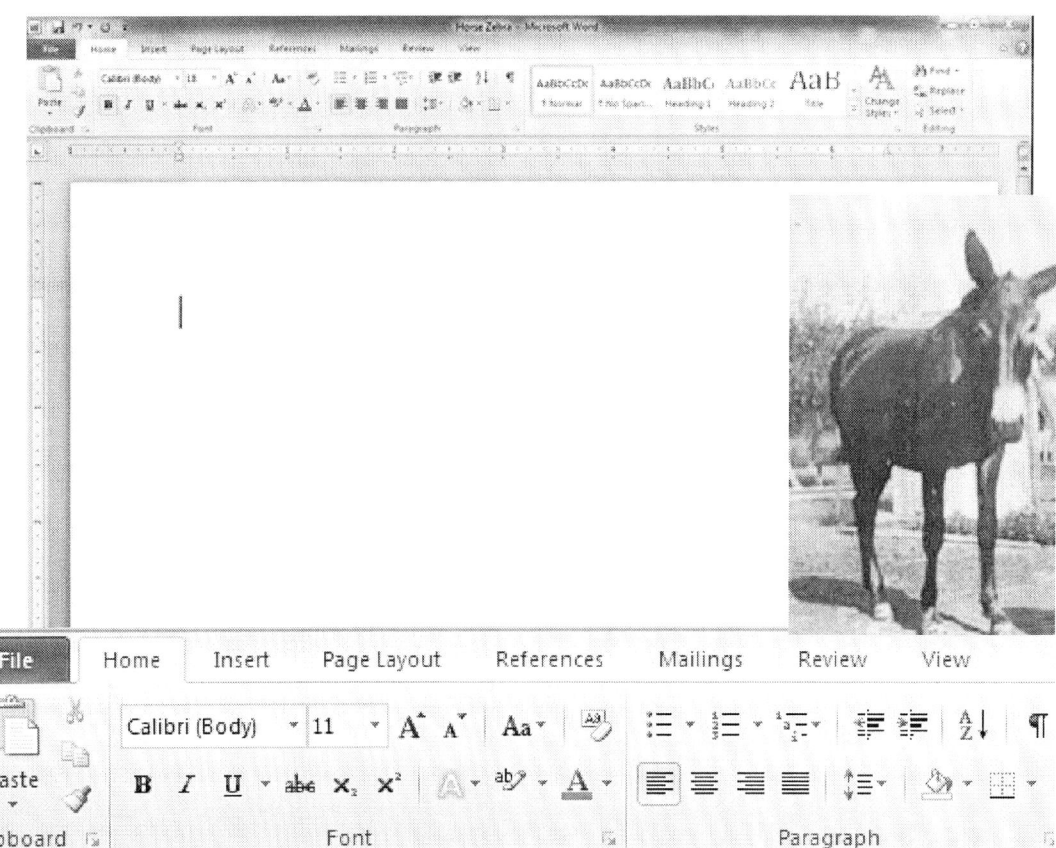

## Format Text

Moving text and graphics from one page to another, or from one document to another, is a fundamental computer task. This lesson begins with text.

**Try It: Format the Font**
**1. Type: Horse**
Type: Zebra

**2. Double click** the word Horse to select it.

**3. Go to Home ->Font**
Select 18 pt, Bold, Red

**Double click** Zebra to select it
Go to **Home ->Font**
Select 18 pt, Bold, Blue

**Memo to Self:** Nothing happens in a computer until you select it first.

**Home ->Font ->Color**

Exam 77-881: Microsoft Word 2010 Core
2. Formatting Content
2-1. Apply font and paragraph attributes: Format font color

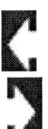

## Copy and Paste

Question: If you format the text big, bold and colorful, will Microsoft Word retain that formatting when you copy and paste the text?

### 1. Try it: Copy the Text

**Double click** Horse to select it

Go to **Home ->Copy**
The Copy command looks like two sheets of paper. Look for it in the Clipboard group.

### 2. Paste the Text

Click your cursor after the word Zebra

Go to **Home ->Paste**

**Paste** the word Horse five more times.

### 3. Repeat the practice

**Double click** Zebra to select it

Go to **Home ->Copy**
Place your cursor after the last word

Go to **Home ->Paste**

**Paste** the word Zebra five more times.

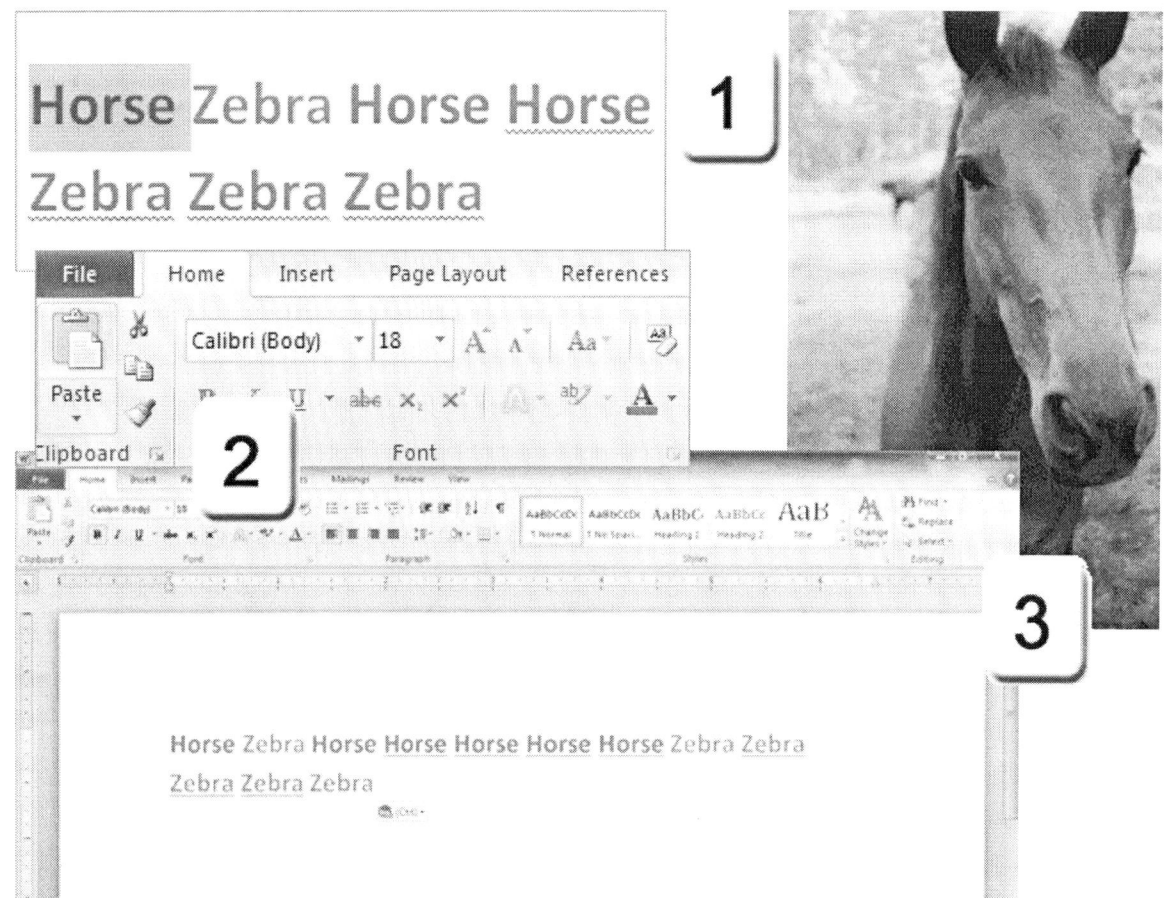

## Drag and Drop Text

Our goal is to edit the words so that they go, "Horse Zebra Horse Zebra." The action is called Drag and Drop.

### Try it: Drag and Drop the Text

**1. Double click** Horse to select it. Click and HOLD your left mouse button The cursor changes from an I-beam to a white headed arrow with a box under it.

**2. Drag and Drop** the word Horse between two Zebras. You can see a little vertical line that follows your mouse as you move it. That's the insertion point. No surprises. When you release your mouse that's where the word you're holding will be dropped.

Play with it a little to get used to drag and drop editing. It works. It's fast. And when you get the hang of it, it's fun.

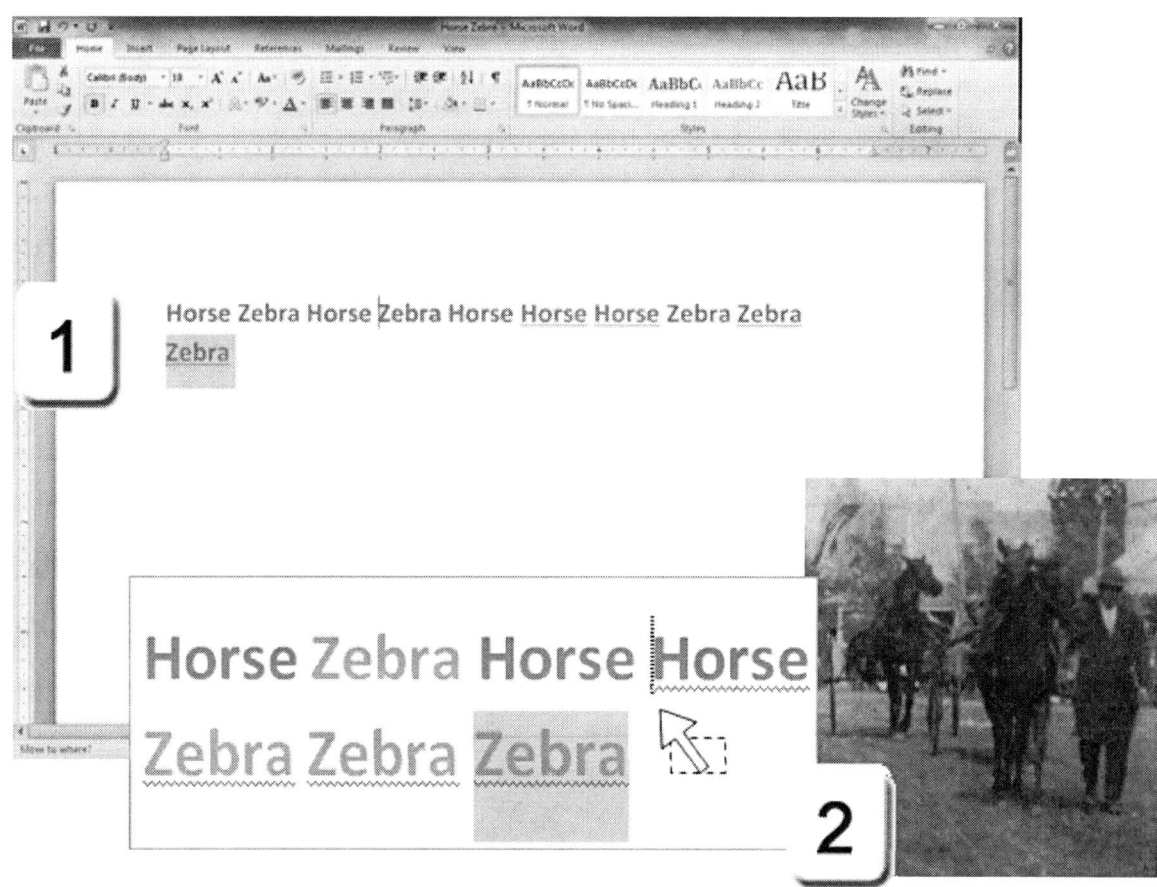

Exam 77-881: Microsoft Word 2010 Core
2. Formatting Content
2-1. Apply font and paragraph attributes

**Insert -> ClipArt**

## Insert ClipArt
This exercise is called Horses and Zebras. The objective is to use the basic commands with pictures as well as text. So, you need horses and zebras.

**Try it: Insert ClipArt**
**1. Go to the Insert tab**
Find the Illustration group.

**2. Click on ClipArt**

**3. What Do You See?** You will see a new **ClipArt Task bar** on the right side of your screen. What options are available?

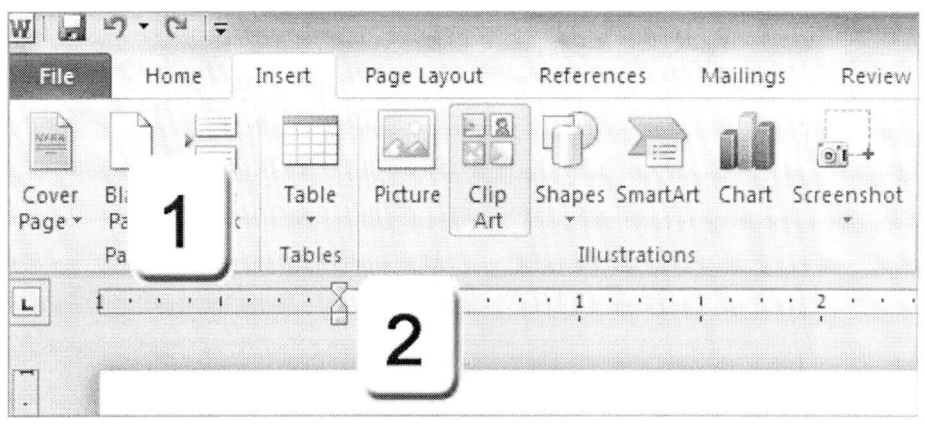

Exam 77-881: Microsoft Word 2010 Core
4. Including Illustrations and Graphics in a Document
4-3. Insert and format Clip Art

# Hellllllo ClipArt!

There are three criteria you can manage when you search for ClipArt: topic, location and media type.

When you look for photos, pictures, or video clips, you are not limited to the media available on your own drive. **Clip Art** can also search online for illustrations, photographs, video and audio sound files at Office.com.

You can choose whether you want to look online from the options found under Search In.

You can also filter your search by checking whether you want some or all of the **media file types**.

**Insert -> ClipArt**

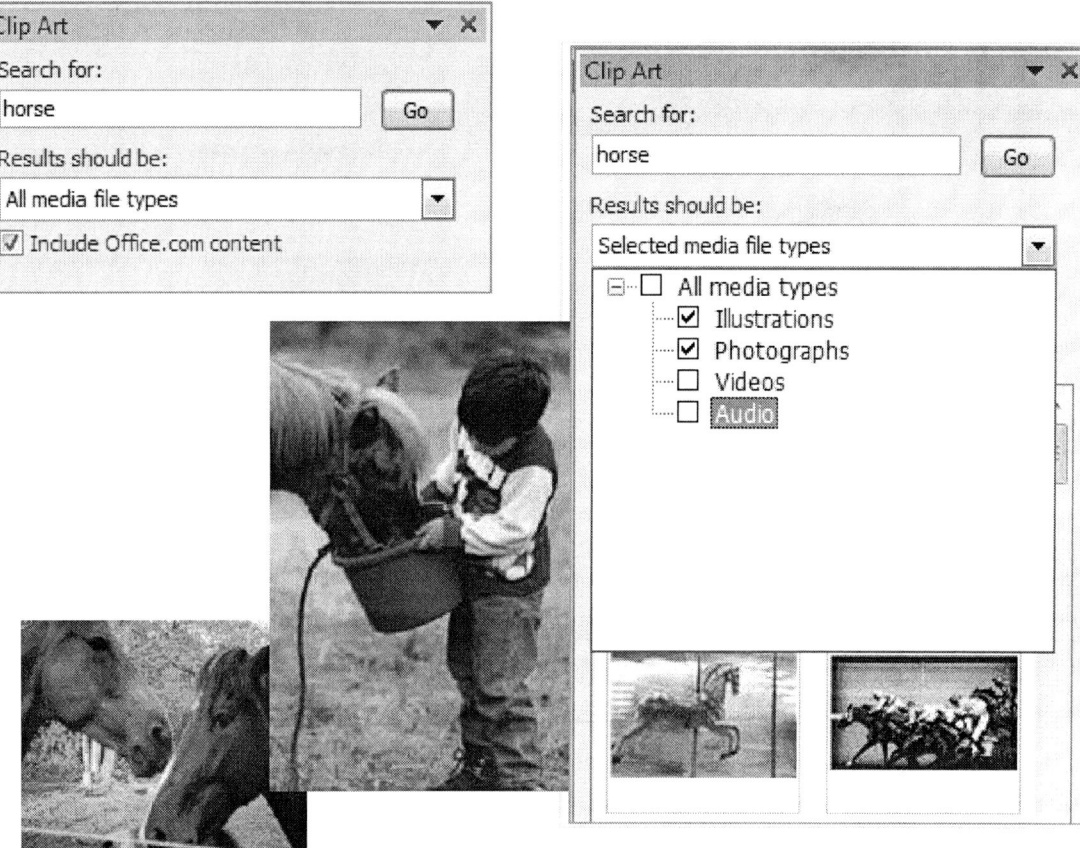

**Exam 77-881: Microsoft Word 2010 Core**
**4. Including Illustrations and Graphics in a Document**
**4-3. Insert and format Clip Art**

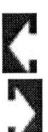

## Pick a Picture

**Try it: Insert ClipArt**

**1. Type** Horse for the Search text.

**2. Click on Go** to make it look for anything that matches your criteria.

**3. What Do You See?** The **ClipArt Gallery** will display a collection of horses.

Click on any picture that you want. It will be inserted into your Word document.

**Insert -> ClipArt**

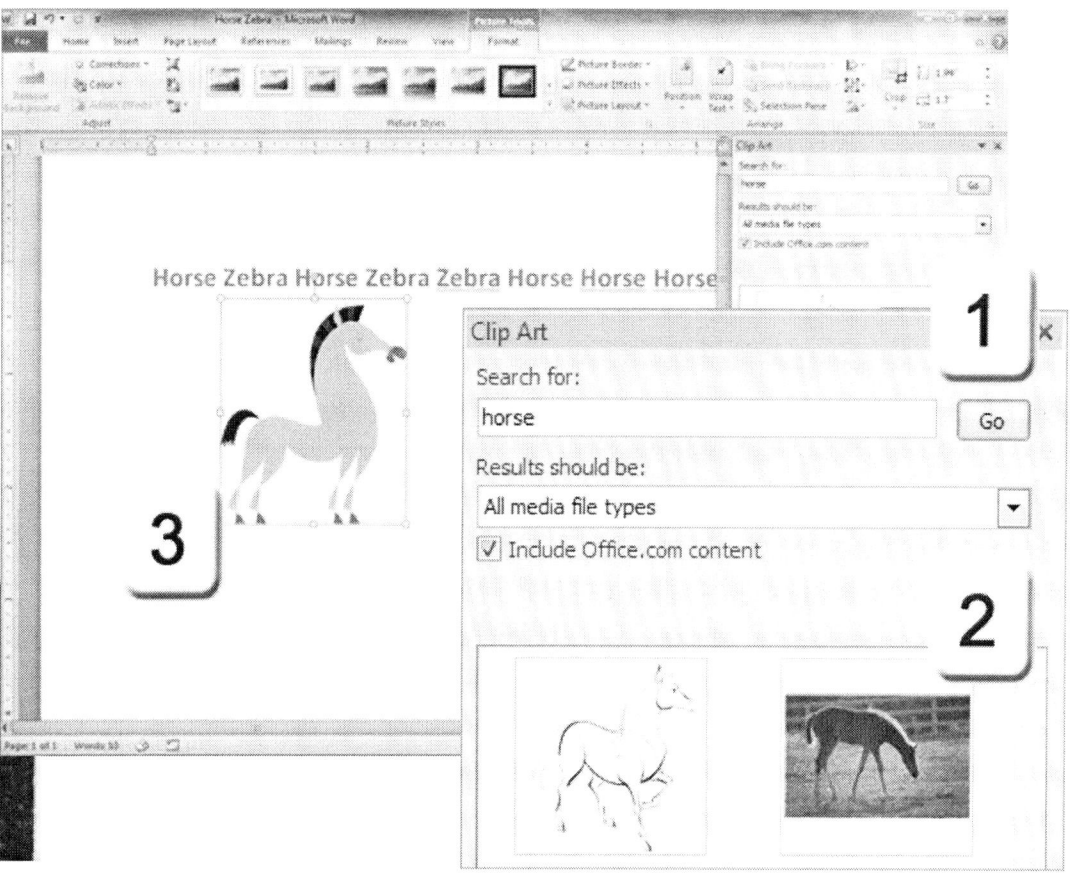

Exam 77-881: Microsoft Word 2010 Core
4. Including Illustrations and Graphics in a Document
4-3. Insert and format Clip Art

## Picture Tools

How does this picture interact with the text? Is it on the words, covering them up? Under the words? What is the **position**?

**Try it: Edit the Picture Position.**
1. **Click once on the picture to select it.** Look for the new **Picture Tools.**

2. **Go to the Format tab.** Look for the **Arrange** group.

3. **Click on Position.** You should see a couple of options. Try different **Positions** by sliding the mouse around.

**Memo to Self:** The phrase **"in Line with Text"** means the picture will behave like a giant letter. When you format a picture **With Text Wrapping**, the picture can be moved freely, as if it was a Sticky Note.

**Picture Tools -> Format -> Position**

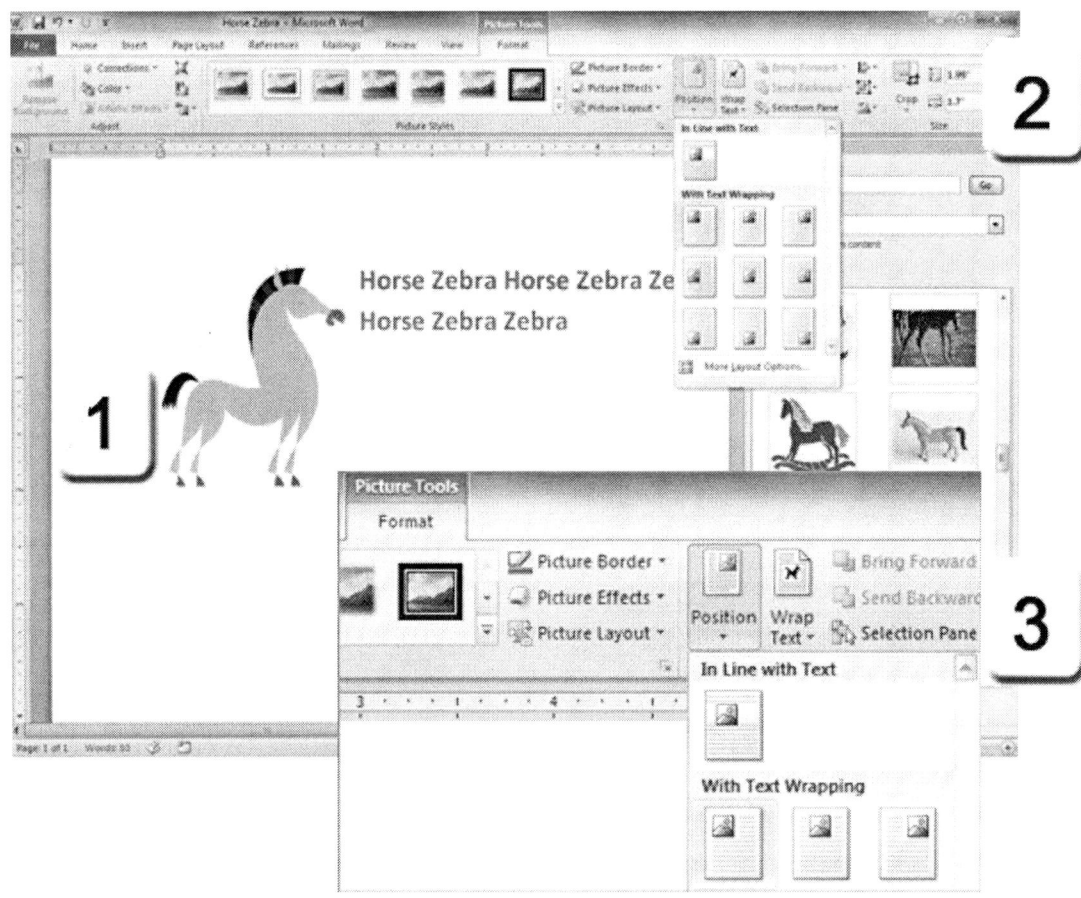

Exam 77-881: Microsoft Word 2010 Core
4. Including Illustrations and Graphics in a Document
4-3. Insert and format Clip Art: Picture Tools

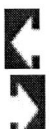

## Resize the Picture

Click once on the picture to select it. See the little circles around the horse picture? Those are the **handles**. If you move your cursor to one the handles, the cursor will turn into a double-headed black arrow.

**Watch your mouse:**

A two-headed arrow means **Resize**.

A four-headed arrow means **Move**.

**Try it: Resize the Picture**

Select the picture.

Run your cursor over any handle.

Watch for a two-headed arrow.

**Click and Hold** your left mouse button to **Resize** the picture.

**Memo To Self:** Pictures, photographs and even graphs are frame-based. The little handles that surround an object when you select it are the edges of the frame. Frames "float," they can be placed anywhere on the document.

**Resize the Picture**

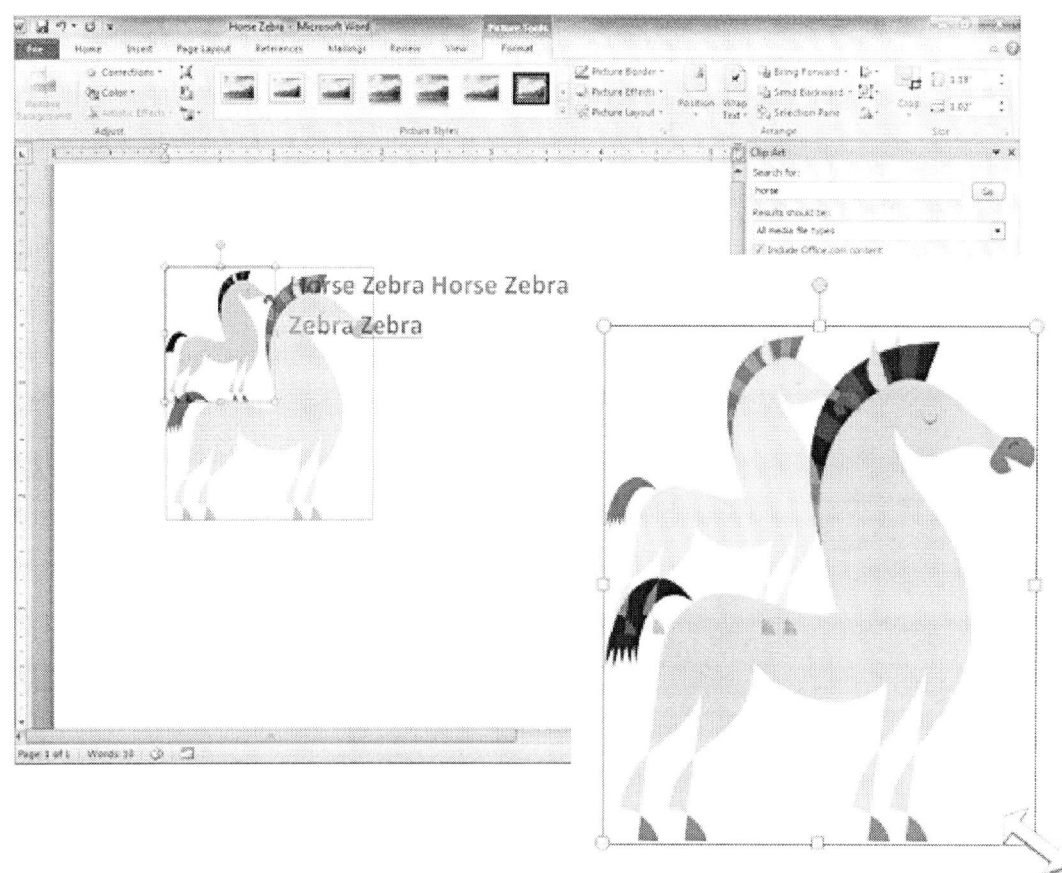

Exam 77-881: Microsoft Word 2010 Core
4. Including Illustrations and Graphics in a Document
4-3. Insert and format Clip Art: Resize a picture

## Copy and Paste the Picture

Sometimes when you copy and paste a picture, the new image may be placed EXACTLY on top of the original image with computer precision. It will be very difficult to see that you do, indeed, have one picture on another.

**Watch your mouse:**
A two- headed arrow means **Resize**.
A four-headed arrow means **Move**.

**1. Try it: Copy and Paste the Picture**
Click once to **select** the picture
Go to **Home ->Copy**
Go to **Home ->Paste**

**2. Try it: Move the Picture**
**Select** the new picture you just pasted
Watch for a four-headed arrow
Click and Hold your left mouse button to **Move** the picture to a new position.

**3. Try it again: Copy, Paste, Move**
Repeat these steps with a Zebra picture.

Home -> Copy

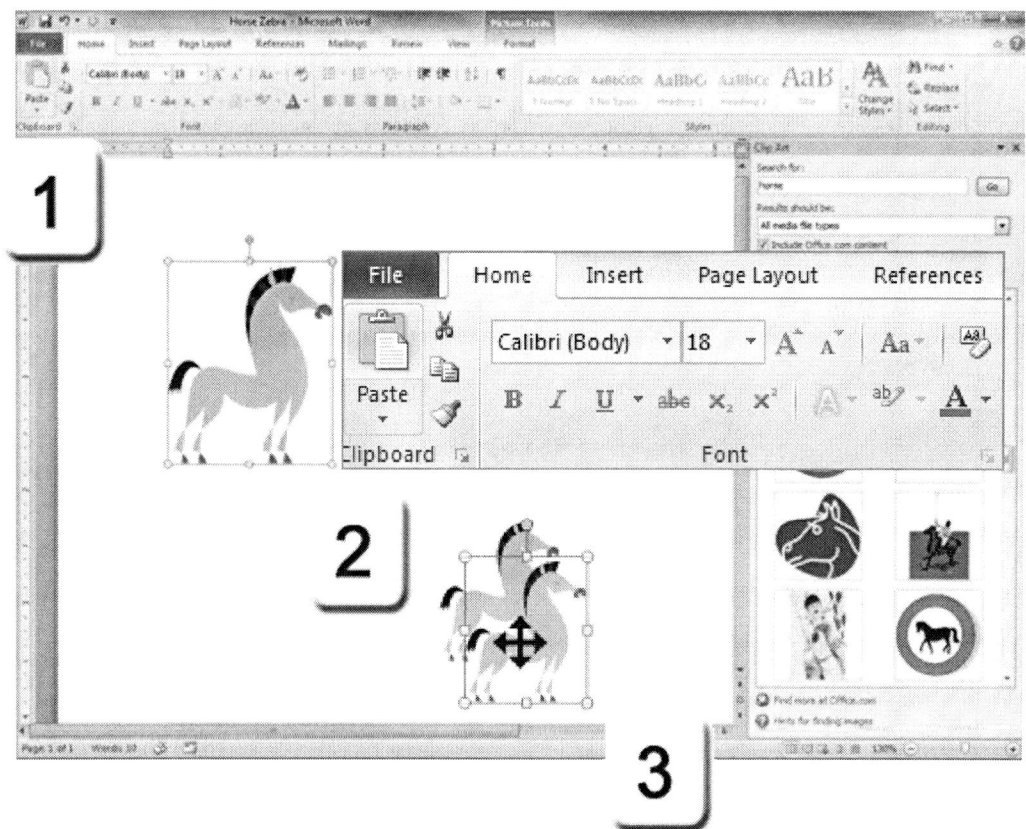

## Formatting Text with Styles

The previous pages introduced basic options for adding text and pictures. The next pages show how to use **Styles** to format the text.

**Before You Begin:** If you were working on the horses and zebras lesson, you can close your document.

Go to **File-> Close.**
When you are prompted to **Save** your document, please click **Don't' Save.**
This was just a practice page.

### 1. Try it: Open a New Document
Go to **File->New.**
Click on **Blank Document.**

Keep going..

File -> New-> Blank Document

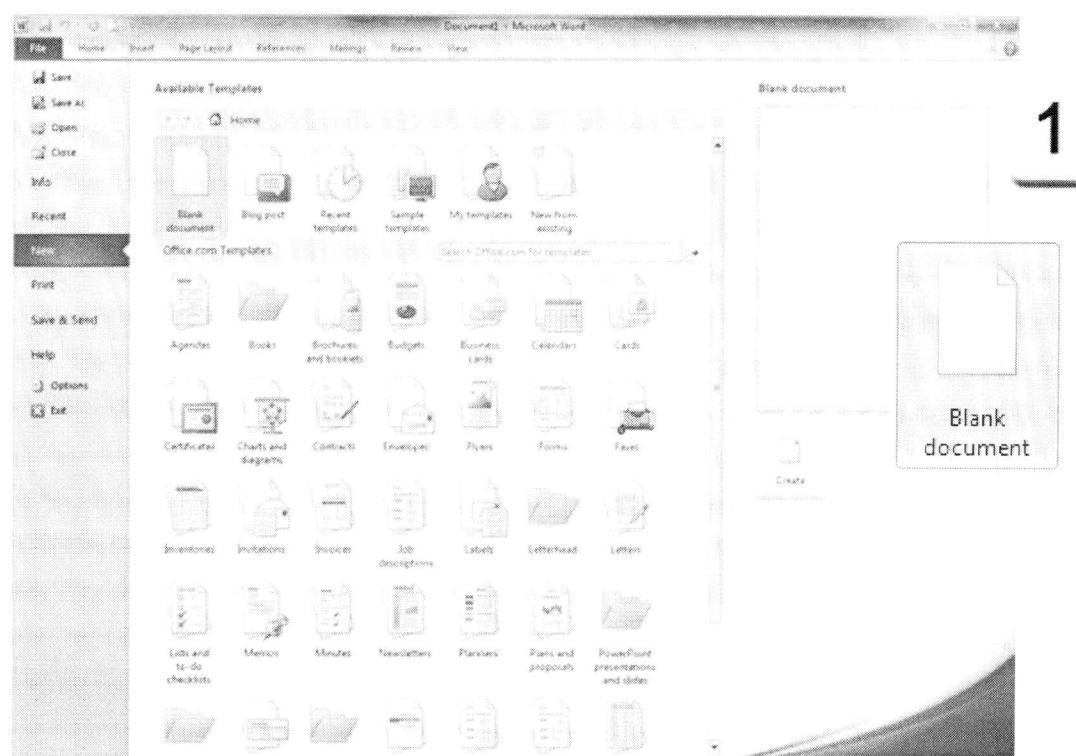

1

Exam 77-881: Microsoft Word 2010 Core
2. Formatting Content
2-1. Apply font and paragraph attributes: Use Styles

## Enter Some Sample Text

**2. Try it: Copy and Paste the Picture**
Please type the following sample text:

Charlotte's Website
123 Main Street
Brighton, Michigan 48116

From the Farm to your Table-That's Fresh!

For Immediate Release
Charlotte's Website, a family owned farm in our community, has announced that they will be launching a virtual Farmers Market online. Please feel free to call us. More information is available at our website.

Keep going...

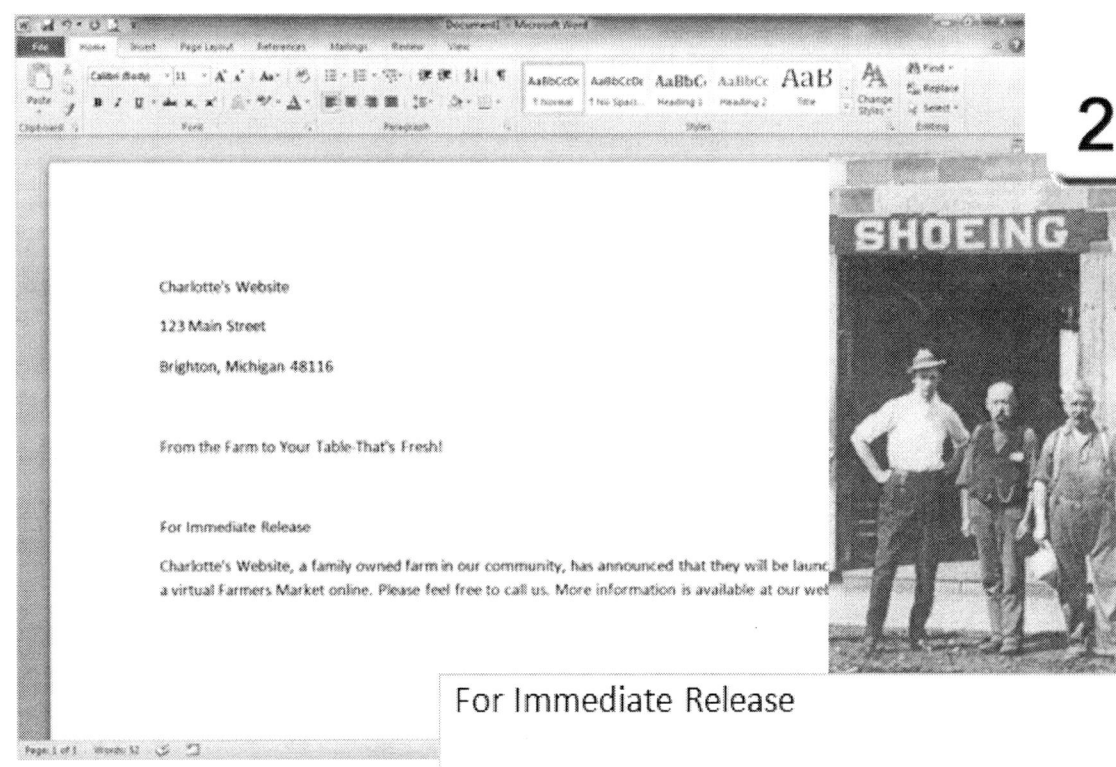

Exam 77-881: Microsoft Word 2010 Core
2. Formatting Content
2-1. Apply font and paragraph attributes: Use Styles

# Format the Text with Styles

The **Styles** can be found on the Home Ribbon. Microsoft Office 2010 has Live Preview: As you run your mouse over the Styles you will see how your text will look.

**3. Try it: Format the Text with Styles**
Select the text: For Immediate Release
Go to **Home ->Style.**
Click on **Heading 1.**

**What Do You See?** The selected text will be formatted as a **Heading 1 Style.** The Style includes the Type Font, Size and Color.

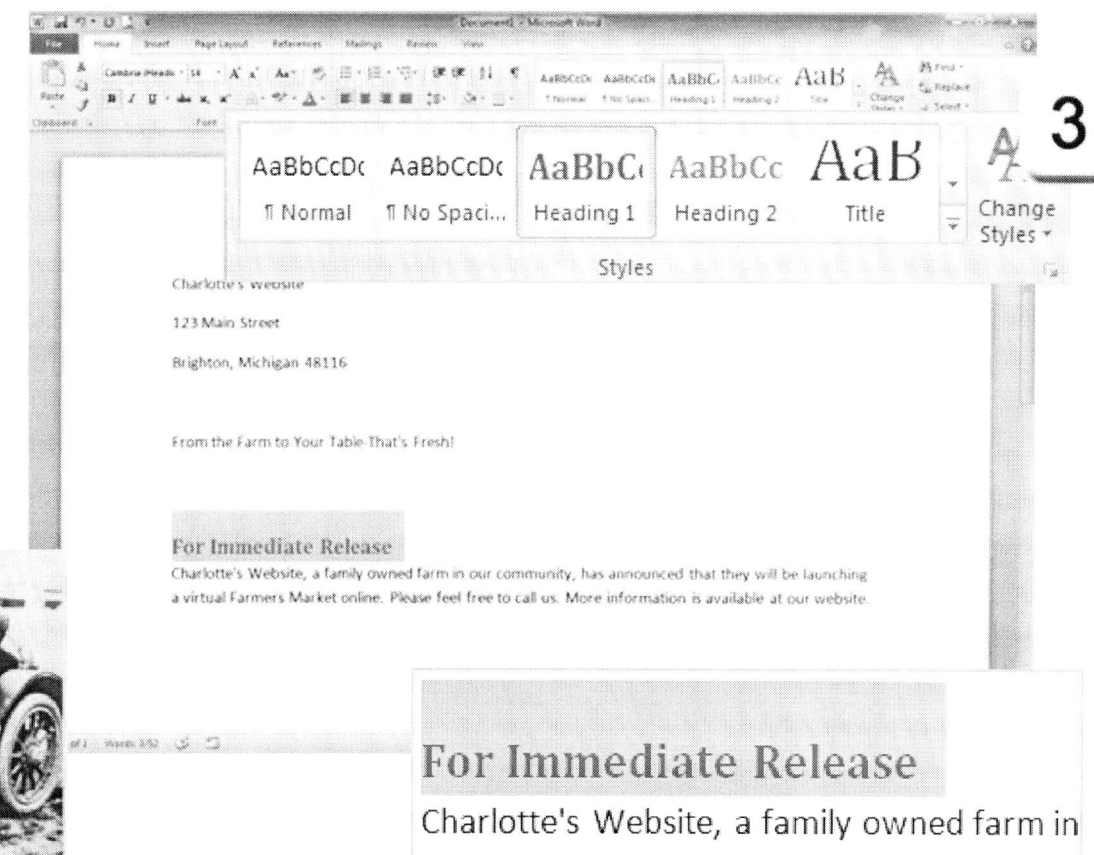

Exam 77-881: Microsoft Word 2010 Core
2. Formatting Content
2-1. Apply font and paragraph attributes: Use Styles

## Additional Styles

**4. Try This, Too: Format the Title**
**Select** the following text:

Charlotte's Website
123 Main Street
Brighton, Michigan 48116

Go to **Home ->Style.**
Select the **Title** style from the library.

**What Do You See?** The selected text will be formatted as a Title Style. The Style-Type Font, Size and Color- is different from the Heading 1 Style.

Home -> Styles-> Title

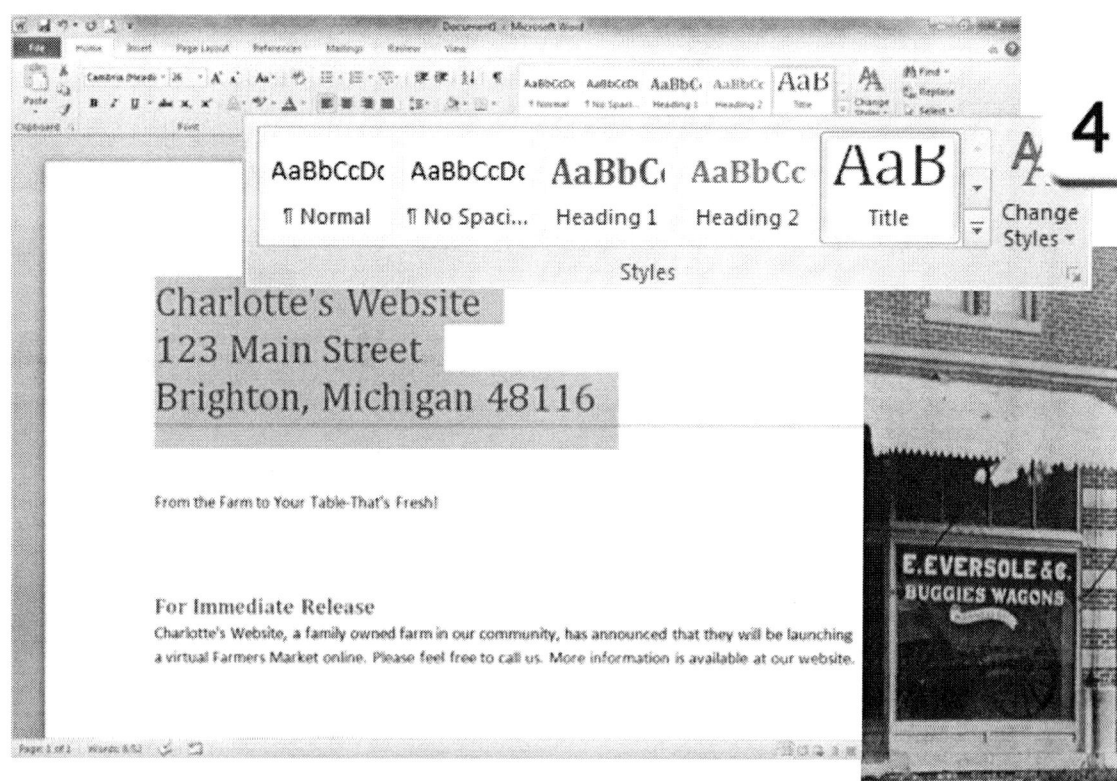

Exam 77-881: Microsoft Word 2010 Core
2. Formatting Content
2-1. Apply font and paragraph attributes: Use Styles

## The Style Library
Microsoft Word 2010 includes many, many more Styles. Here is how you can find and use the **Style Library**.

**Before You Begin:** Look on the right side of the Styles for the Arrows. As you hover your mouse over the down arrow, you should see the word **More.**

### 5. Try it: Find More Styles
**Select** the Text: From the Farm to Your Table- That's Fresh.

Go to **Home ->Styles**.

Click on **More**.

Select the **Intense Quote** style**.**

**What Do You See?** The **Style Library** displays about a dozen different **Styles**. Each Style in the Library shows an preview of the formatting.

For example, the **Intense Quote** is formatted 11 pt Bold, Italic and Blue. This Style includes an underline as well.

Home -> Styles-> More

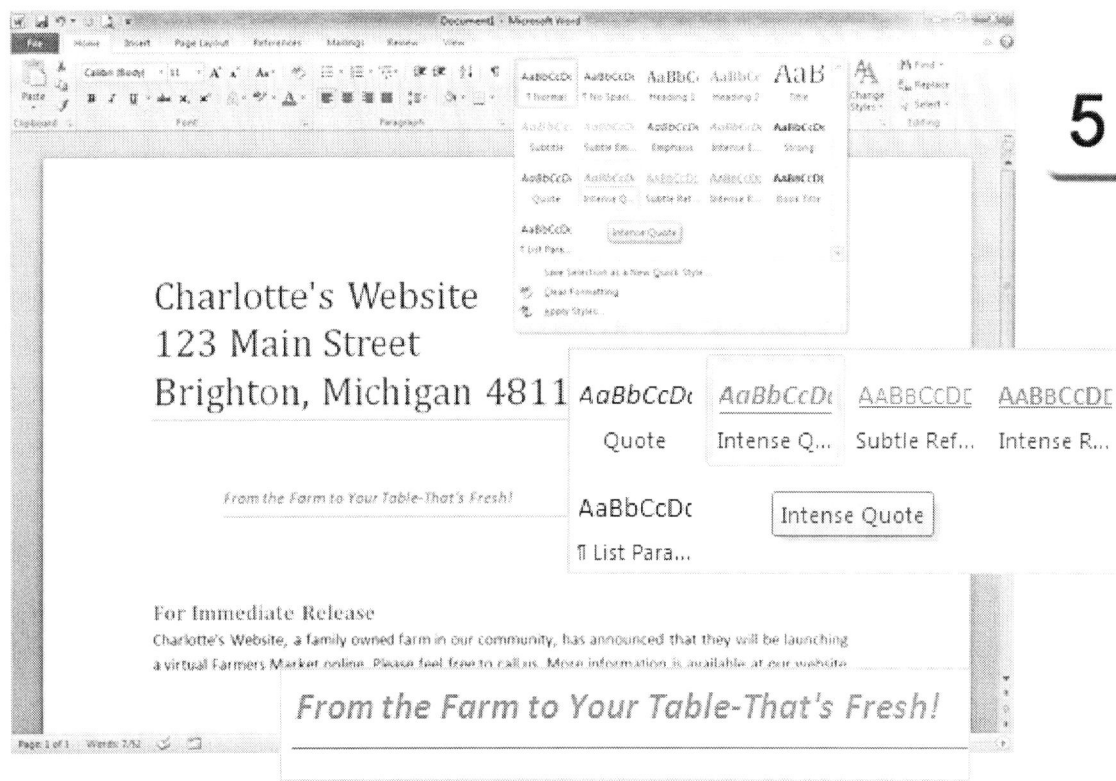

5

Exam 77-881: Microsoft Word 2010 Core
2. Formatting Content
2-1. Apply font and paragraph attributes: Use Styles

## Summary for Working with Text and Pictures

The goal of this beginning lesson was to become familiar with the text and graphic tools. The focus was on the Home Ribbon, and the basic options in the **Clipboard** (Copy and Paste), and **Font** Groups. (Big, Bold and Blue).

**Please close this file.** You do NOT have to save this practice document when you are prompted.

You done good.
You get the cookie.

Home -> Styles

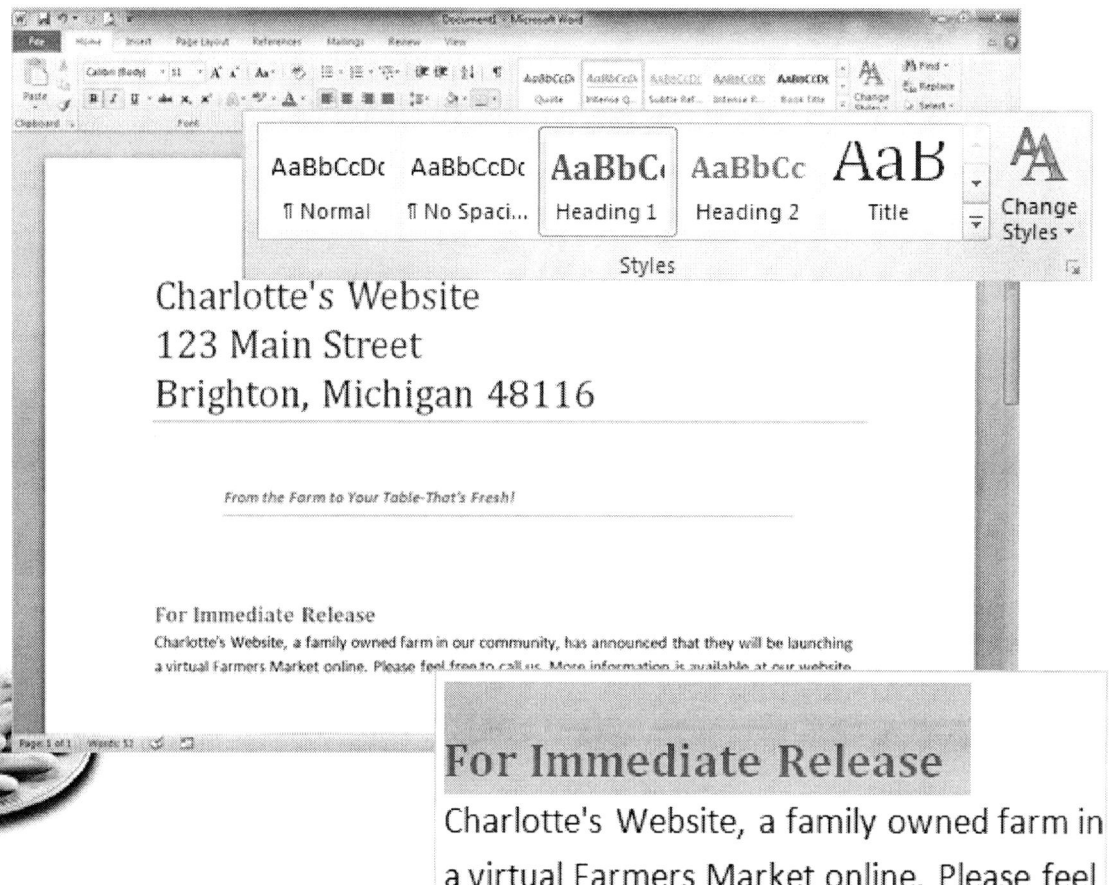

# Practice Activities

## Lesson: Horses and Zebras

**Before You Begin:** Start Microsoft Word 2010. You should see a new, blank document.

**Try This: Do the following steps**
1. Insert a photo of a cat from the ClipArt gallery.
2. Insert an illustration of a mouse from the ClipArt gallery.
3. Insert a picture of a dog from the ClipArt gallery
4. Format the Position of dog to be Top Left with Square Wrapping
5. Format the Text Wrapping around the mouse and dog to be Middle with Square Wrapping.
6. Format the Text Wrapping around the dog to be In Line with Text.
7. Resize the pictures so the dog is the largest and the mouse is the smallest.
8. Copy the mouse and paste it three times.
9. Add the following text: The dog ran after the cat who was chasing the mouse.
10. Copy and paste your text three times.
11. Add the text: The mouse just wanted some cheese.
12. Drag and drop the sentence "The mouse just wanted some cheese" to be after the first sentence.
13. Close Microsoft Word. When you are prompted, click Don't Save.
This is a practice document that you do not have to submit.

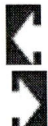

# Test Yourself

1. How do you turn on (activate) the Picture Tools Ribbon?
a. Go to File→ Ribbon→ Picture Tools
b. Select a picture
c. Go to Insert→ Ribbon and select More Options

Tip: Beginning Word, page 52

2. Which type of arrow means resize?
a. 4- headed
b. 2- headed
c. Normal arrow

Tip: Beginning Word, page 53

3. Which of the following can be copied and pasted?
(Select all correct answers)
a. Text
b. Pictures

Tip: Beginning Word, page 54

4. You can format the position of a picture to a designated place on the page, such as bottom center or top right.
a. True
b. False

Tip: Beginning Word, page 52

5. Which group includes the commands Copy and Paste?
a. Home
b. Clipboard
c. Copy and Paste

Tip: Beginning Word, page 47

6. What media types are available in Microsoft's Clip Art Gallery?
(Select all that apply)
a. Illustrations
b. Photographs
c. Videos
d. Audio

Tip: Beginning Word, page 50

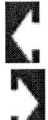

 **Word 2010: Working with Text**

# Mice and Men

## Beginning Word Objectives

**In this lesson, you will learn how to:**

1. Identify and use the Mini Toolbar

2. Identify and use Paste Options

3. Use Spelling and Grammar checking tools

4. Use AutoText, AutoCorrect, Spelling & Grammar Tools

5. Save a document using Office2007-2010 format

6. Save a document as a Office2003 format

7. Use the Save As command to create a copy of a document

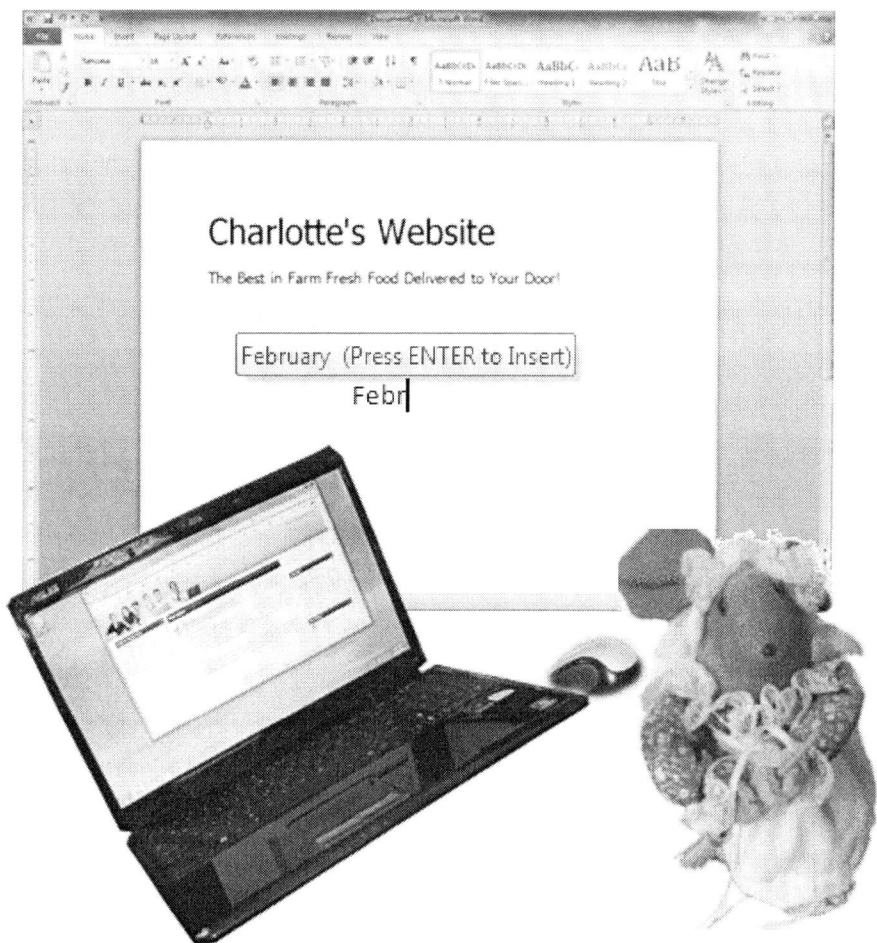

# Lesson 4: Mice and Men

## 1. Readings
Read Lesson 4 in the Beginning Word guide, page 63-92.

## Project
A sample document that you do not need to save.

## Downloads
There are NO downloads for this lesson.

## 2. Practice
Complete the Practice Activity on page.91

## 3. Assessment
Review the Test questions on page 92.

**Home**

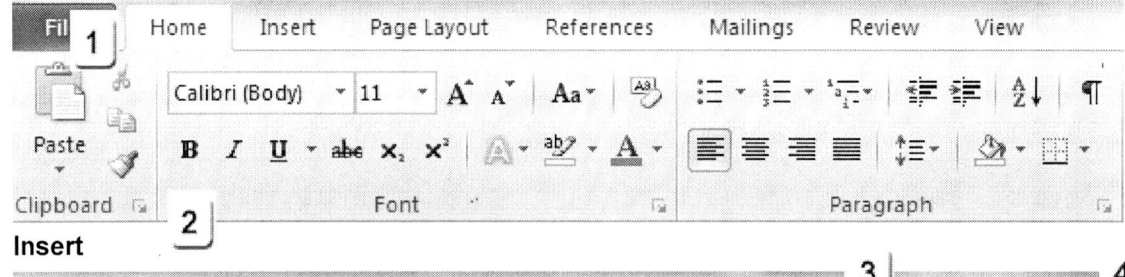

**Insert**

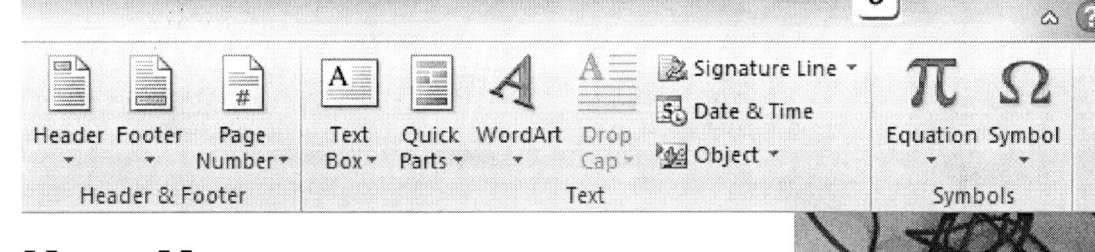

# Menu Maps
This lesson demonstrates options on the **Home** Ribbon.
1. Home->Paste, page 68
2. Home-> Clipboard, page 69

This lesson introduces options on the **Insert** Ribbon.
3. Insert->Equation, page 74
4. Insert-> Symbol, page 75

# Mice and Men

You have to talk with your computer. In one way or form, you need to use an interface to change your words into actions in the digital world. Microsoft Office can be used for dictation, but the majority of our computer interaction is with a **mouse**. In this lesson, the focus will be on what you can think and do with the mouse. **Start** the **Program** Microsoft **Word**.

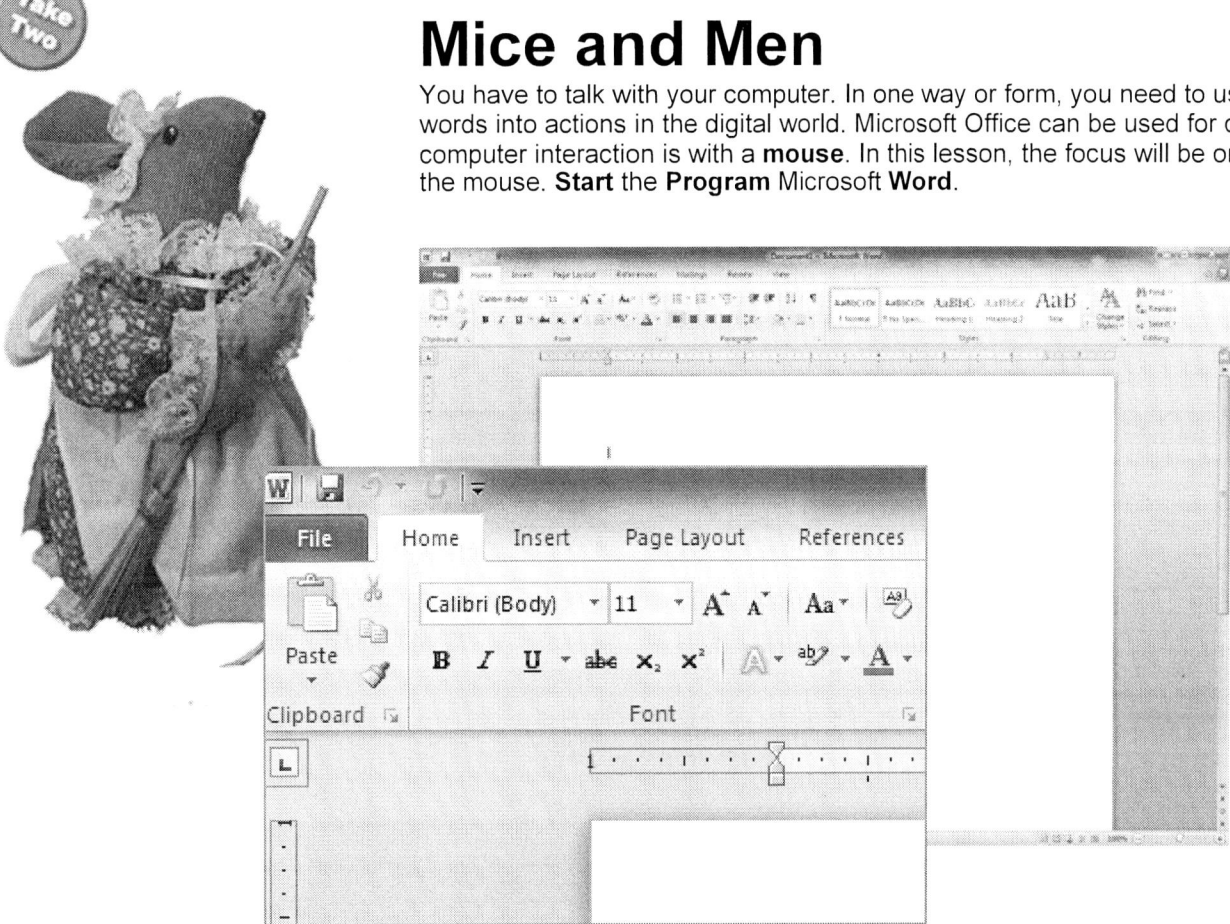

**What do you see from the top of the screen?** Is there a Title Bar that says Microsoft Word? Yes.

Is there a **Home** Ribbon with the **Clipboard, Font and Paragraph** Groups? Yes.

If your screen looks similar to the example on this page, then you are ready to get started.

## Begin with the text
Enter the following sample text.

### 1. Enter the name
**Type**: Charlotte's Website
**Select** the text.
Go to **Home** and select Tahoma, 36 pt

### 2. Enter the marketing text
**Type**: The Best in Farm Fresh Food
Delivered to Your Door!
**Select** the text
Go to **Home** and select Tahoma, 16 pt

Home -> Font

Exam 77-881: Microsoft Word 2010 Core
2. Formatting Content
2-1. Apply font and paragraph attributes

## The Mini Toolbar

When you select text, you may see a **Mini Toolbar.** It looks transparent until you rub your mouse over any of the formatting commands.

You can use this toolbar to edit the Font, text size, alignment, color, indents and even bullets.

**Try it: Format the text**
**Select** the text: Charlotte's
Look for the **Mini Toolbar**
**Change** the size and color: Tahoma, 36 point, Bold and Blue.

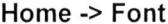

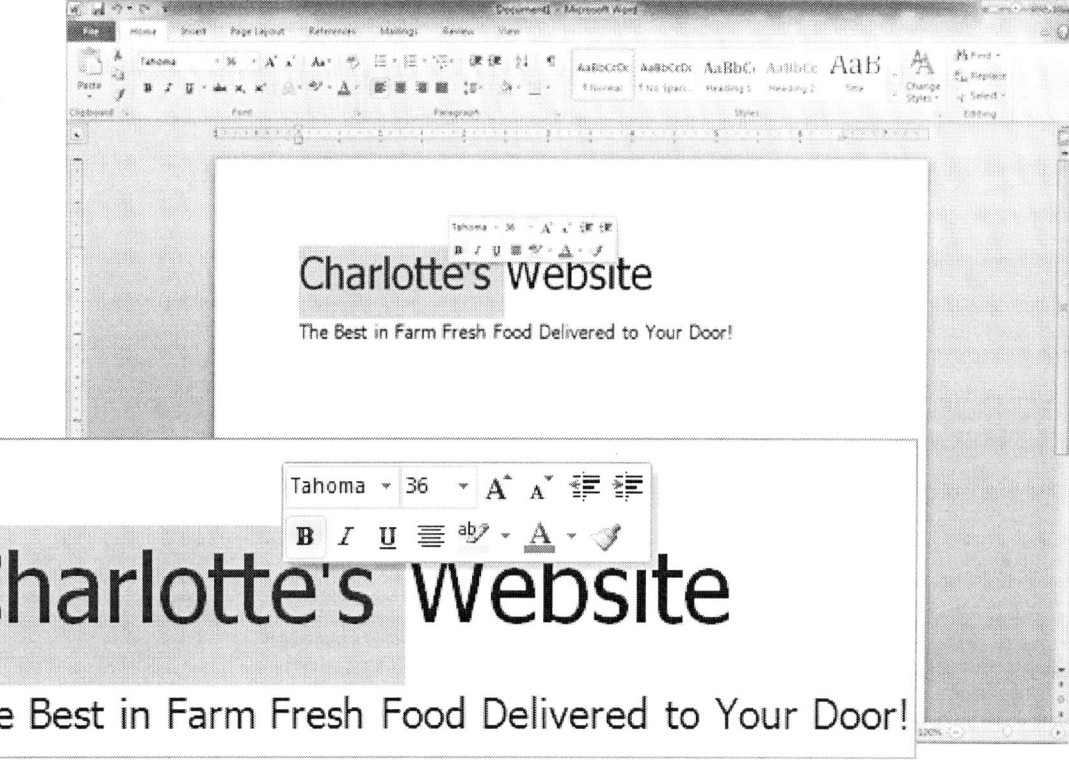

Exam 77-881: Microsoft Word 2010 Core
2. Formatting Content
2-1. Apply font and paragraph attributes

## Paste Options

When you copy and paste text, you may see a small **Clipboard** pop up. There are three formatting choices in these **Paste Options**.

### Try it: Paste Options

Select the text: Charlotte's Website

The Best in Farm Fresh Food Delivered to Your Door!
Copy and Paste the text. (Look for the Clipboard pop up.)

 **Keep Source Formatting:**

In the example on this page, the word "Charlotte" would paste with all of the formatting that you copied: big, bold and colorful.

 **Match Destination Formatting:**

The word "Charlotte" would paste with the default font, size and color for Microsoft Word: Calibri, 11 pt, black.

 **Keep Text Only:**

This option strips away any formatting you may have copied. This is a good way to simplify the text you copy from the Internet.

**Home ->Paste**

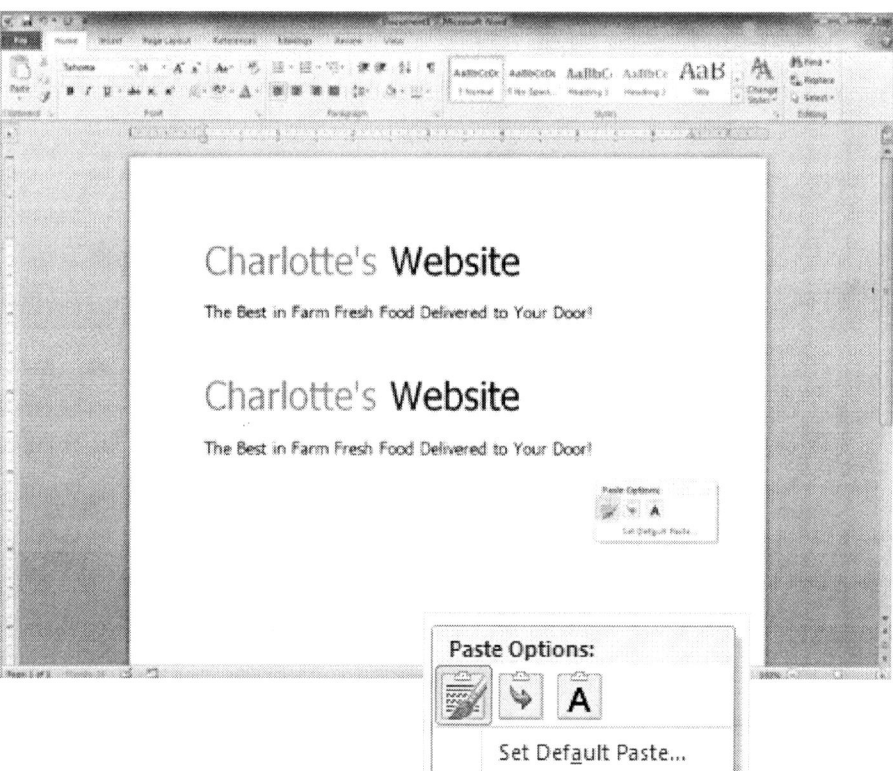

Exam 77-881: Microsoft Word 2010 Core
2. Formatting Content
2-1. Apply font and paragraph attributes

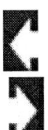

## Paste One, Paste All

The **Clipboard** is one of the oldest helper applications in the computer. You can use the Clipboard to copy and paste a paragraph or a picture from one program to another.

**1 Try it: Use the Clipboard**
Double click the word: Charlotte's.
Go to **Home -> Clipboard**. Click on the small option arrow to the right of the label for the Clipboard.

**2. What Do You See?** A new pane will open on the left side of Microsoft Word. Each item that you copied will be listed here. Click on any item to paste it. You can also **Paste All**, if you wish.

**3. What Else Do You See?** The Clipboard can display the text that you copy as well as the pictures. Sometimes, the image is too large. In that case, you may see an alert in the corner of your screen

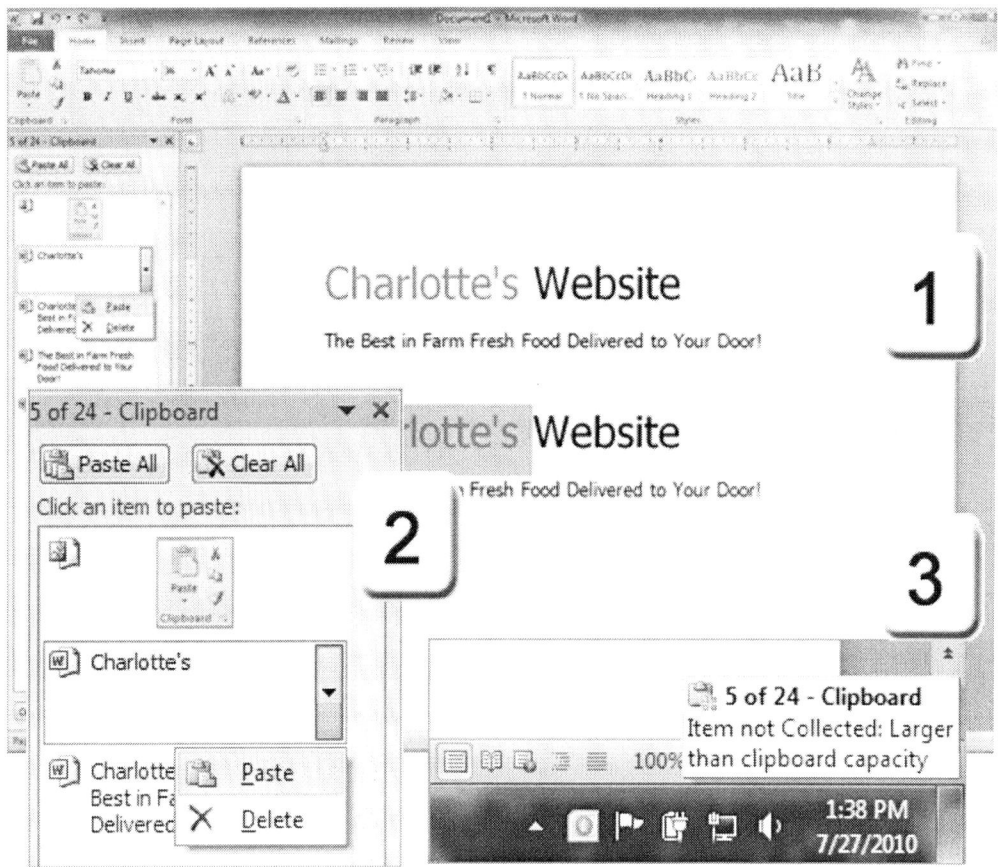

Exam 77-881: Microsoft Word 2010 Core
2. Formatting Content
2-1. Apply font and paragraph attributes

## Spelling and Grammar

Microsoft Office includes a dictionary. It compares your spelling and grammar as you are typing. If your words do not match ones in the dictionary, you will see a red wavy line. That's the **Spell Checker**.

If your sentence has a structural problem with the grammar, say the subject and the verb do not match, then you will see a green wavy line. That's the **Grammar Checker.**

**Try it: Spell and Grammar Check**
**Type** the following two sentences:
We was going to school.
We saw Charlotte Sergayiff.

Please include all of the punctuation!

Click **Enter** on your keyboard. What do you see?

**Review ->Spelling and Grammar**

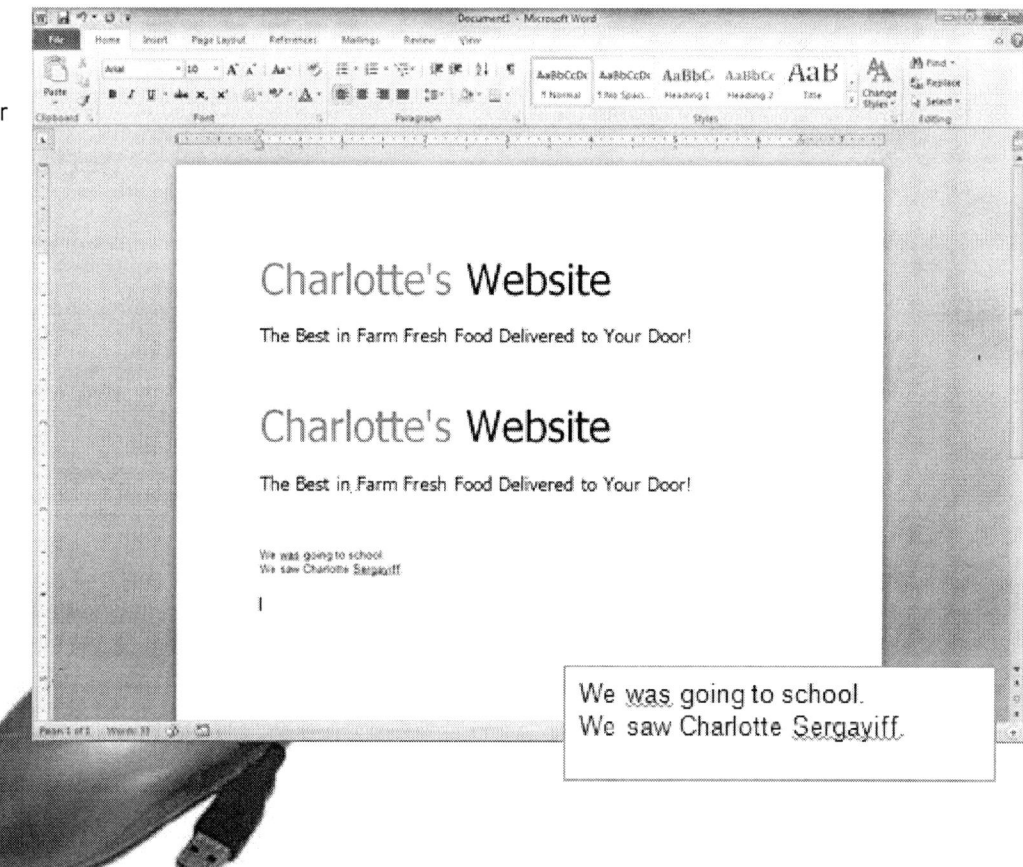

Exam 77-881: Microsoft Word 2010 Core
5. Proofreading documents
5-1. Validate content by using spelling and grammar checking options

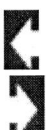

## Spelling and Grammar

Everything in a computer has a left and a right mouse action. What does the left mouse button do?

What mouse button to you use to **click** on Start?
Say left.
What mouse button do you use to **double click**?
Say left.
What mouse button do you use to **drag and drop**?
Say left.

**Left gives you action:** Select, open, and move.
**Right gives you options:** A short list of choices.

**Try it: Right click the Grammar**
Select **were**, the correct grammar from the list of options, by clicking on it with your Left mouse.

**Try it: Right click the Spell Check**
Sometimes, you will see a few suggestions from the dictionary. If the name is spelled correctly but does not appear on the list of options, click on **Add to dictionary** with your Left mouse.

Keep going...

**Review ->Spelling and Grammar**

Exam 77-881: Microsoft Word 2010 Core
5. Proofreading documents
5-1. Validate content by using spelling and grammar checking options

File ->Options ->Proofing ->AutoCorrect

## AutoText, AutoCorrect and Other Fancy Mouse Options

**AutoText:** Microsoft Office also notices common words and offers to fill them in for you. The most obvious example is the names of the months.

**Try This: Play With the AutoText**

What do you see as you type the word February?

AutoText also inserts formatted symbols. If you type (tm), Microsoft Office will format the text as a superscript. If you type :) Microsoft Office will substitute a smiley face. It is the Computer Mama's understanding that the symbol next to the smiley face means SmartAss, which would be accurate for her.

**AutoCorrect:** Microsoft Office automatically corrects a long, long list of the most common spelling mistakes. Prove it to yourself. Type: hte and watch the letters when you press the space bar.

Keep going...

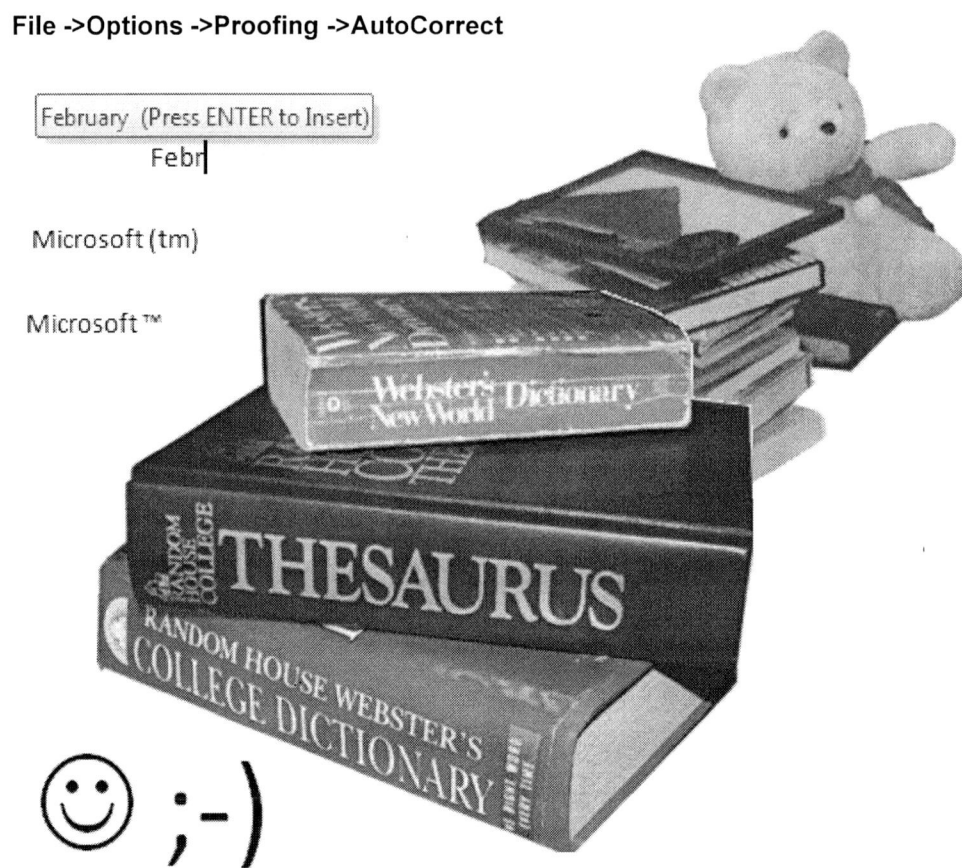

February (Press ENTER to Insert)

Febr

Microsoft (tm)

Microsoft ™

Exam 77-881: Microsoft Word 2010 Core
5. Proofreading documents
5-1. Validate content by using spelling and grammar checking options

## Math AutoCorrect

There are several ways to document your math equations in Word. Microsoft Office 2010 has an extensive library of equations and symbols.

### 1. Try it: Type a Math Symbol
Please open a blank document.
Type the following examples:
\angle
\approx
\degree
\Alpha
\Omega

**2. What Do You See?** Word substituted the right math symbol as you typed the text.

**What If It Doesn't Work?** There is an option that turns the Math AutoCorrect on or off. This option is demonstrated in a few more pages. Keep going, please...

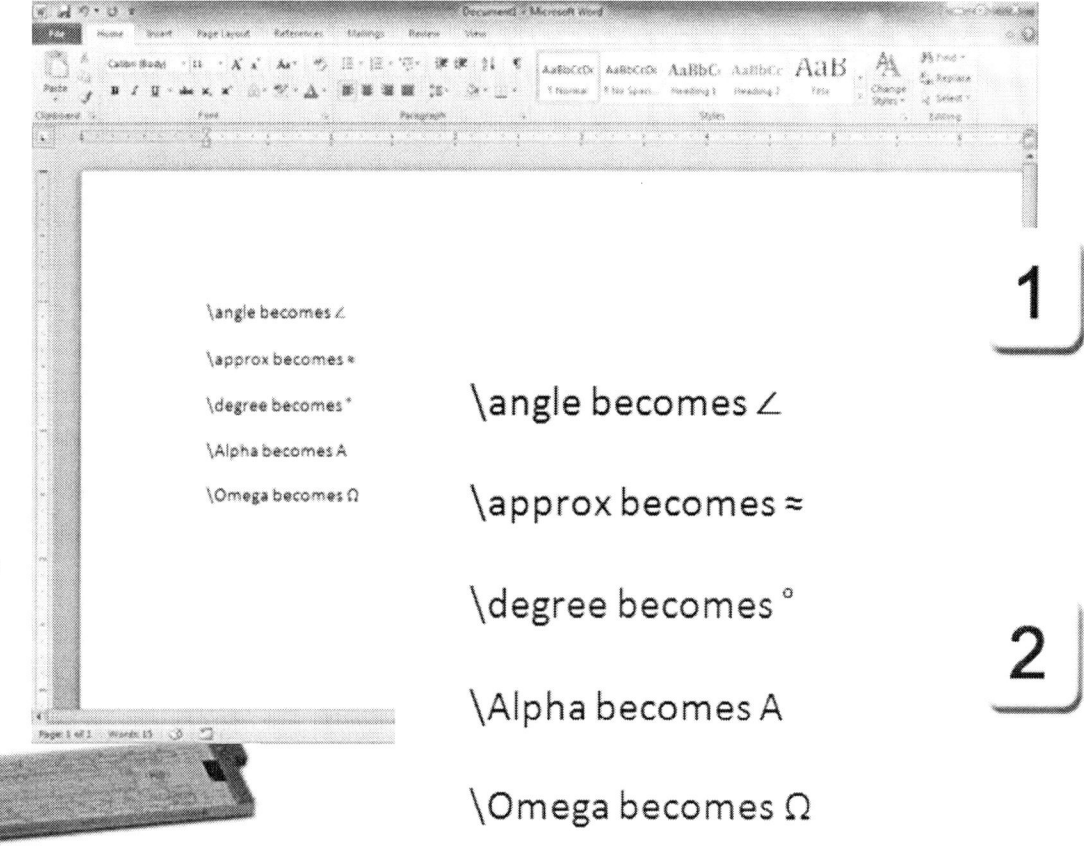

\angle becomes ∠

\approx becomes ≈

\degree becomes °

\Alpha becomes A

\Omega becomes Ω

Exam 77-881: Microsoft Word 2010 Core
5. Proofreading documents
5-1. Validate content by using spelling and grammar checking options

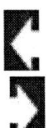

## Insert Equations

In addition to the math symbols that substitute as you type, Microsoft Word 2010 offers equations that you can edit.

**1. Try This: Insert An Equation**
Go to **Insert-> Symbols->Equation.**

**2. What Do You See?** There should be a list of equations including the Area of a Circle, Binomial Theorem and, yes indeed, it is the Pythagorean Theorem for triangles.

**3. Try This, Too: Insert An New Equation**
Go to **Insert-> Symbols->Equation.**
Click on **Insert New Equation.**

**What Do You See?** There should be a new **Equation Block** that you can edit.

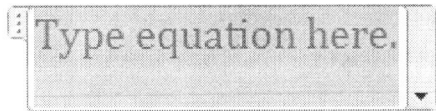

**Insert-> Symbols->Equation**

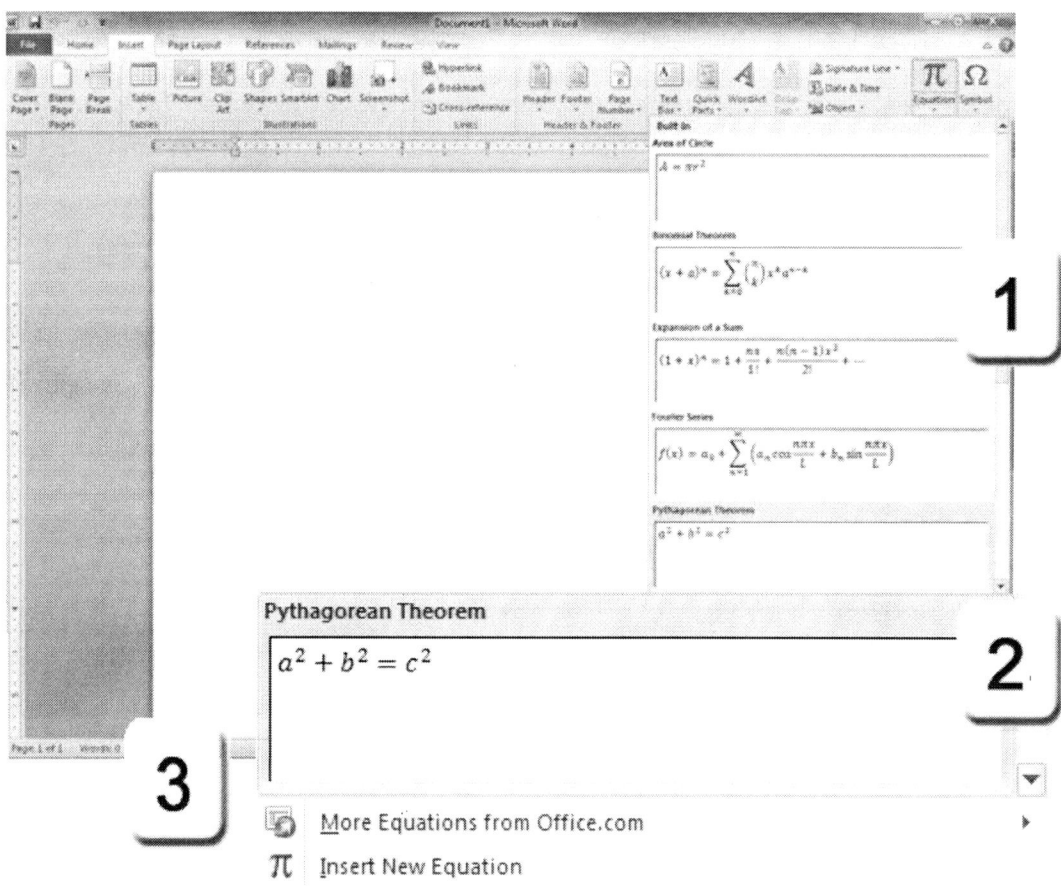

Exam 77-881: Microsoft Word 2010 Core
5. Proofreading documents
5-1. Validate content by using spelling and grammar checking options

## Insert Symbols

Many of the math and business symbols can be found in the **Symbol** library.

**1. Try This: Insert A Symbol**
Go to **Insert-> Symbol.**

**2. What Do You See?** There should be math symbols, Greek letters, as well as copyright, trademark and bullets.

\angle becomes ∠

\approx becomes ≈

\degree becomes °

\Alpha becomes A

\Omega becomes Ω

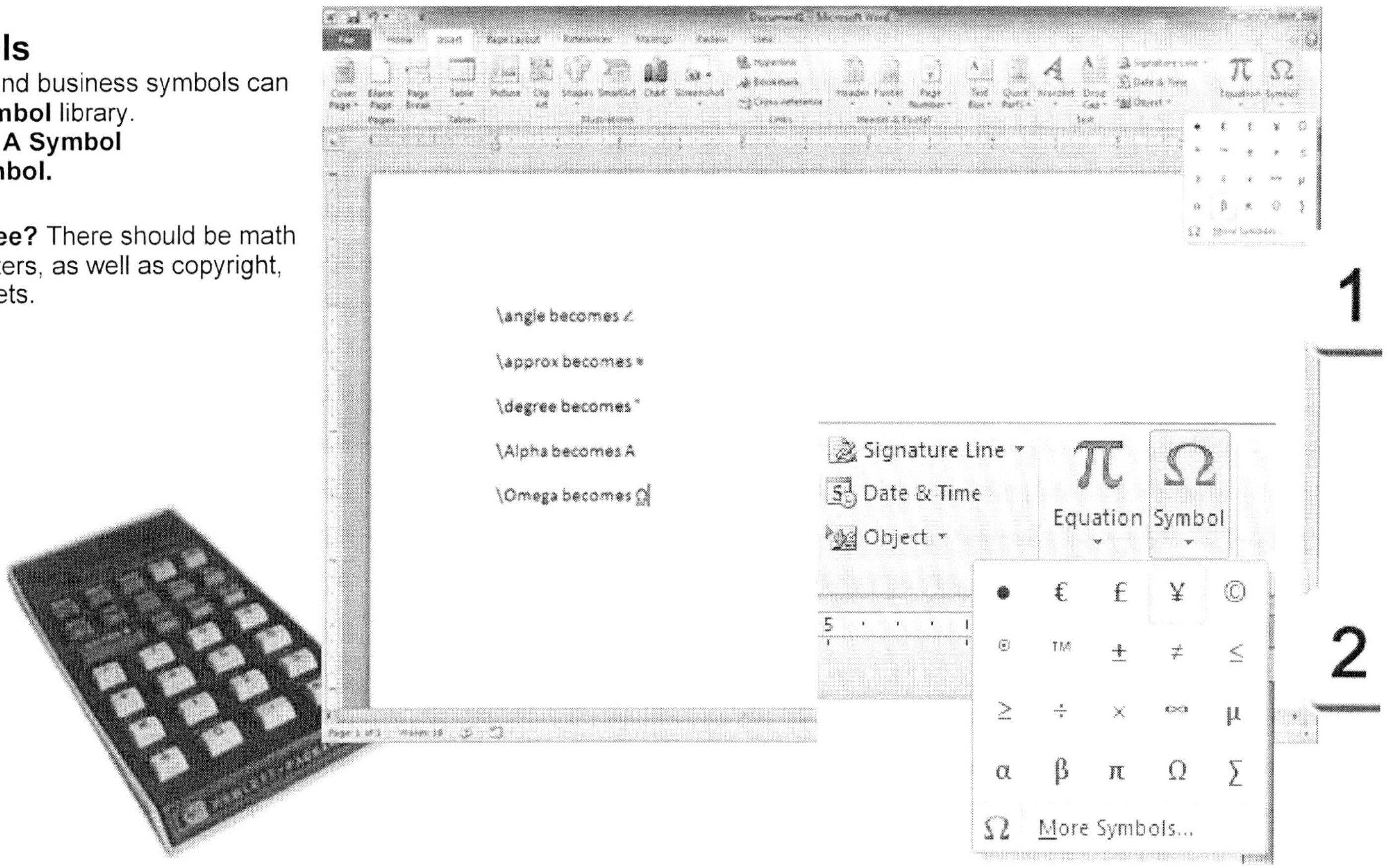

Exam 77-881: Microsoft Word 2010 Core
5. Proofreading documents
5-1. Validate content by using spelling and grammar checking options

File ->Options

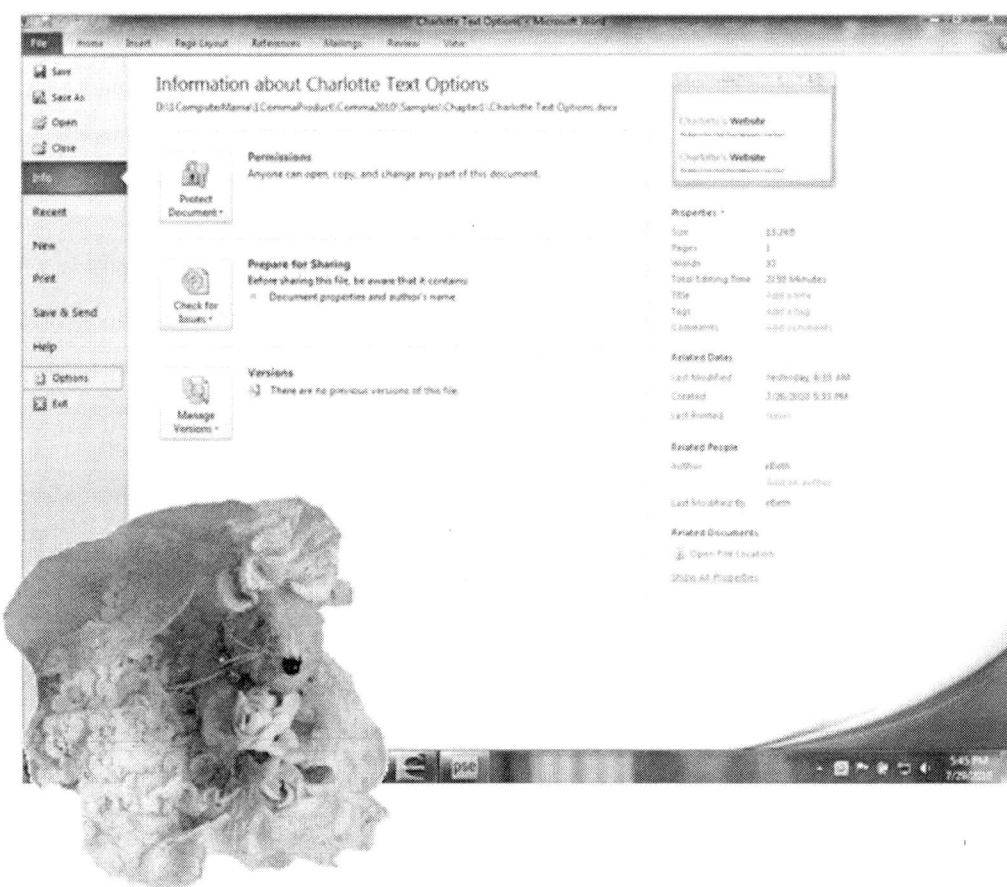

# Word Options

Where does Microsoft Word keep these AutoCorrect words, AutoText entries, Formulas and Symbols?

**Try it: Review the Word Options**

Go to **File** in the upper left corner of the Home Ribbon and click on **Options.**

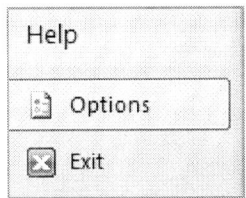

You will be taken to the **Word Options**:

Popular

Display

Proofing

Save

Advanced

Select **Proofing** and review the defaults.

Exam 77-881: Microsoft Word 2010 Core
5. Proofreading documents
5-2. Configure AutoCorrect settings

## AutoCorrect Options

By Default, Microsoft Word 2010 has several options that help you create professional documents.

**Try it: Review the AutoCorrect Options**
Word is programmed to ignore:
UPPERCASE
Word with numbers
Internet addresses

Word will automatically look for:
Spelling
Grammar
Repeated words

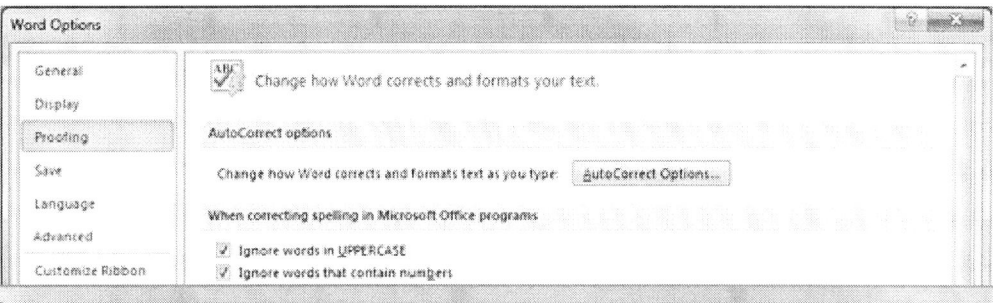

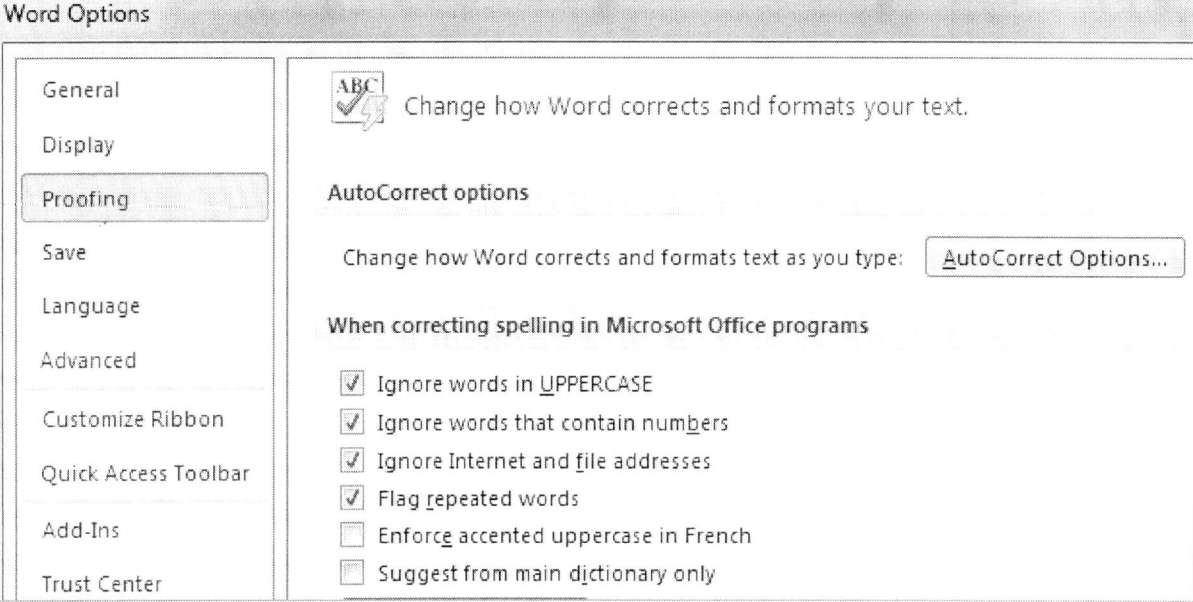

Exam 77-881: Microsoft Word 2010 Core
5. Proofreading documents
5-2. Configure AutoCorrect settings

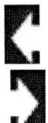

## AutoCorrect Options

At the top of the **AutoCorrect** page is a list of **Capitalization** options. Microsoft Word capitalizes:

First letter of sentences

First letter in a table cell

Names of days

**Try It: Replace text as you type:**

Earlier in this lesson we played with a few symbols and emoticons. This is the page that lets you add and change the AutoCorrect words. For example, if you type ;) it will be replaced with a smiley face.

You can add a phrase to AutoCorrect and have Microsoft Office spell it out for you automatically. The buttons are pretty obvious: you can **ADD** or **REMOVE** any text in this list.

**Memo to self: AutoCorrect is a productivity tool.** AutoCorrect quickly replaces "hte" with "the." However, as with all programming, it is a good idea to review the corrections and make sure that it makes sense.

**File ->Options -> Proofing ->AutoCorrect Options**

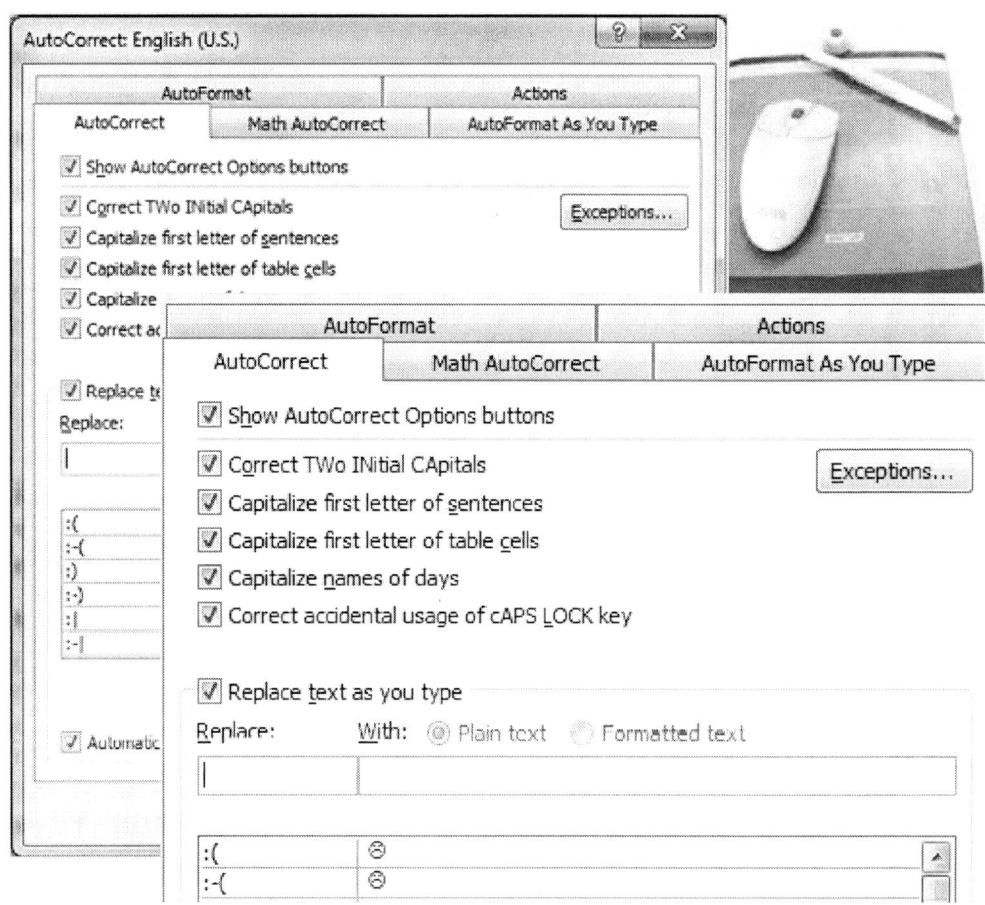

## AutoCorrect Exceptions

There are always exceptions to the rule. AutoCorrect can include a list of word you do NOT want automatically corrected. .

**Try it: Review the Exceptions**
If you are not already on this page, please...
Go to **File->Options-> Proofing,**
Click on the **AutoCorrect** tab.
Click on **Exceptions**.

**What Do You See?** Microsoft Word 2010 has a long list of AutoCorrect exceptions. For example, the software is programmed to skip the capital letters after common abbreviations such as abbr, tbs., and tbsp.

**File ->Options -> Proofing ->AutoCorrect Options ->Exceptions**

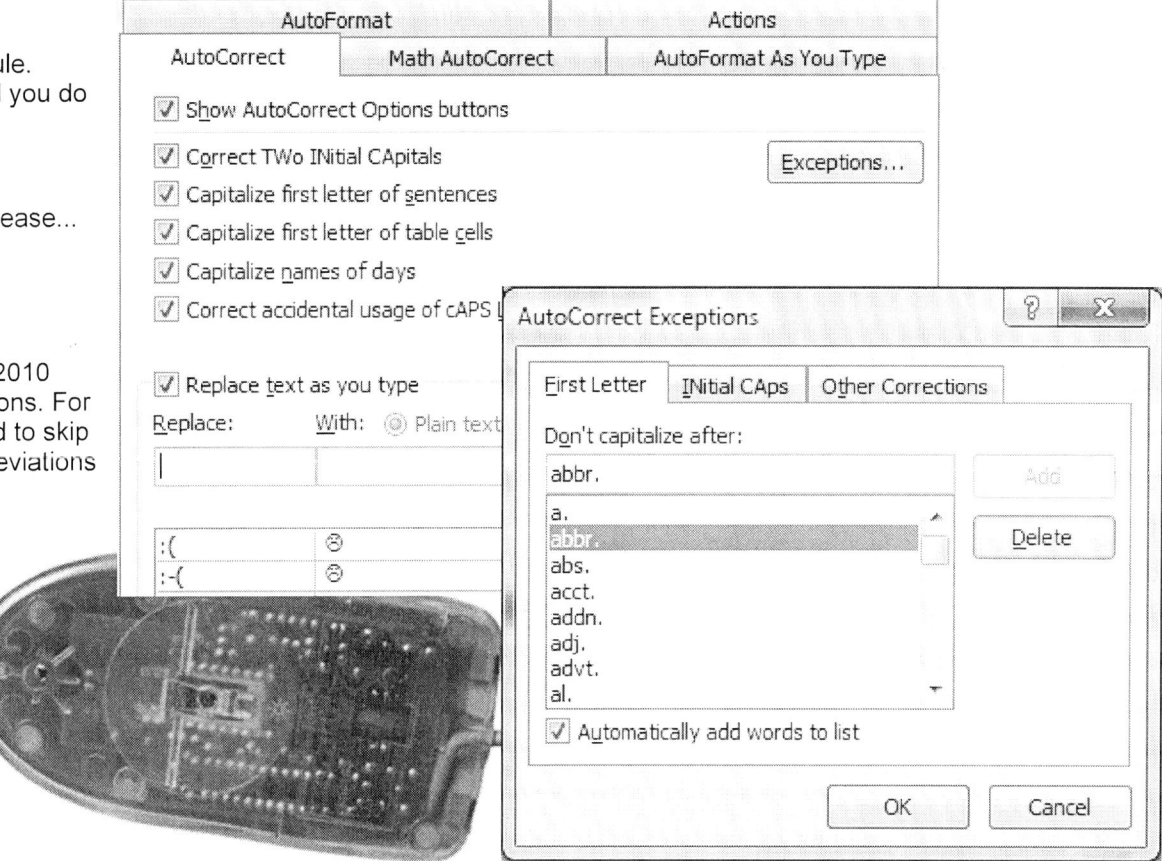

Exam 77-881: Microsoft Word 2010 Core
5. Proofreading documents
5-2. Configure AutoCorrect settings

File ->Word Options -> Proofing ->AutoCorrect

## Math AutoCorrect Options

Earlier, we reviewed the Math Equations and Functions. Many professions use mathematical symbols in reports and documentation. Prior to Office 2007, you had to **Insert** a **Symbol** and select a letter from a set of custom Fonts named Dingbats or Symbols.

**Math AutoCorrect** has an extensive list of replacements for math, chemistry and engineering. This list is adaptable, too. You can add or edit your own entries, same as with AutoCorrect.

Look for the check box to **Use Math AutoCorrect outside of the math regions**. This is an important option if you wish to type formulas and equations.

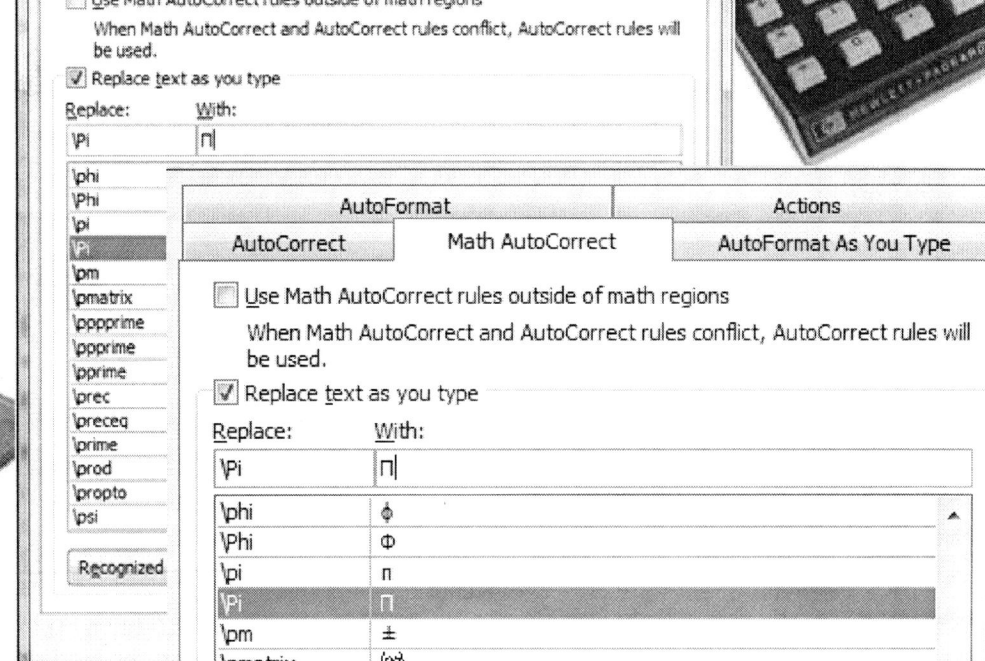

Exam 77-881: Microsoft Word 2010 Core
5. Proofreading documents
5-1. Validate content by using spelling and grammar checking options

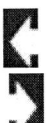

**File ->Options -> Proofing**

## Grammar Options

Microsoft Word 2010 has options for the **Grammar Checker** as well. You can choose if you are going strictly by the rules or not. For example, the phrase "A rose is a rose is a rose" is not misspelled, but it would probably be flagged by the Grammar Checker.

**1. Try it: Find the Grammar Options**
Go to **File ->Options -> Proofing**

**2. What Do You See?** The Grammar Checker will check the grammar as well as the spelling as you type. The **Writing Style** is marked **Grammar Only**.

Click on **Settings** to choose a different Writing Style.  Keep going...

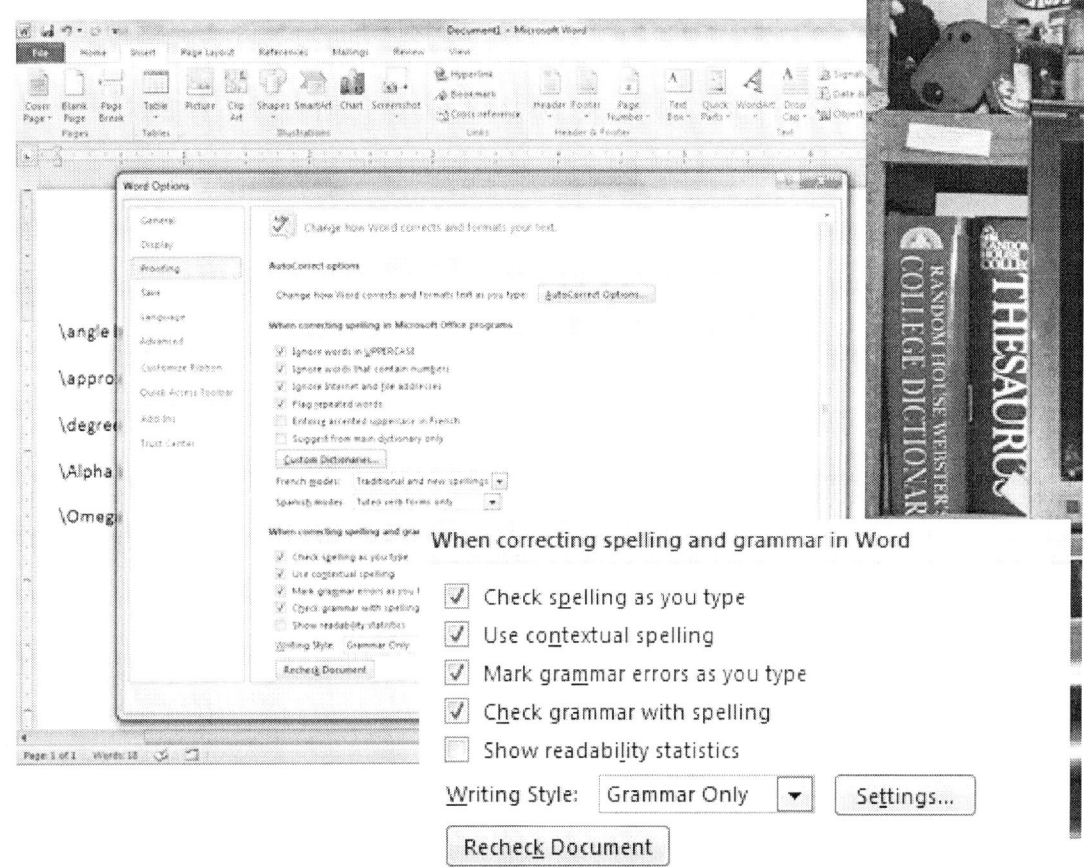

**When correcting spelling and grammar in Word**

- ☑ Check spelling as you type
- ☑ Use contextual spelling
- ☑ Mark grammar errors as you type
- ☑ Check grammar with spelling
- ☐ Show readability statistics

Writing Style: Grammar Only ▼ | Settings...

Recheck Document

Exam 77-887: Microsoft Word Expert 2010
1. Sharing and Maintaining Documents
1.1. Configure Word options.

## Grammar Settings

**Try it: Edit the Grammar Settings**
Go to **File ->Options -> Proofing.**
Find the Spelling and Grammar options.
Click on **Settings.**

**What Do You See?** By default, Microsoft
Word checks **Grammar Only**. Grammar
includes Capitalization, Fragments, Noun
phrases, even Questions and Punctuation

**Grammar and Style** checks for clichés and
jargon (Watch that tech talk!) and sentence
length (more than sixty words...hmmm that
leaves out Earnest Hemmingway.)

**File ->Options -> Proofing ->Settings**

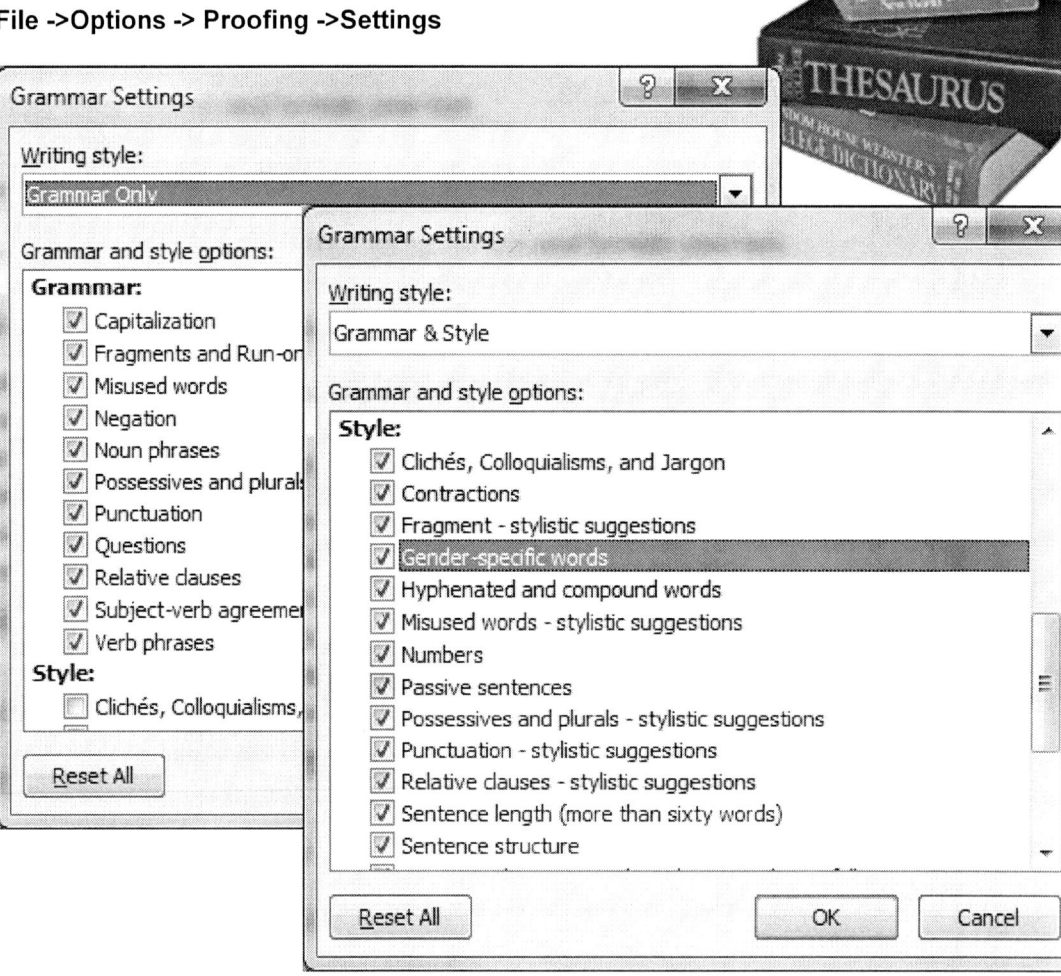

Exam 77-887: Microsoft Word Expert 2010
1. Sharing and Maintaining Documents
1.1. Configure Word options.

## Save Your Work

One of the most important things a newbie learns is how to save a file. The following pages demonstrate how to save a document.

Microsoft Word 2010 and 2007 have a different file format than the previous versions of Word. This lesson also shows how to use **Save As** to create version of your document that can be opened in Word 97-2003.

**Get A Clue:** Look at the top of the Title Bar. New documents are named Document 1, 2, etc. They are NOT saved. When you save a file you type a name and choose a place to save your work.

Keep going...

**File ->Save**

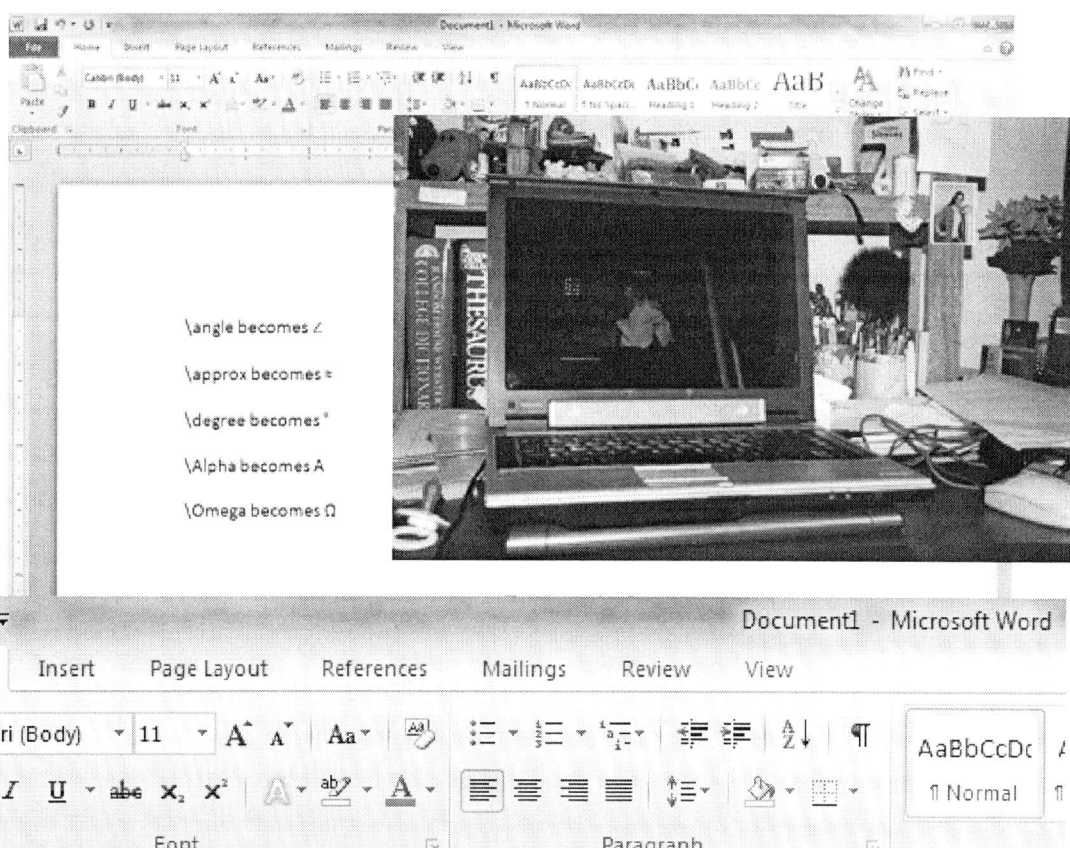

\angle becomes ∠

\approx becomes ≈

\degree becomes °

\Alpha becomes A

\Omega becomes Ω

Exam 77-881: Microsoft Word 2010 Core
1. Sharing and Maintaining Documents
1-5. Save a Document

## Save Your Document
**There are three parts to saving a file:**
1. Where are you saving it?
2. What are you naming it?
3. What are you doing? SAVE!

These are the steps to save your work and find a folder to keep it in.

**Try This: Save a document**
**Start Microsoft Word**
**Type your name**
Go to **File ->Save.**

Keep going...

**File ->Save**

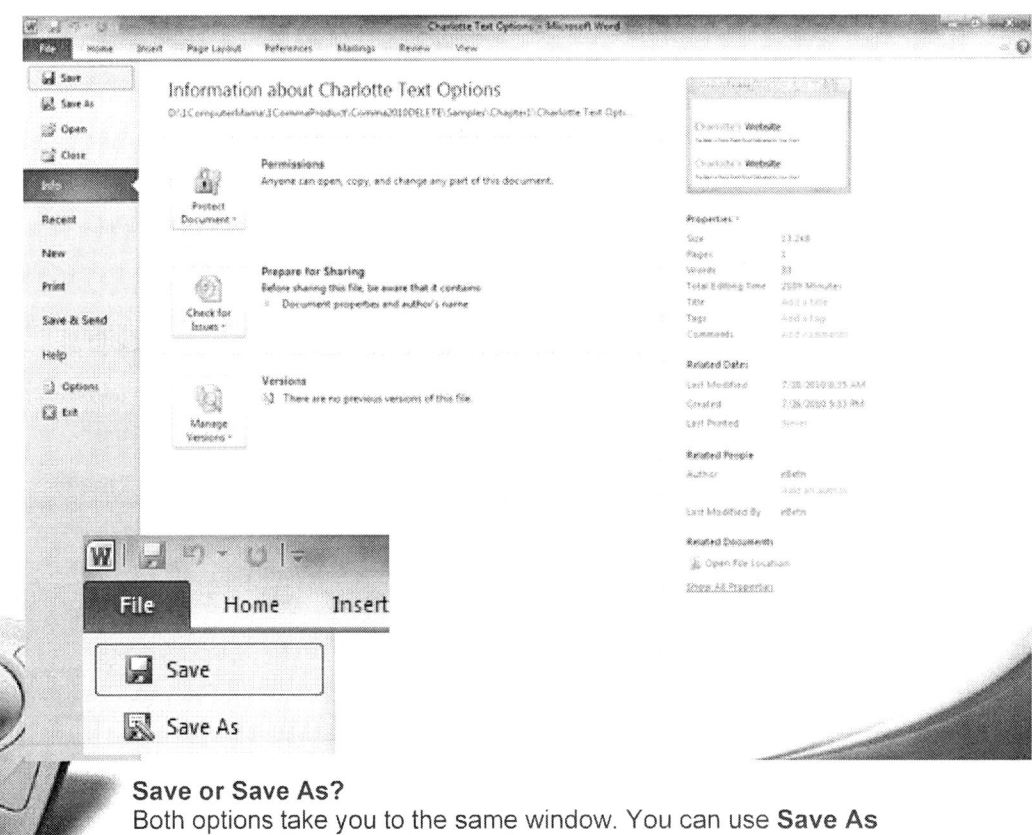

**Save or Save As?**
Both options take you to the same window. You can use **Save As** to create a different version of a document.

Exam 77-881: Microsoft Word 2010 Core
1. Sharing and Maintaining Documents
1-5. Save a Document

## Save Options

### 1. Where Are You Saving It?
By default, Microsoft Office offers your **Documents** folder on your computer's hard drive as a place to save it. You can use the Documents folder if you wish.

### 2. What Are You Naming It?
Type the File Name: Charlotte

### What Do You See?
The new **file type** in Microsoft Word 2007 and Word 2010 is the **docx** format. The docx format conforms to the new international Open Office standard.

### 3. What Are You Doing?
Click on **Save**.

When you click on **Save**, your document will be named, date stamped, and stored in the Documents folder.

File ->Save

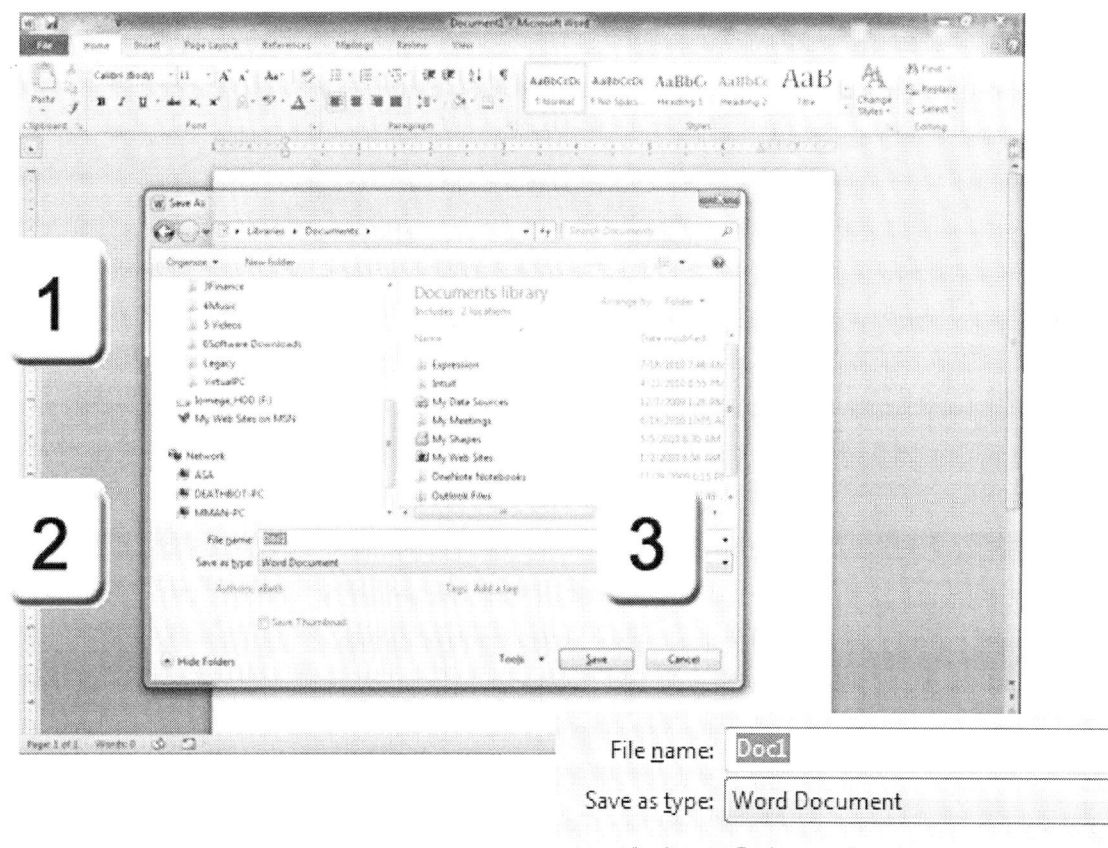

File name: Docl

Save as type: Word Document

Authors: eBeth

**Exam 77-881: Microsoft Word 2010 Core**
**1. Sharing and Maintaining Documents**
**1-5. Save a Document**

## Save As Office 97-2003

When you save a new document in Microsoft Word 2007 or Word 2010, you should be aware that this is a **new file format** and that companies with a previous version of Microsoft Word might not be able to open or edit your work.

Here are the steps you can take to create a **copy** in Word 97-2003.

**Try it: Save As Previous Version**
Go to **File ->New**.
Create a blank document.
Type: Dr. Green
Go to **File ->Save As**.
Select: **Word 97-2003 Document**.

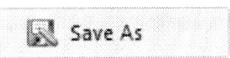

Keep going...

**File ->Save As -> Word 97-2003**

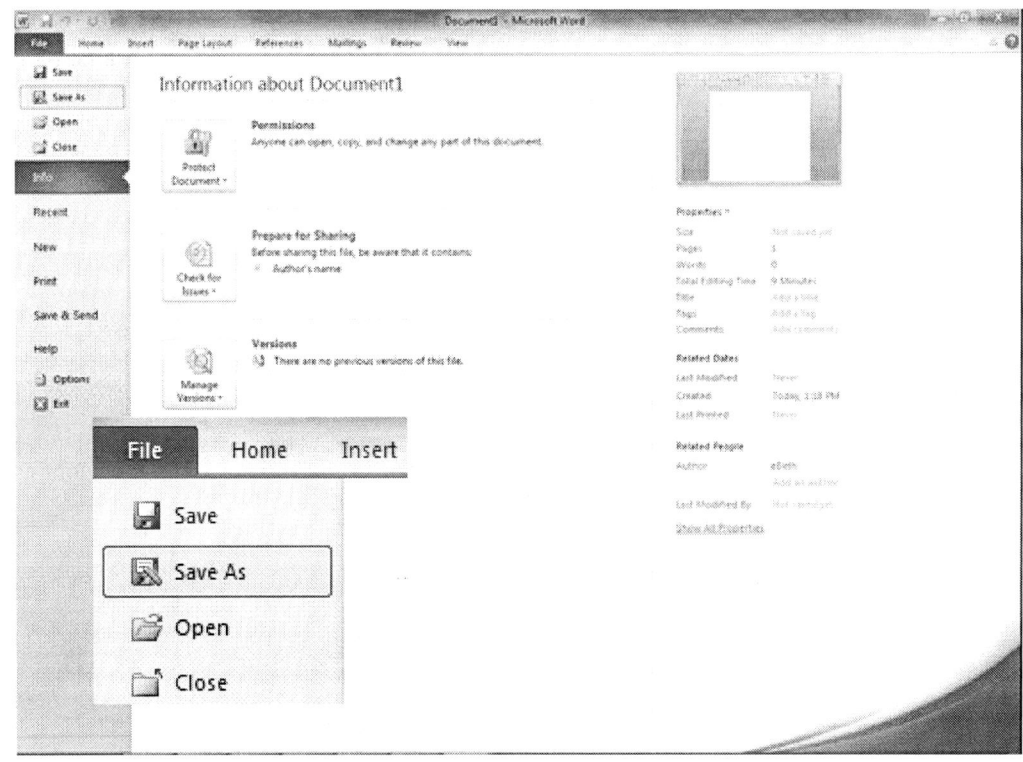

**Memo to Self:** If you can't remember when you had to consider which version of Microsoft Office you are using, then you are not as old as the Computer Mama. The last time anyone had to ask, "Which Word?" was in 1997.

**Exam 77-881: Microsoft Word 2010 Core**
**1. Sharing and Maintaining Documents**
**1-5. Save a Document**

# Save As Office 97-2003

**1. Where Are You Saving It?**
You can use the Documents folder if you wish.

**2. What Are You Naming It?**
Type the File Name: Dr Green

**What Do You See?**
The file type is Microsoft Word 97-2003. It is the **doc** format. This is the file type that is compatible with most businesses, schools and government departments.

**3. What Are You Doing?**
Click on **Save.**

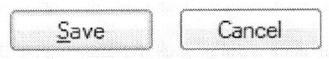

When you click on **Save**, your document will be named, date stamped, and stored in the Documents folder.

File ->Save As -> Word 97-2003

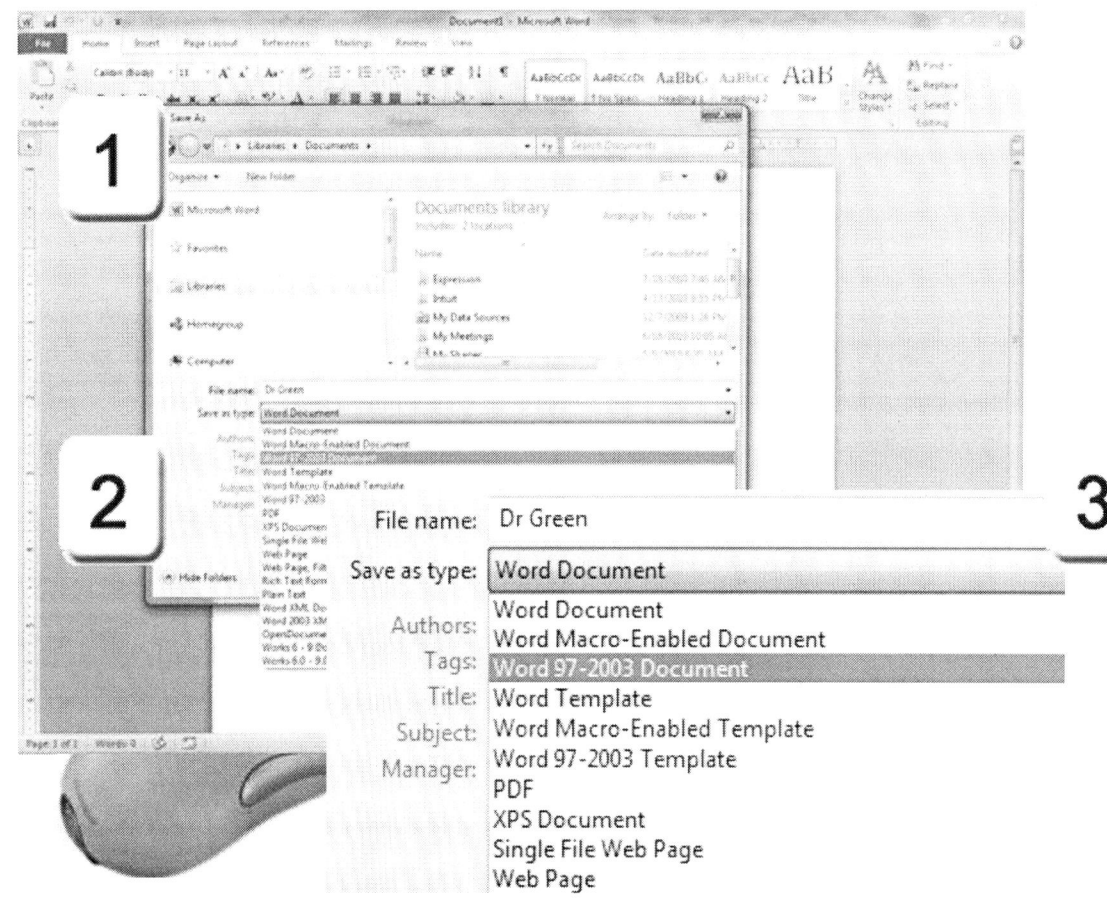

Exam 77-881: Microsoft Word 2010 Core
1. Sharing and Maintaining Documents
1-5. Save a Document

## Save As a Different Copy

Say you needed to consult with two doctors:
Dr. Green and Dr. Cooper. Say the letter you
typed to Dr. Green will be the same as letter
to Dr. Cooper except you need to edit the
name and address. You can use **Save As** to
create **another copy, or version** of your
letter.

### Try it: Use Save As to Make A Copy
**1.Edit the text**
Open the file saved as: Dr Green.
Delete the name Green and type Cooper.

### 2, Where are you going?
Go to **Office -> Save As**.

Where are you saving it: Documents.

What is the File Name: Doctor Cooper.

### 3. What are you going to do?
Go to **Save as Type** and choose the Word
97-2003 Document. Click **Save**.

**Memo to Self:** When you use Save As to
create another copy of a Word 97-2003 file,
Word uses the same file type as the original.

File ->Save As

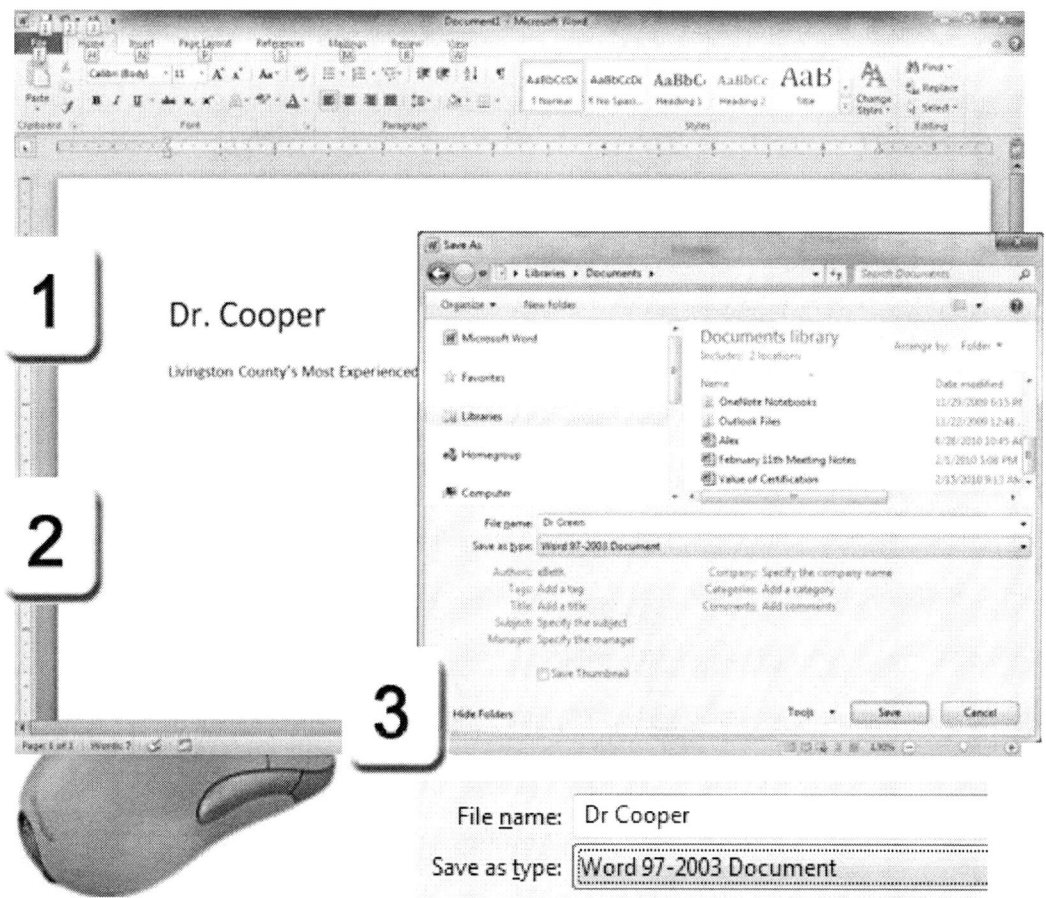

Exam 77-881: Microsoft Word 2010 Core
1. Sharing and Maintaining Documents
1-5. Save a Document

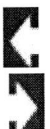

# Where Did You Save It?

All of the **Microsoft Office** programs save files in the Documents folder. You can change the default location if you wish. This setting is under the **File** menu, with the AutoText options and other tidbits.

## Review the Default Location for Saving Your Documents
Go to **File ->Options**.
Select the category: Save.

**What Do You See?** You can use the **Browse** button to find and select a different folder to be the default location when you Save a file.

Please **Cancel** out of these Word Options without changing the default file location.

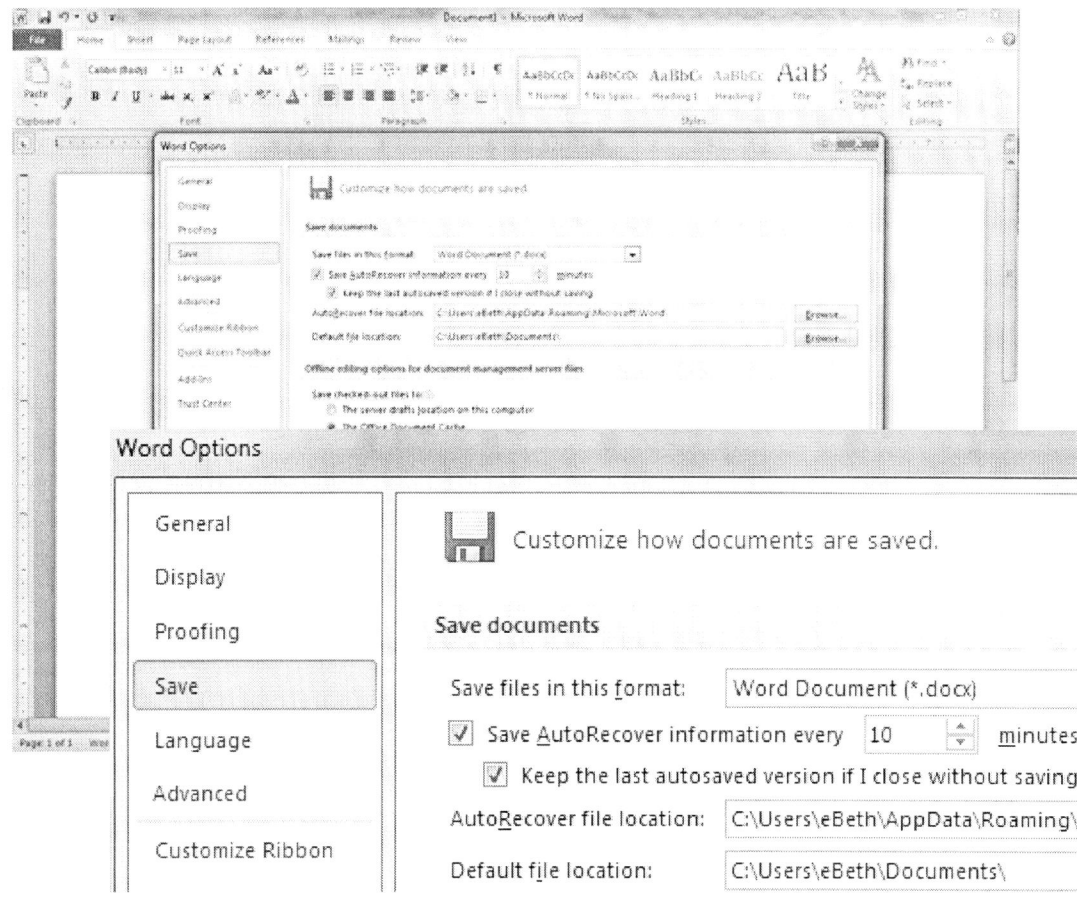

Exam 77-881: Microsoft Word 2010 Core
1. Sharing and Maintaining Documents
1-5. Save a Document

## Beginning Word

These pages demonstrated many of the options you might see as you learn Microsoft Word 2010. It is important to consider who has upgraded to the new Word 2007/2010 format, and how you can use **Save As** to create a version that is compatible with Word 97-2003.

Finally, this lesson introduced the concept of different versions. This page shows two copies of the same letter, one for each consultant in the Word 97-2003 document (doc) format..

Well, you done good.
You can have two cookies.

**Start ->Documents**

| Word Options | |
|---|---|
| General | |
| Display | |
| **Proofing** | ABC Change how Word corrects and formats your text. |
| Save | **AutoCorrect options** |
| Language | Change how Word corrects and formats text as you type: |
| Advanced | **When correcting spelling in Microsoft Office programs** |
| Customize Ribbon | ☑ Ignore words in UPPERCASE |
| Quick Access Toolbar | ☑ Ignore words that contain numbers |
| Add-Ins | ☑ Ignore Internet and file addresses |
| Trust Center | ☑ Flag repeated words |
| | ☐ Enforce accented uppercase in French |
| | ☐ Suggest from main dictionary only |

Save As

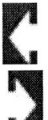

# Practice Activities

## Lesson: Mice and Men

**Before You Begin:** Start Microsoft Word 2010. You should see a new, blank document.

**Try This: Do the following steps**

1. Type: January. Watch for the AutoText and click ENTER on the keyboard to insert the word.
2. Type: Monday. Watch for the AutoText and click ENTER on the keyboard to insert the word.
3. Type (tm). Watch for the AutoText convert the text into the symbol for trademark.
4. Type (c). Watch for the AutoText convert the text into the symbol for copyright.
5. Go to File->Options-> Proofing. Click on AutoCorrect Options.
6. Go to Math AutoCorrect.
7. Select Use Math AutoCorrect rules outside of math regions. Close the AutoCorrect window.
8. Type: \approx. Watch for the AutoText convert the text into the symbol for approximate.
9. Go to Insert->Symbol. Click on the Copyright symbol.
10. Go to Insert->Symbol. Click on the Trademark symbol.
11. Go to Insert->Equation. Click on Pythagorean Theorem
12. Close Microsoft Word. When you are prompted, click Don't Save.

This is a practice document that you do not have to submit.

# Test Yourself

1. When does the Mini Toolbar appear?
a. When text is selected
b. When you double click on the ribbon
c. When you start typing
 Tip: Beginning Word, page 67

2. The clipboard holds items copied:
a. Just from the current program you're using
b. Only from Microsoft programs
c. From any program on your computer that allows copying
 Tip: Beginning Word, page 69

3. What does Paste All do?
a. Pastes all items from the clipboard into the current document
b. Pastes all items copied that day into the current document
c. Pastes only the last copied item into document
 Tip: Beginning Word, page 69

5. Where are the commands for Copy and Paste located?
A. On the Insert Ribbon
B. On the Edit Ribbon
C. On the Home Ribbon
 Tip: Beginning Word, page 69

6. Word 2010 includes Math Autocorrect, which replaces certain commands with symbols.
a. TRUE
b. FALSE
 Tip: Beginning Word, page 73

7. It is possible to create personalized AutoCorrect commands.
a. TRUE
b. FALSE
 Tip: Beginning Word, page 78

8. Microsoft Word 2010 uses a new file format that is different from Word 1997-2003.
a. TRUE
b. FALSE
 Tip: Beginning Word, page 83

9. Which of the following is a Paste Option? (select all correct answers)
a. Keep source formatting
b. Match destination formatting
c. Keep text only
 Tip: Beginning Word, page 68

10. Which of the following is true about mouse buttons?
(Select all correct answers)
a. Left gives you actions like select, open and move
b. Right gives you options in a short menu list of choices
 Tip: Beginning Word, page 71

11. Which of the following can be inserted into a Word document?
(Select all correct answers)
a. Equations
b. Symbols
c. Clip Art
 Tip: Beginning Word, page 74, **75**

**Word 2010: Graphics and Quick Parts**

# Fancy Colors

**Beginning Word Objectives**

In this lesson, you will learn how to:

1. Access the Picture Tools Ribbon

2. Apply Pictures Styles and Effects

3. Apply Borders to a Picture

4. Use the Picture Corrections Tool

5. Apply Artistic Effects to a Picture

6. Compress a Picture for optimal size

7. Remove the background of a Picture

8. Crop a Picture and Crop to Shape

# Lesson 5: Fancy Colors

## 1. Readings
Read Lesson 5 in the Beginning Word guide, page 93-118.

## Project
A sample document that you do not need to save.

## Downloads
Graphic files used in the lesson:
Durand1.jpg, Durand2.jpg, Durand3.jpg, Durand4.jpg, Durand5.jpg, Michigan-Balloonfest-4.gif, Michigan-Balloonfest-18.gif, Michigan-Balloonfest-22.gif Michigan-Balloonfest-26.gif (not cropped)

## 2. Practice
Complete the Practice Activity, page.117

## 3. Assessment
Review the Test questions, page 118.

**Picture Tools->Format**

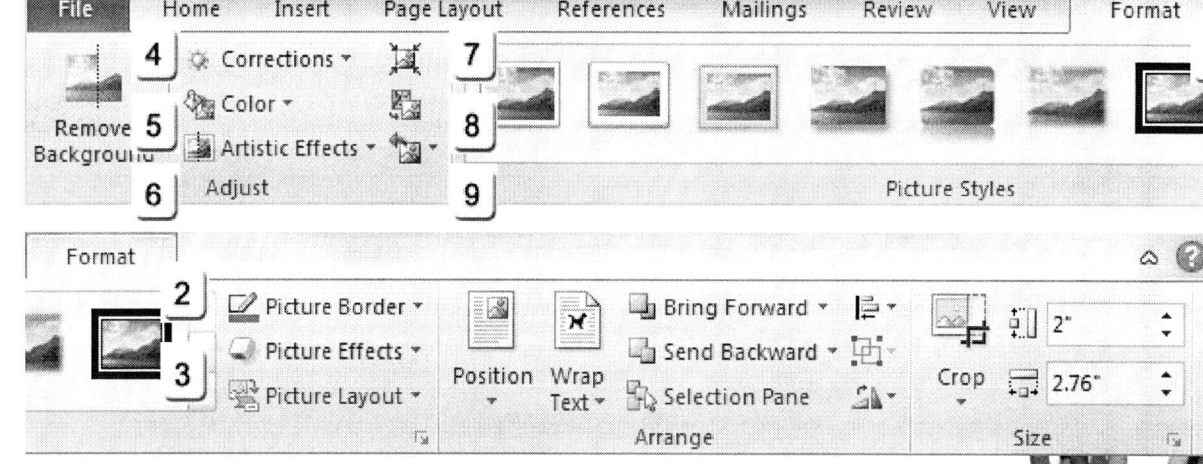

# Menu Maps
This lesson shows options on the **Picture Tools Format** Ribbon.
1. Picture Tools-> Format-> Styles, page 99
2. Picture Tools-> Format-> Picture Border, page 102
3. Picture Tools-> Format-> Picture Effects, Page 101
4. Picture Tools-> Format -> Adjust-> Corrections, page 103
5. Picture Tools-> Format -> Adjust-> Color, page 105
6. Picture Tools-> Format -> Adjust-> Artistic Effects, page 107
7. Picture Tools-> Format -> Adjust-> Compress, page 109
8. Picture Tools-> Format -> Adjust-> Change Picture, page 110
9. Picture Tools-> Format -> Adjust-> Reset Picture, page 111

# A New Box of Crayons

Getting a new box of crayons is always fun: whether you are a child in grade school or a big kid in an office. There's nothing like the feeling of opening the box and seeing all of the crayons arranged by color: so many shades of red, orange, green and yellow. Silver and gold that glitter!

Microsoft Office 2010 has a wonderful set of tools for working with pictures and graphics. In this lesson, the focus will be on formatting pictures. So, if you are ready, please **Start** the **Program** Microsoft **Word**.

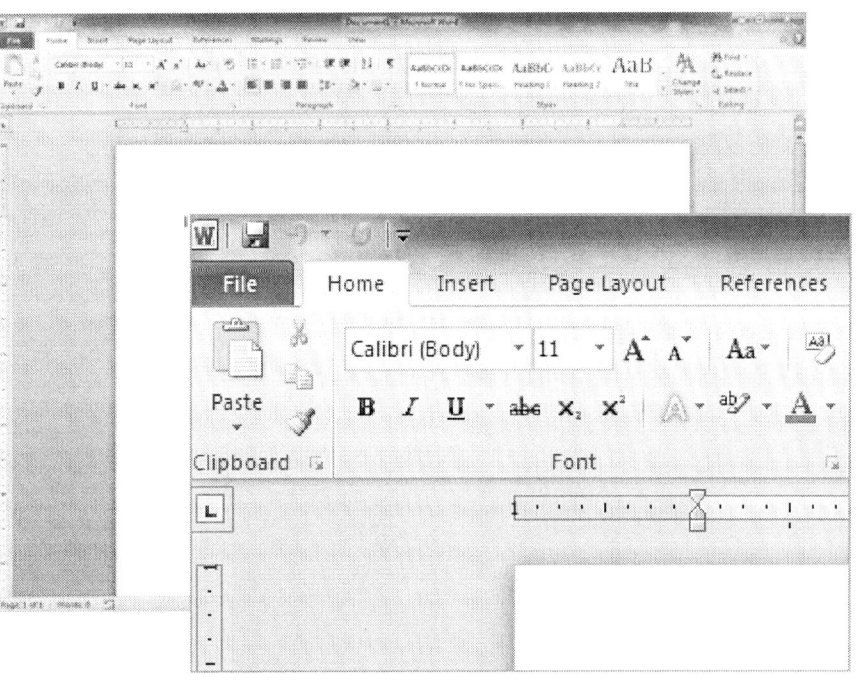

What do you see from the top of the screen? Is there a **Title Bar** that says Microsoft Word? Yes.

Is there a **Home** Ribbon with the Clipboard, Font and Paragraph Groups? Yes.

If your screen looks similar to the example on this page, then you are ready to get started.

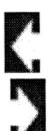

## Insert a Picture

Our lesson begins by adding a picture. There are several sample pictures available with this course online. You can also use your own pictures if you wish.

**Try it: Insert a Picture**
**1. Go to the Insert tab.**
Find the Illustrations group on the Insert Ribbon.

**2. Click on Picture**
Keep going, please...

Insert -> Picture

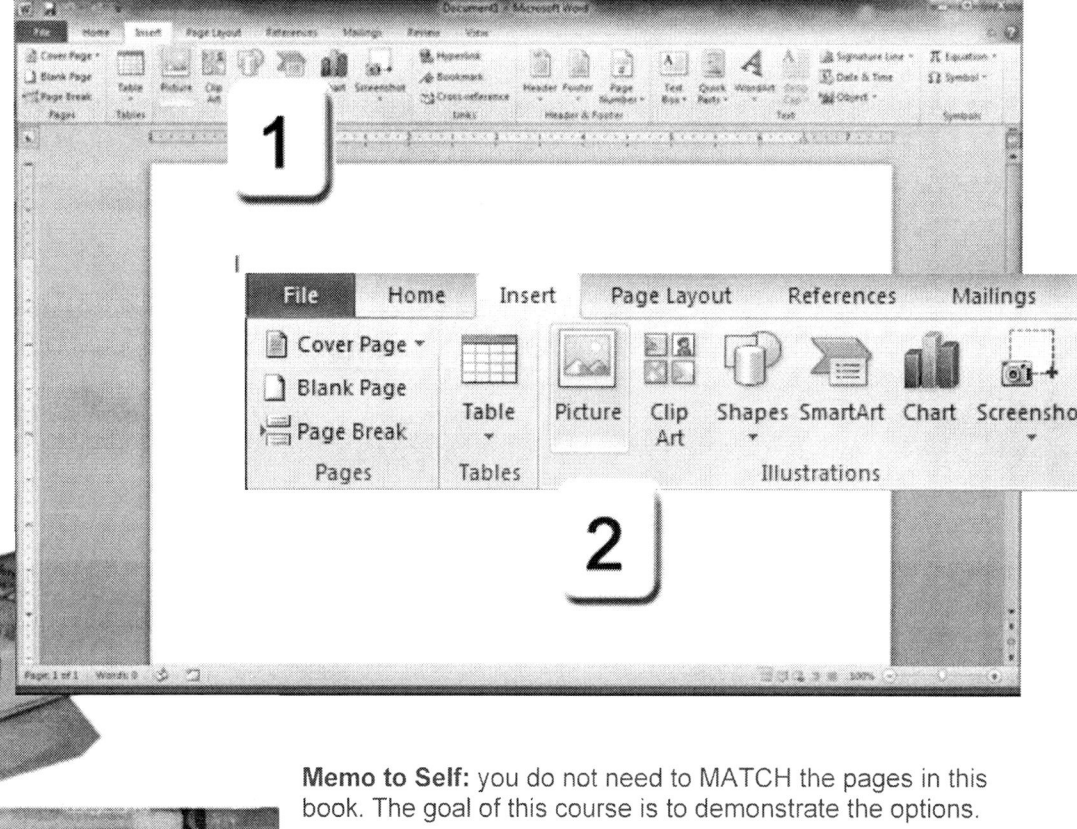

**Memo to Self:** you do not need to MATCH the pages in this book. The goal of this course is to demonstrate the options.

**Exam 77-881: Microsoft Word 2010 Core**
**4. Including Illustrations and Graphics in a Document**
**4-1. Insert and format Pictures in a document**

Insert -> Picture

## Insert a Picture, continued

**3. What Do You See?** You will be prompted to browse for a folder. The default location is the **Pictures** Library in Windows Vista and Windows 7, however you can create your own folders to organize your work.

**Choose your picture: Double click on a picture** and it will be inserted into your document.

Exam 77-881: Microsoft Word 2010 Core
4. Including Illustrations and Graphics in a Document
4-1. Insert and format Pictures in a document

**Picture Tools**

# The Picture Ribbon

When you click on a picture, you will see the picture frame and handles. That is your clue that the picture has been selected.

You should also see the **Picture Tools.** The Picture Tools appear when you select a picture They disappear when the picture is no longer selected.

**Try it: Now You See It, Now You Don't.** Click on the picture. The Picture Tools are available. Click on the blank page so that the picture in not selected (it no longer has handles) and the Picture Tools hide.

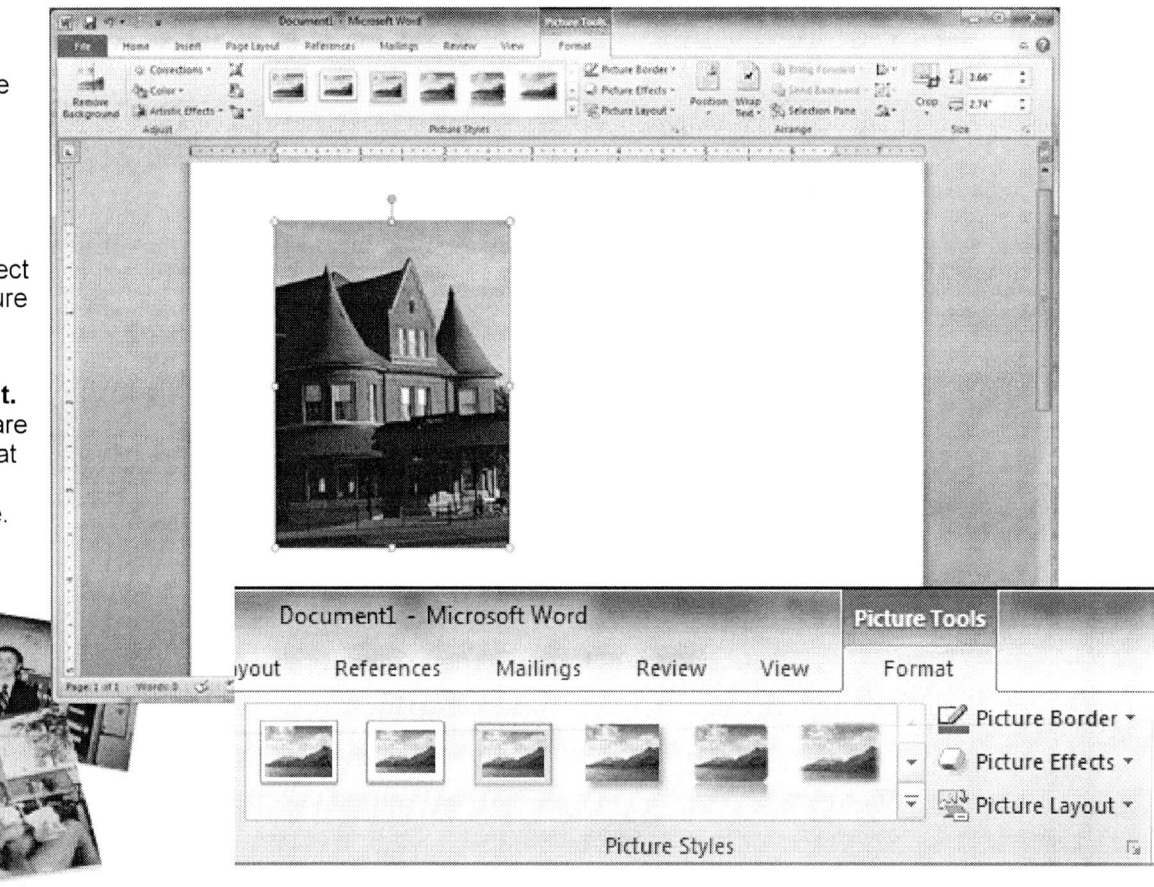

Exam 77-881: Microsoft Word 2010 Core
4. Including Illustrations and Graphics in a Document
4-1. Insert and format Pictures in a document: The Picture Ribbon

## Picture Styles

Microsoft Word 2007 and 2010 offer a rich gallery of **Picture Styles**. You can see a Live Preview of the Style when you run your mouse over the options.

The Picture Styles include shadows, frames, and reflections. Keep going...

**Picture Tools -> Format -> Picture Styles**

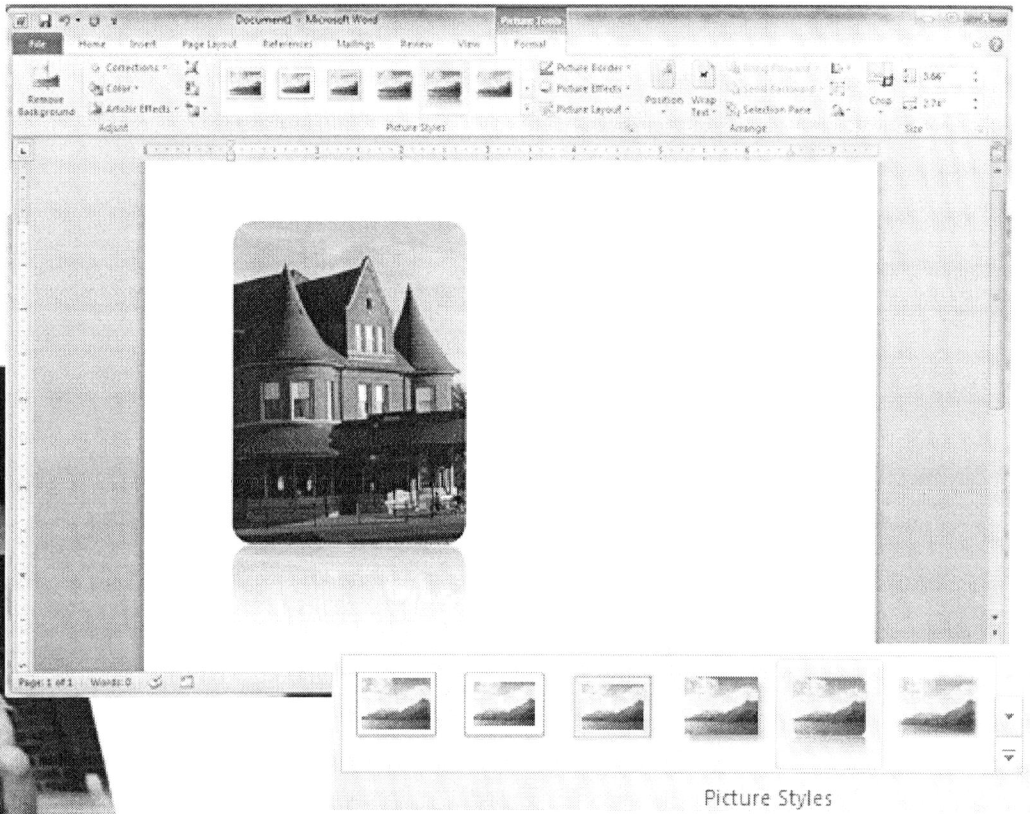

Exam 77-881: Microsoft Word 2010 Core
4. Including Illustrations and Graphics in a Document
4-1. Insert and format Pictures in a document: Picture Styles

## More Picture Styles

Look carefully on the bottom right corner of the Picture Styles Gallery. There is an arrow pointing down with a line above the arrow. When you run your mouse over that arrow, it says simply, "More." That's exactly what it is: more Picture Style options.

**Try It: Find More Picture Styles**
1. Go to **Picture Tools -> Format.**
Go to **Picture Styles.**

2. Click on the down arrow for **More**
There are Styles with different frames, shapes and reflections.

Way cool, isn't it?
Keep going....there's even more.

Picture Tools -> Format -> Picture Styles ->More

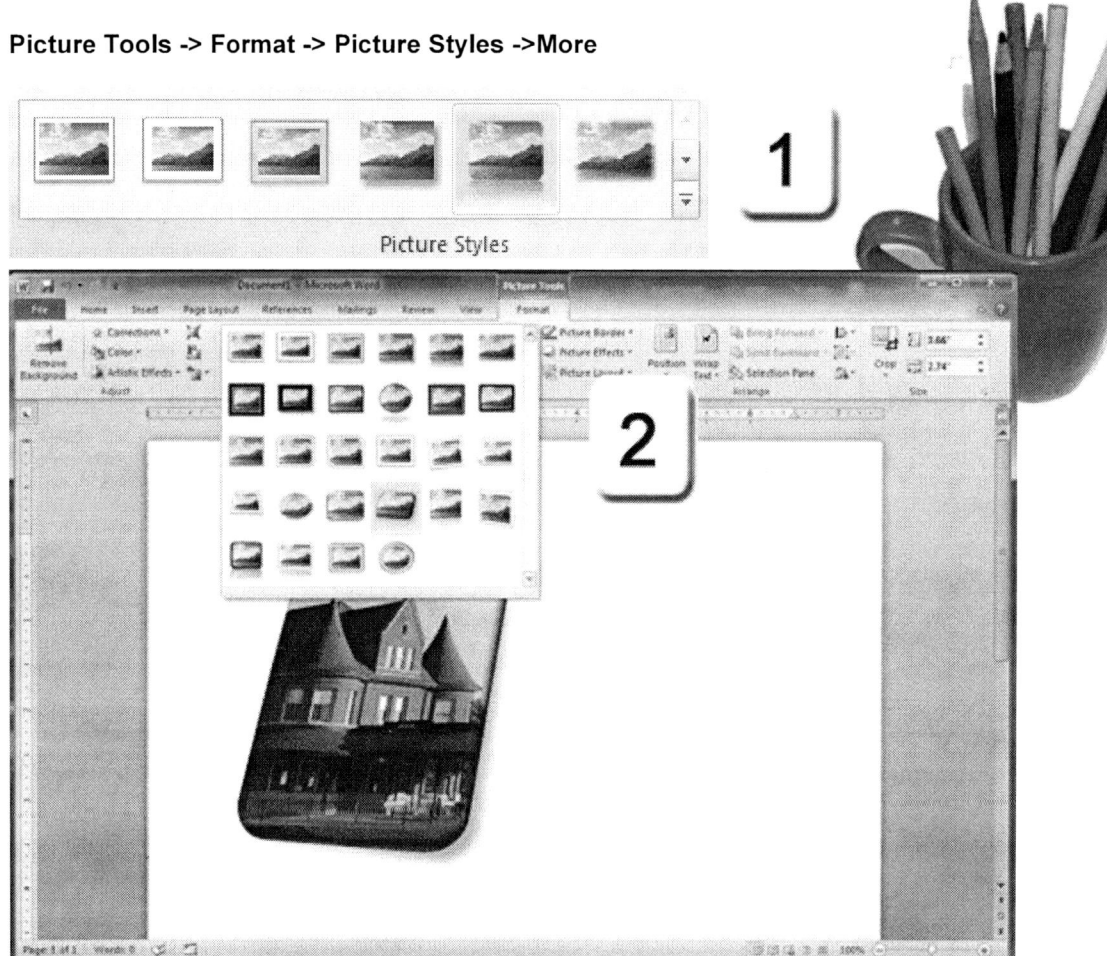

Exam 77-881: Microsoft Word 2010 Core
4. Including Illustrations and Graphics in a Document
4-1. Insert and format Pictures in a document: Picture Styles

## Picture Effects

The options in the **Picture Style** gallery can be created with the **Picture Effects** as well. The Picture Style Gallery combines many effects into each option.

You can use the **Picture Effects** to choose some, or all of the options if you wish. The effects include:
Shadow
Reflections
Glow
Soft Edges
Bevel
3-D Rotation

**Try It: Play with the Picture Effects**
1. Go to **Picture Tools -> Format.**
Go to **Picture Effects.**

**2. Choose Some Picture Effects**
Notice that you can add more than one Picture Effect to create your own design..

**Picture Tools -> Format -> Picture Effects**

Exam 77-881: Microsoft Word 2010 Core
4. Including Illustrations and Graphics in a Document
4-1. Insert and format Pictures in a document: Picture effects

**Picture Tools -> Format -> Picture Styles -> Picture Border**

## Picture Borders

You can format the **Picture Border** as well. The Border options include line width, style and color.

**Try it: Edit the Picture Border**
1. Go to **Picture Tools -> Format**.
Go to **Picture Styles -> Borders**

**2. Preview the Picture Borders**
The **Color** palette presents Theme colors as well as the Standard colors.

The **Weight** and **Dashes** menus show a short list of formats. There are **More options** at the bottom of these lists.

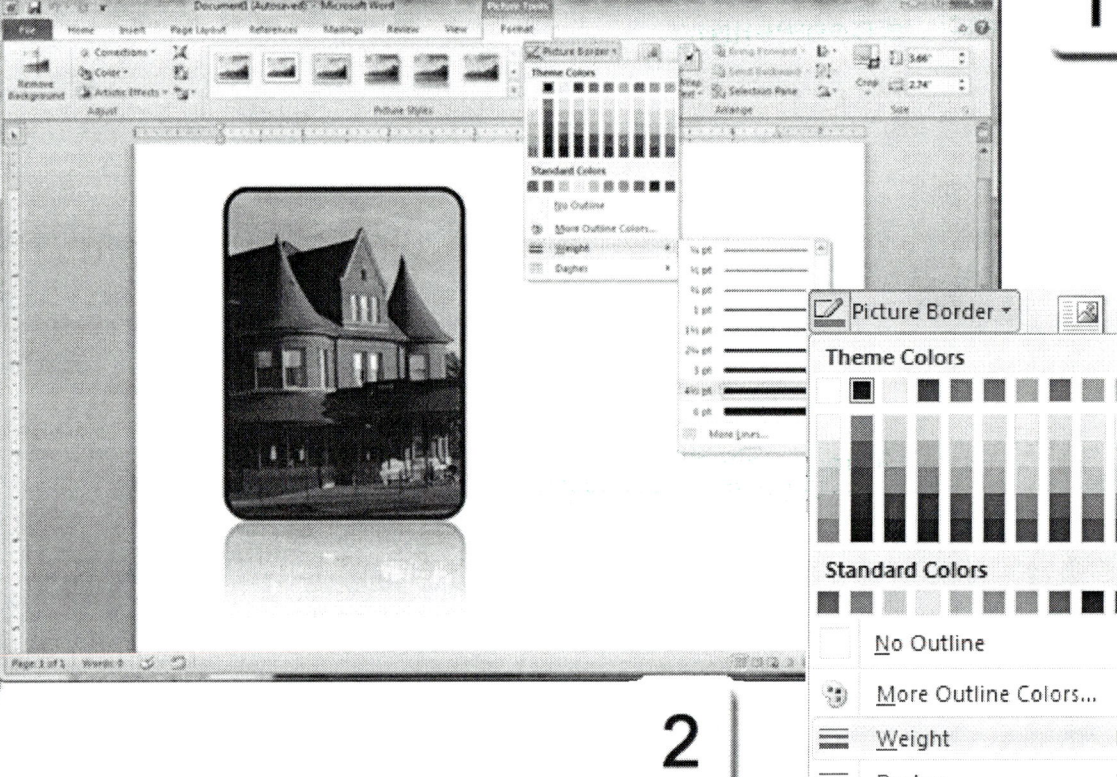

Exam 77-881: Microsoft Word 2010 Core
4. Including Illustrations and Graphics in a Document
4-1. Insert and format Pictures in a document: Picture borders

## Picture Corrections

Today's digital cameras mount the flash on the front of the camera. This works reasonably well with the automatic settings that most people use. However, the in-your-face flash often creates dark pictures with flat lighting. You can correct the picture by adjusting the **Brightness** and **Contrast**.

**Try it: Adjust the Brightness and Contrast**
1. Go to **Picture Tools -> Format.**
Go to **Adjust -> Corrections.**

**2. What Do You See?**
You can **Sharpen** or **Soften** the edges in an image. The **Brightness** and **Contrast** adjust the Brightness (the amount of light) and the Contrast (the difference between absolute white to absolute black.) Each little square preview is a different percentage.

**Picture Tools -> Format -> Adjust -> Corrections**

Exam 77-881: Microsoft Word 2010 Core
4. Including Illustrations and Graphics in a Document
4-1. Insert and format Pictures in a document: Picture corrections

## More Correction Options

You can adjust the Picture Corrections manually in addition to the preset Brightness and Contrast ratios. The advanced settings are available at the bottom of the Corrections menu.

**Try it: Adjust the Brightness and Contrast Manually**
1. Go to **Picture Tools -> Format.**
Go to **Adjust -> Corrections.**
Click on **Picture Correction Options.**

**2. Review the Picture Corrections**
You can Sharpen or Soften the edges in an image by using the slider bar or typing a percent. The Brightness and Contrast can be adjusted as well.

**Picture Tools -> Format -> Adjust -> Corrections**

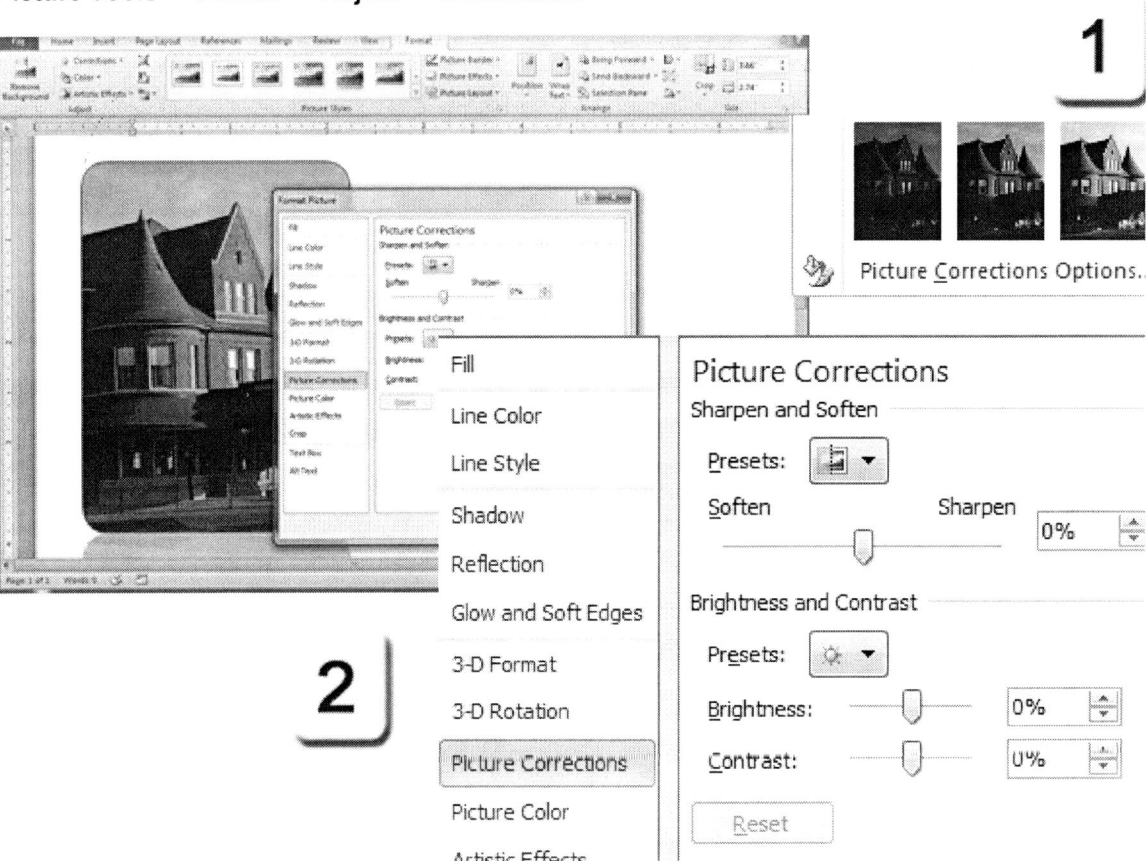

Exam 77-881: Microsoft Word 2010 Core
4. Including Illustrations and Graphics in a Document
4-1. Insert and format Pictures in a document: Picture corrections

## Adjust the Color

Color can alter the basic feeling of an image. Changing a picture from warm red to high contrast black and white can change the mood from a sunny afternoon to the dark house in a scary movie like Psycho!

**Try it: Adjust the Color**
1. Go to **Picture Tools -> Format.**
Go to **Adjust -> Color.**

**2. Review the Color Options**
There a three different categories of Color adjustments. **Color Saturation** infuses the image with more or less color.

**Color Tone** works with yellow and blue filters to warm or cool an image. Color Tone corrects for the yellowing that can occur with indoor lighting.

**Recolor** applies a tint to an image, such as the "Olde Time" **sepia** brown pictures.

**Picture Tools -> Format -> Adjust -> Color**

Exam 77-881: Microsoft Word 2010 Core
4. Including Illustrations and Graphics in a Document
4-1. Insert and format Pictures in a document: Adjust picture color

## More Color Adjustments

All of the Microsoft Office Picture Tools have advanced options. Here are the steps to find the Color options.

**Try it: Adjust the Color Manually**
1. Go to **Picture Tools -> Format.**
Go to **Adjust -> Color.**
Click on **Picture Color Options.**

**2. Review the Picture Corrections**
You can edit the **Color Saturation** as well a the **Color Tone**. You can edit the Color with the slider bar or type a number if you wish.

**3. What Do You See?** Did you notice that you can add several effects? For example, you can format the Color Saturation to high contrast and then Recolor the image red?

**Picture Tools -> Format -> Adjust -> Color**

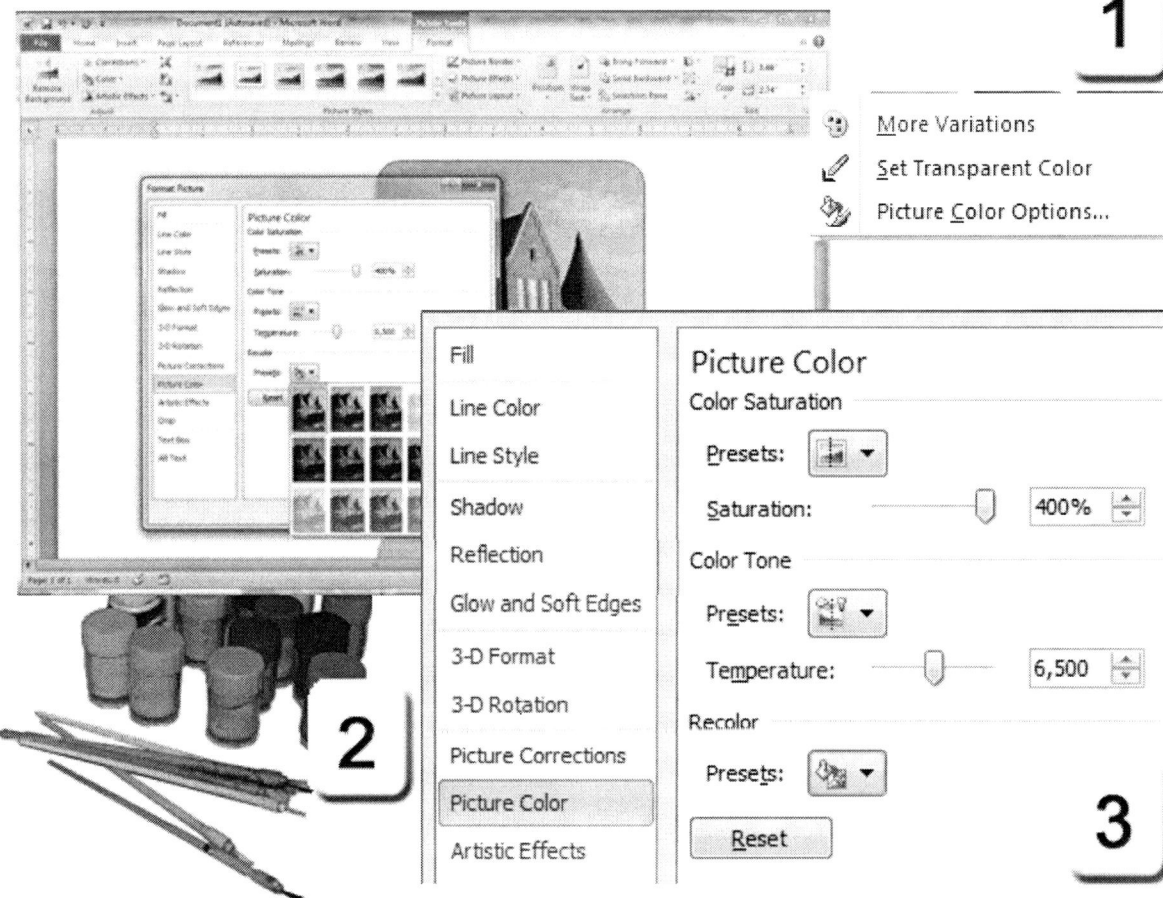

Exam 77-881: Microsoft Word 2010 Core
4. Including Illustrations and Graphics in a Document
4-1. Insert and format Pictures in a document: Adjust picture color

## Artistic Effects

Older versions of Microsoft Office included a Picture Editor. It is fun to note that Office 2010 includes a new edition of this cool editor.

The **Artistic Effects** are photographic filters that are applied to your image. The Effects include pencil, pastel, chalk and even shiny plastic wrap.

**Try it: Apply Artistic Effects**
1. Go to **Picture Tools -> Format.**
Go to **Adjust -> Artistic Effects.**

**2. Review the Artistic Effects**
As you pass your mouse over the **Artistic Effects** gallery you can see the results in Live Preview.

Keep going,...of course there's more.

**Picture Tools -> Format -> Adjust -> Artistic Effects**

Exam 77-881: Microsoft Word 2010 Core
4. Including Illustrations and Graphics in a Document
4-1. Insert and format Pictures in a document: Artistic effects

## More Artistic Effects

Each effect has its own unique adjustments. Here are the steps to the advanced options.

**Try it: Edit the Artistic Effects**
1. Go to **Picture Tools -> Format.**
Go to **Adjust ->  Artistic Effects.**
Click on **Artistic Effects Options.**

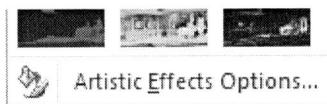

**2. Adjust the Artistic Effects**
Say you selected the Pencil Sketch Effect. Changing the **Transparency** adds and removes the color. Adjusting the **Pressure** makes the strokes bigger.

**Picture Tools -> Format -> Adjust -> Artistic Effects**

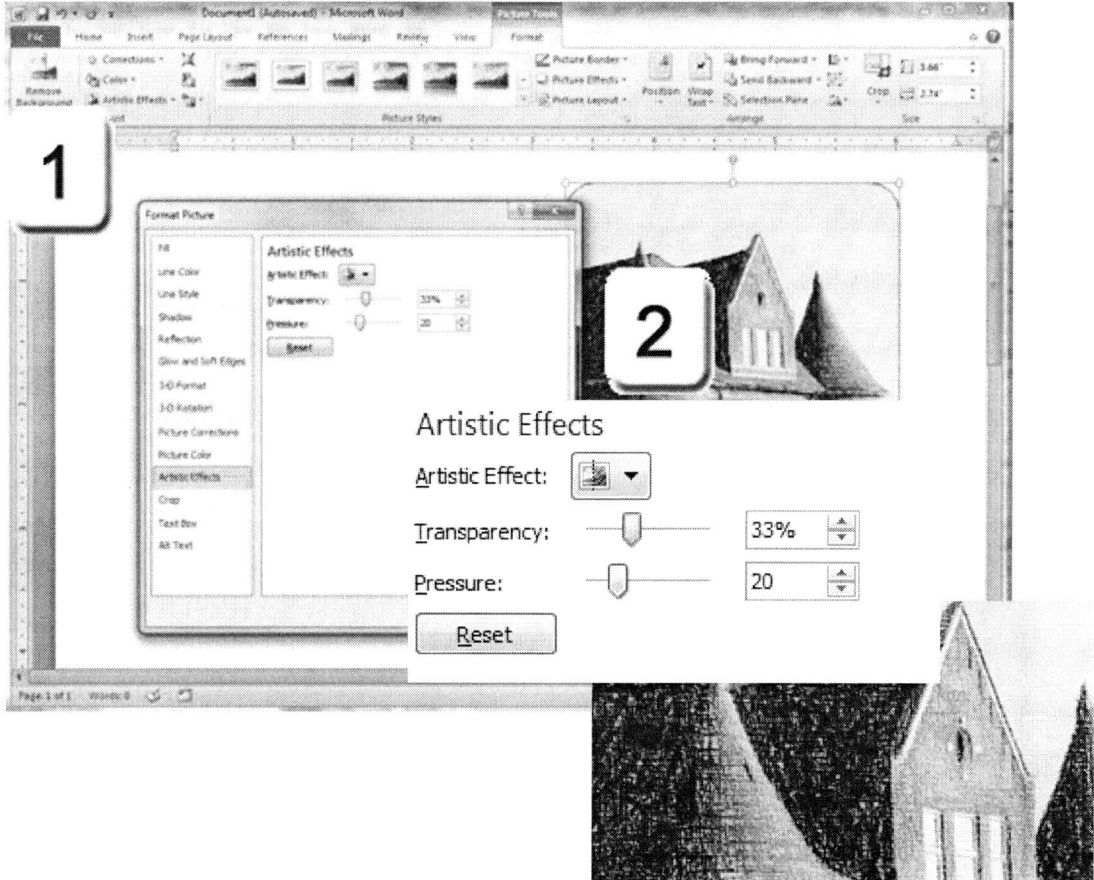

Exam 77-881: Microsoft Word 2010 Core
4. Including Illustrations and Graphics in a Document
4-1. Insert and format Pictures in a document: Artistic Effects

## Compress the Picture

The Adjustment group has a useful tool for reducing the size of your pictures. There are times when you need to make a document smaller so that it can be easily shared on the Internet via email or uploaded to a forum.

**Try it: Compress the Picture**
1. Go to Picture Tools -> Format.
Go to **Adjust -> Compress**.

**2. What Do You See?**
Microsoft Word prompts you to choose whether this image should be reduced to 150 ppi, which is good for web pages, or 96 ppi, which is smaller for email.

You can choose to compress just the picture you selected, or all of the pictures in this document.

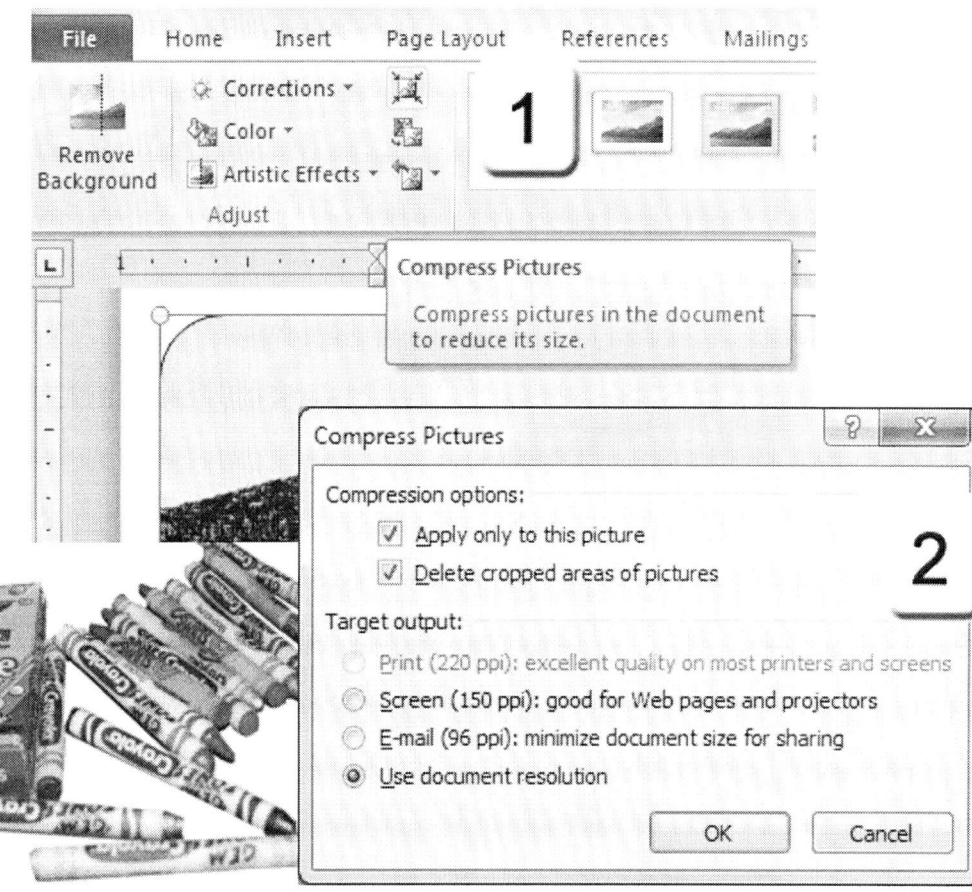

Exam 77-881: Microsoft Word 2010 Core
4. Including Illustrations and Graphics in a Document
4-1. Insert and format Pictures in a document: Compress picture

## Change the Picture

**Change Picture** lets you switch a picture, but keep all of the Styles, Borders and Effects that you edited.

**Try it: Change the Picture**
1. Go to **Picture Tools -> Format**. Go to **Adjust -> Change**.

**2. What Do You See?**
Microsoft Word 2010 prompts you to browse for the new picture. You can double click to select the picture that you want.

**3. What Do You See?** The new picture replaces the original one, however the picture formatting has been retained.

Picture Tools -> Format -> Adjust -> Change

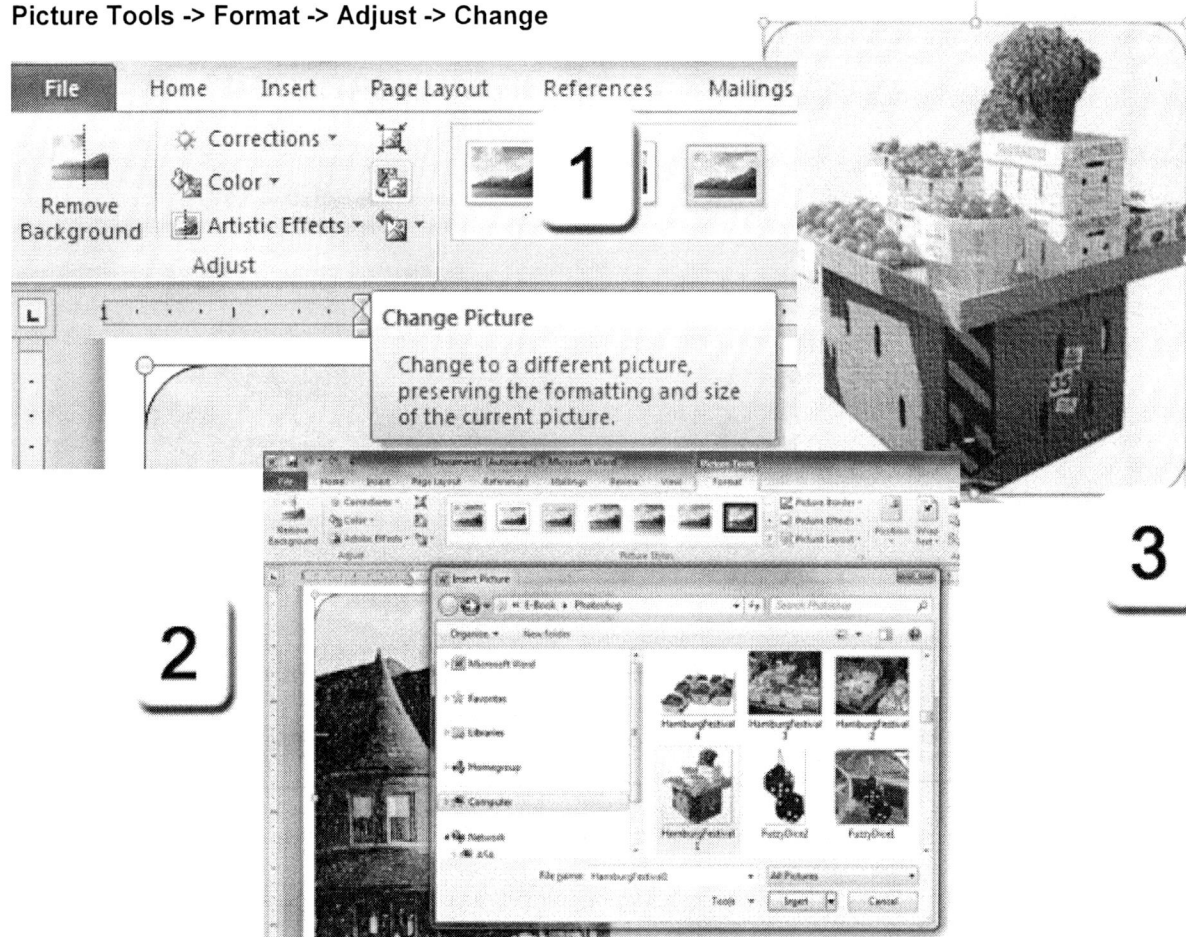

**Exam 77-881: Microsoft Word 2010 Core**
**4. Including Illustrations and Graphics in a Document**
**4-1. Insert and format Pictures in a document: Change picture**

## Reset!

Sometimes you get way too many effects layered one on top of each other. In that case, you may wish to **Reset** the image and return your picture back to the original appearance and formatting. Here are the steps.

**Try it: Reset the Picture**
1. Go to **Picture Tools -> Format.**
Go to **Adjust -> Reset.**

**2. What Do You See?**
Microsoft Word 2010 has two **Reset** options: **Reset Picture** and **Reset Picture & Size** which returns your picture to the original size...which may be very large depending on your camera's settings.

**Picture Tools -> Format -> Adjust -> Reset**

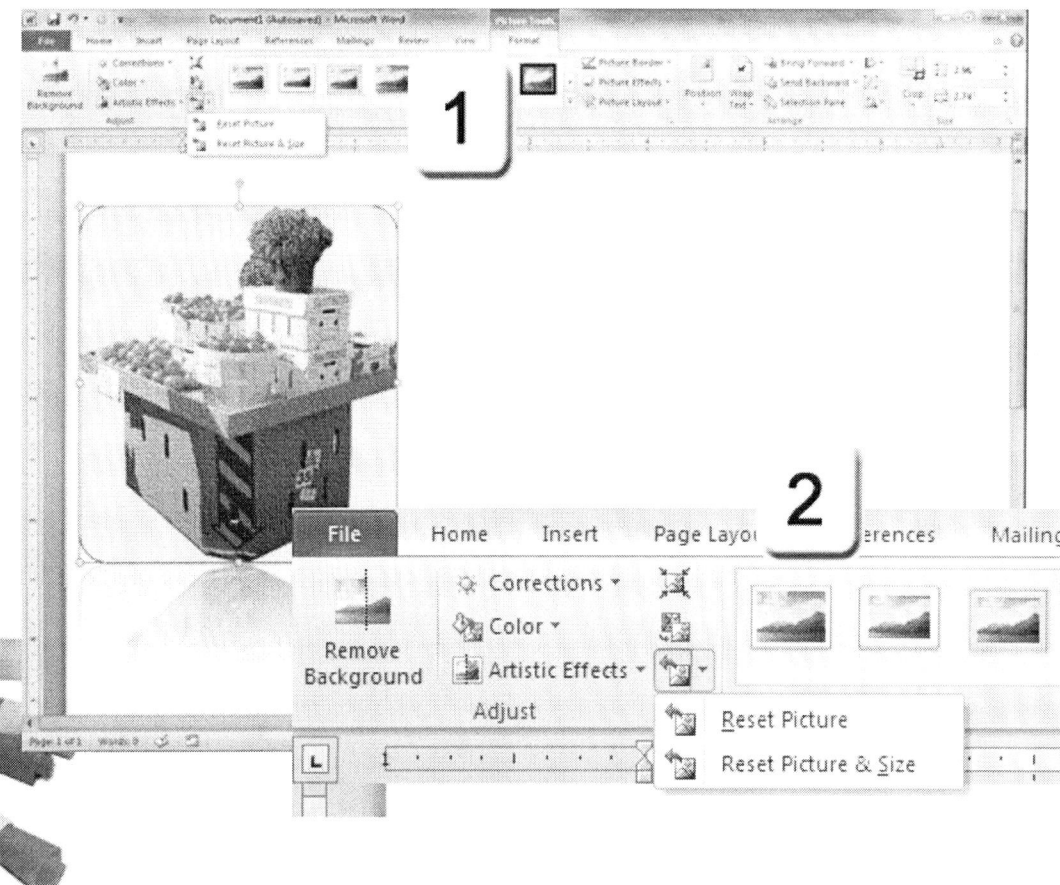

Exam 77-881: Microsoft Word 2010 Core
4. Including Illustrations and Graphics in a Document
4-1. Insert and format Pictures in a document: Reset

# Remove Background

Here is an interesting option. You can use the **Picture Tools** to remove the background on a picture. The example on this page has a complex background: the various plants are different shades of green. Will it work? You can try this with any picture if you wish.

**Try it: Remove the Background**
1. Go to Picture Tools -> Format.
Go to **Adjust -> Remove Background.**

Keep going...

**Picture Tools -> Format -> Adjust -> Remove Background**

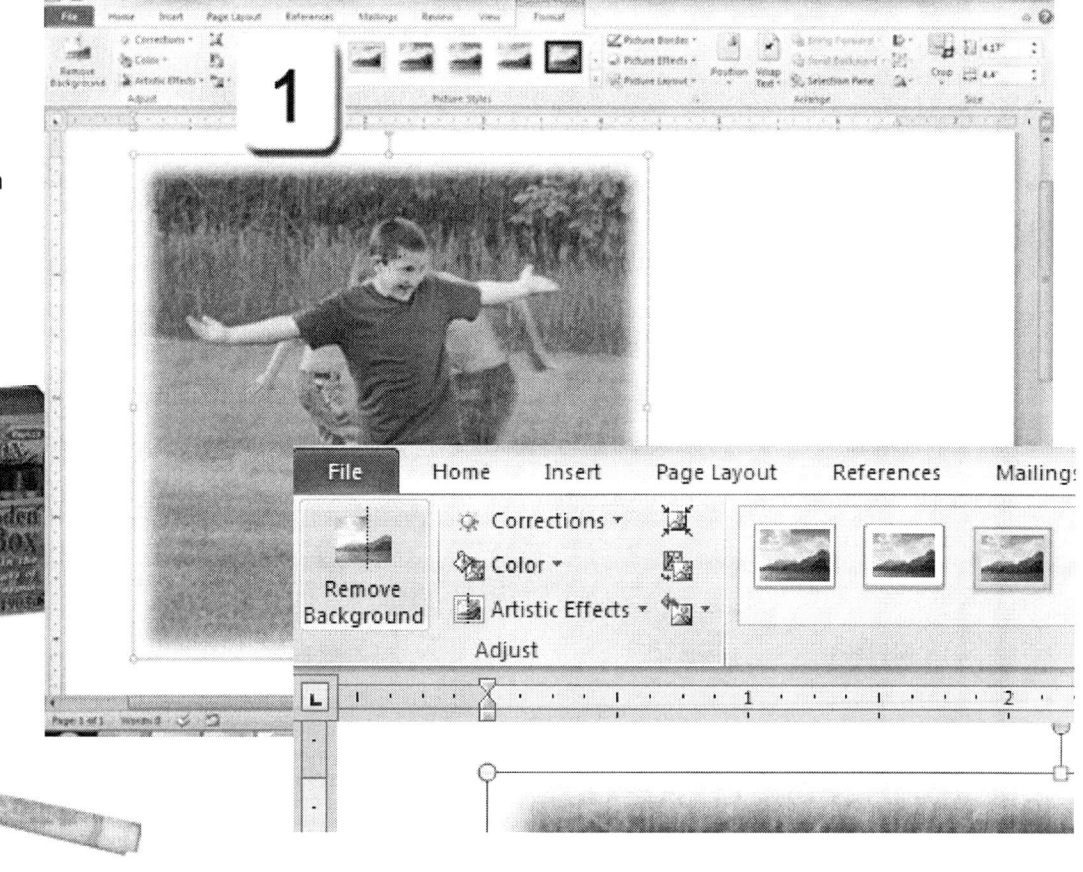

Exam 77-881: Microsoft Word 2010 Core
4. Including Illustrations and Graphics in a Document
4-1. Insert and format Pictures in a document: Remove background

# Remove Background

## 2. Mark the Areas

Microsoft Word 2010 compares the colors in your picture and makes a reasonable guess. The suggested background is displayed in a pink mask. The areas that will be kept are shown in full color.

## 3. Edit the Marks

Look carefully at your picture. In this example, I noticed that some of the children's socks and shoes needed to be marked **Areas to Keep**.

## 4. Keep the Changes

When you click on **Keep Changes**, you will see your picture without the background. You can change your Marked Areas by clicking again on Remove Background. Your background marks will still be there if you wish to add or remove some areas.

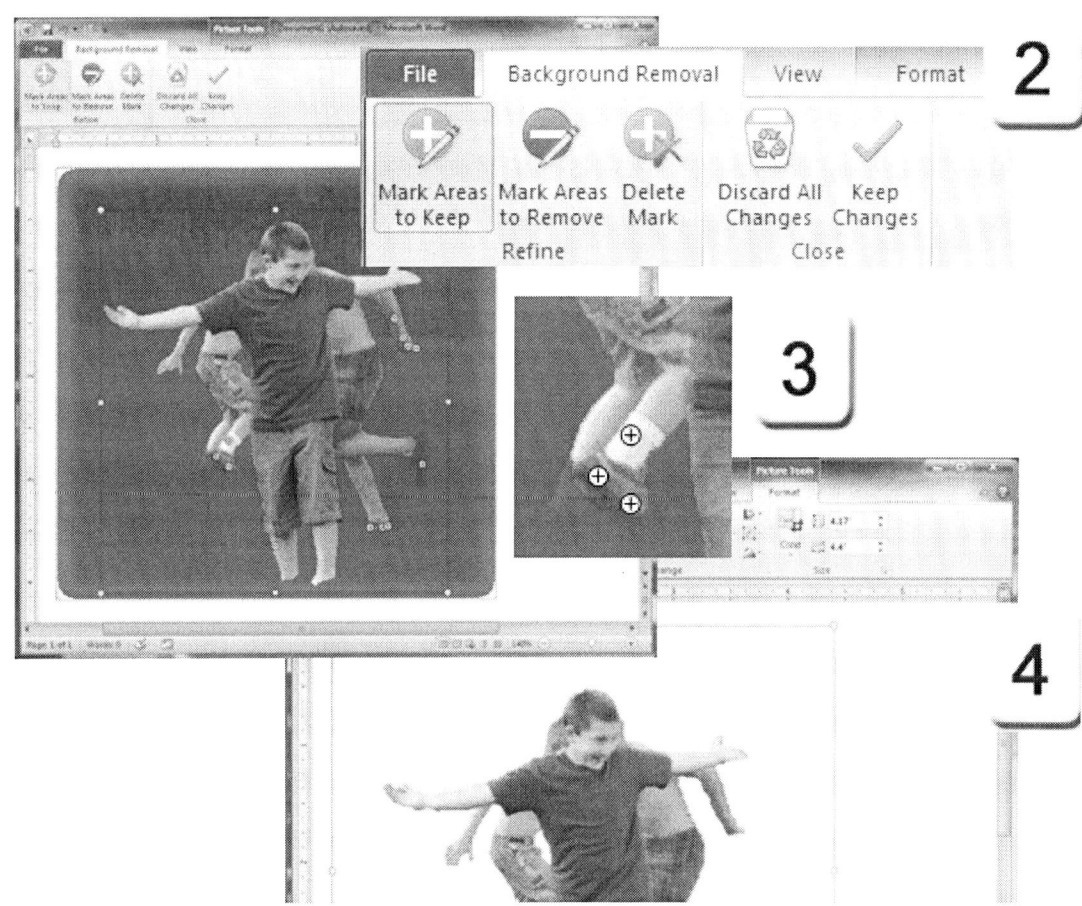

Exam 77-881: Microsoft Word 2010 Core
4. Including Illustrations and Graphics in a Document
4-1. Insert and format Pictures in a document: Remove background

## Crop the Picture

Here is another essential Picture Tool: Cropping. You can use the Cropping tools to cut out distracting background images and focus on the best part of the picture. Here are the steps.

**Try it: Crop the Picture**
1. Go to **Picture Tools -> Format.**
Go to the **Size** group.
Click on **Crop.**

**2. What Do You See?** The picture will have a new frame with black crop marks. Place your cursor on any crop mark, then click and hold your mouse to drag the crop marks and edit the picture. When you are ready, click on **Crop** again to accept your new marks.

**Picture Tools -> Format -> Size -> Crop**

Exam 77-881: Microsoft Word 2010 Core
4. Including Illustrations and Graphics in a Document
4-1. Insert and format Pictures in a document: Crop picture

## Crop to Shape

OK, Ok, one more Picture Tool, just because it is so much fun. You can **Crop** a picture and make it a different shape.

**Try it: Crop the Picture Shape**
**1. Go to Picture Tools -> Format.**
Go to the **Size** group.
Click on **Crop -> Crop to Shape.**

**2. What Do You See?** Microsoft Word 2010 has an impressive library of picture shapes. When you select any one of the shapes, your picture will be formatted as the shape.

**Picture Tools -> Format -> Size -> Crop -> Crop to Shape**

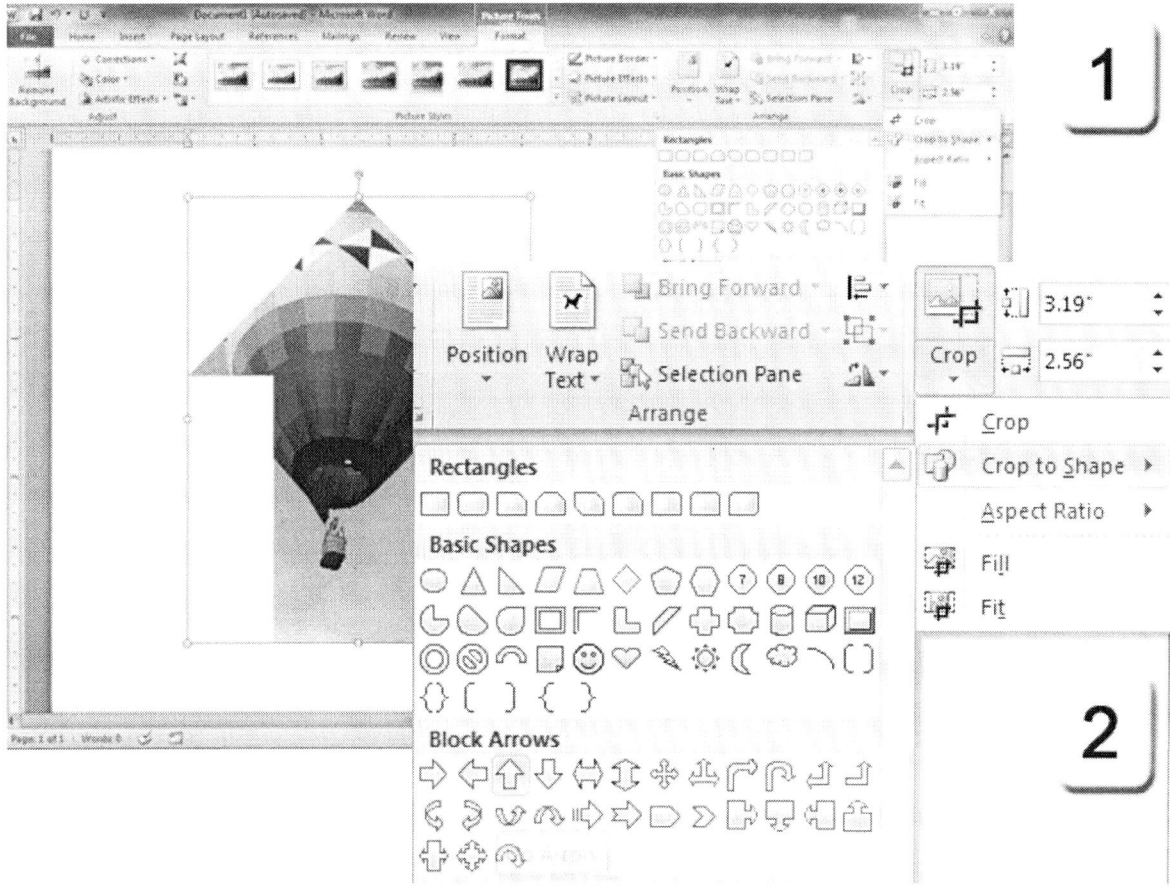

Exam 77-881: Microsoft Word 2010 Core
4. Including Illustrations and Graphics in a Document
4-1. Insert and format Pictures in a document: Crop to shape

## Summary

This lesson demonstrated many of the Picture Tools available in Word 2010. Playing with the pictures is very creative and fun...like a new box of crayons. In the next lesson we will put it all together and create professionally designed business letterhead.

Well you done good.
You get the cookie.

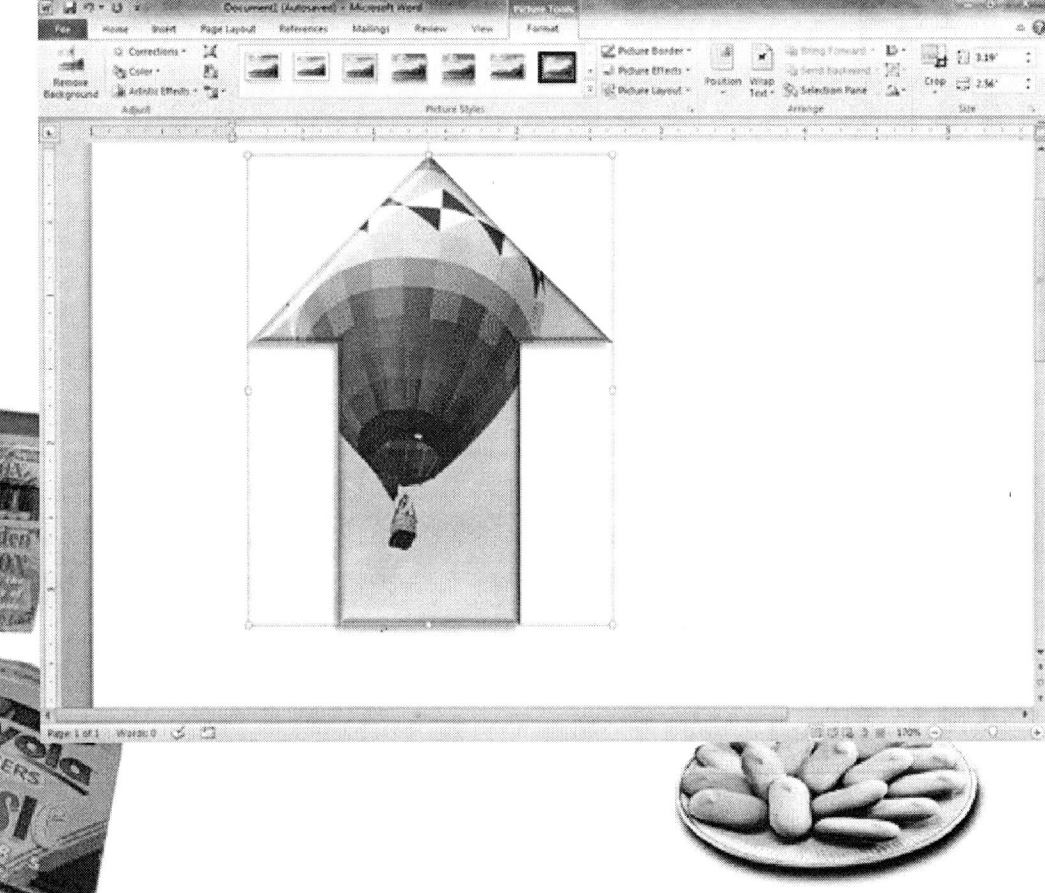

# Practice Activities

## Lesson: Fancy Colors

**Before You Begin:** Start Microsoft Word 2010. You should see a new, blank document.

**Try This: Do the following steps**

1. Insert a picture from your computer using the Insert Picture command.
2. Apply Picture Style Metal Frame.
3. Insert a 2nd picture from your computer.
4. Apply Soft Edges at 10 pt.
5. Insert a 3rd picture from your computer.
6. Use the Recolor Tool and apply Accent Color 2 Light. Apply Picture Border 3 pt Weight in Red.
7. Insert a 4th picture from your computer.
8. Format the Picture: Saturation, 3D Rotation, Effects (Glow), Accent Color 2, 18 pt
9. Insert a 5th Picture from your computer.
10. Crop the Picture to Shape using either an arrow or heart shape.
11. Pick 1 of the 5 pictures and use Reset Picture.
12. Save this document as Your Name Practice 4.

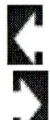

# Test Yourself

1. Insert Picture adds which of the following?
a. Clip Art from the Clip Art gallery
b. Clip Art from the online gallery
c. A photo or image on your computer
Tip: Beginning Word, page 96

2. To turn on the Picture Tools Ribbon, select a picture in the document.
a. True
b. False
Tip: Beginning Word, page 98

3. What Ribbon are the Pictures Styles found on?
a. Home
b. Picture Tools->Format
c. Styles
Tip: Beginning Word, page 99

4. You can add more than one picture effect.
a. True
b. False
Tip: Beginning Word, page 101

5. When you use the Change Picture command, all formatting applied to the original picture is applied to the replacement picture.
a. True
b. False
Tip: Beginning Word, page 110

6. Which of the following is an option under the Color command?
(Select all correct answers.)
a. Color saturation
b. Color tone
c. Recolor
d. Brightness
Tip: Beginning Word, page 105

7. Which of the following is NOT a picture correction option?
A. Sharpen
B. Soften
C. Brighten
D. Contrast
E. Recolor
Tip: Beginning Word, page 103

8. Which of the following is a Picture Border option?
(Select all correct answers)
a. Width
b. Color
c. Style
d. Length
Tip: Beginning Word, page 102

9. Which of the following is true about Artistic Effects?
(Select all correct answers)
a. They are photographic filters applied to an image
b. Effects include pencil, pastel, and chalk
c. The effects can be adjusted manually
Tip: Beginning Word, page 107

10. Picture Effects and Borders commands are located in what group on the Picture Tools Ribbon?
A. Format
B. Adjust
C. Picture Styles
D. Effects
Tip: Beginning Word, page 101

## Word 2010: Graphics and Quick Parts
# First Prize

### Beginning Word Objectives
**In this lesson, you will learn how to:**

1. Insert a Shape

2. Apply Styles, Quick Styles and other formatting to a Shape

3. Resize Shapes

4. Add Text to and modify text in a Shape

5. Insert SmartArt

6. Add text to and modify text in SmartArt

7. Access the Smart Art Tools Ribbon

8. Format and Modify SmartArt shapes, layout, and colors

9. Identify and Use different document views, including Reading, Split Screen and Side by Side

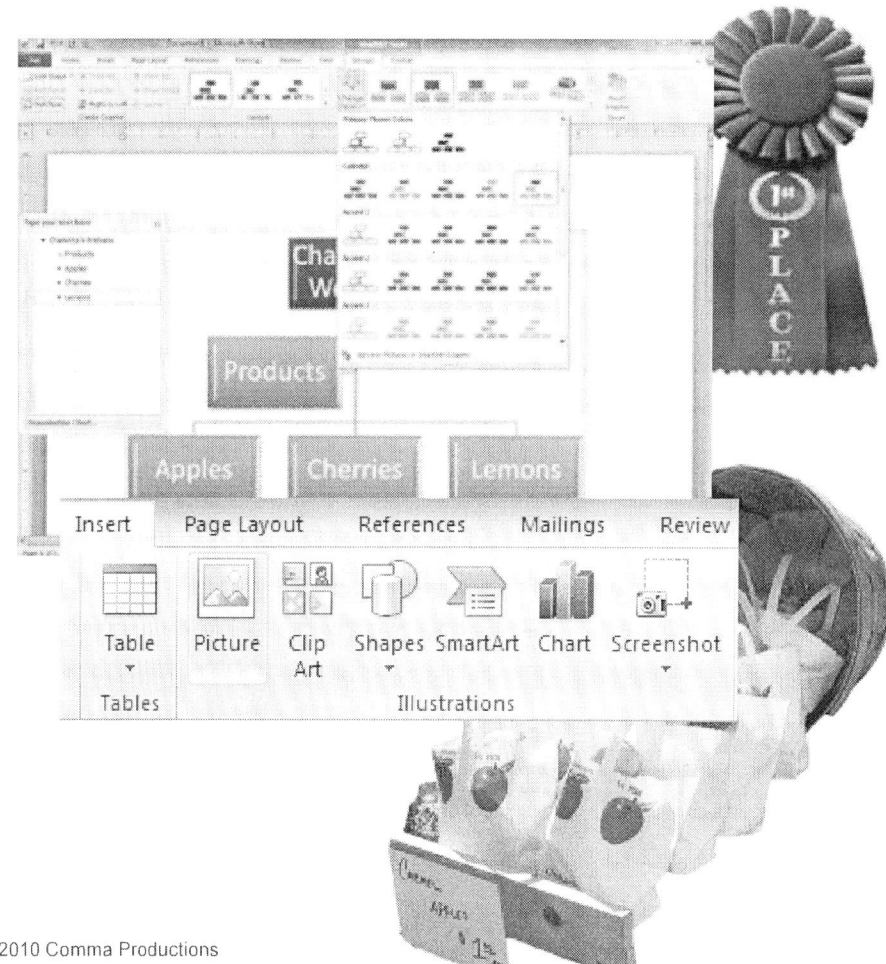

© 2010 Comma Productions

# Lesson 6: First Prize

## 1. Readings

Read Lesson 6 in the Beginning Word guide, page 119-156.

## Project

A marketing flier using Shapes, Quick Styles, Picture Tools and Smart Art.

## Downloads

Graphic files used in the lesson:
Logo, American Flag, HamburgFestival3, HamburgFestival4, HamburgFestival5

## 2. Practice

Complete the Practice Activity for this lesson, page 155.

## 3. Assessment

Review the Test questions, page 156.

**Drawing Tools->Format**

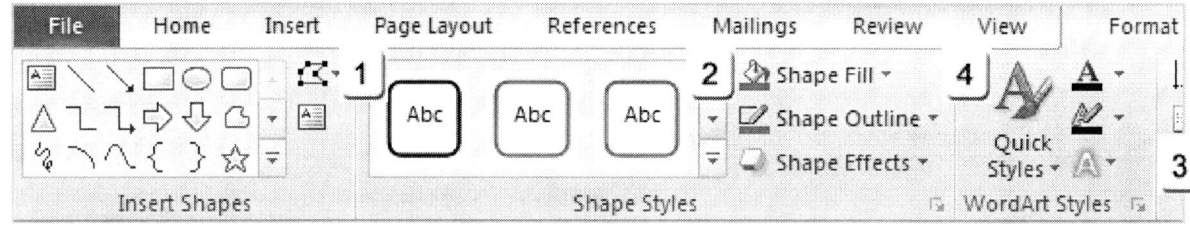

**SmartArt Tools->Design**

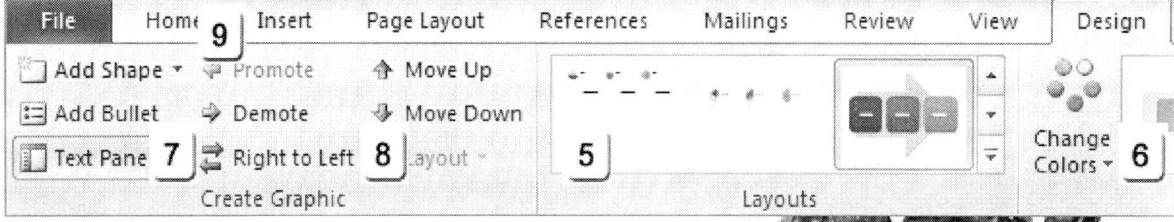

# Menu Maps

This lesson shows options on the **Drawing and SmartArt Tools**.
1. Drawing Tools-> Format ->Shape Styles, page 127
2. Drawing Tools-> Format-> Shape Fill, page 128
3. Drawing Tools-> Format WordArt Styles-> Text Effect, page 131
4. Drawing Tools-> Format-> Quick Styles, page 133
5. SmartArt Tools-> Design ->SmartArt Styles, page 136
6. SmartArt Tools-> Design->Change Colors, page 138
7. SmartArt Tools-> Design->Create Graphic-> Text Pane, page 141
8. SmartArt Tools-> Design->Create Graphic->Right to Left, page 142
9. SmartArt Tools-> Design->Create Graphic->Add Shape, page 143

# First Prize

Every business and even every department is in a race to win my time and money. Marketing is allowed to "color outside the lines" to get my attention. In addition to setting up formal stationery, you need to promote your products and services. As you create this little marketing flier, watch how the Picture Tools compare with the Shape Tools. If you are ready, **Start** the **Program** Microsoft **Word**.

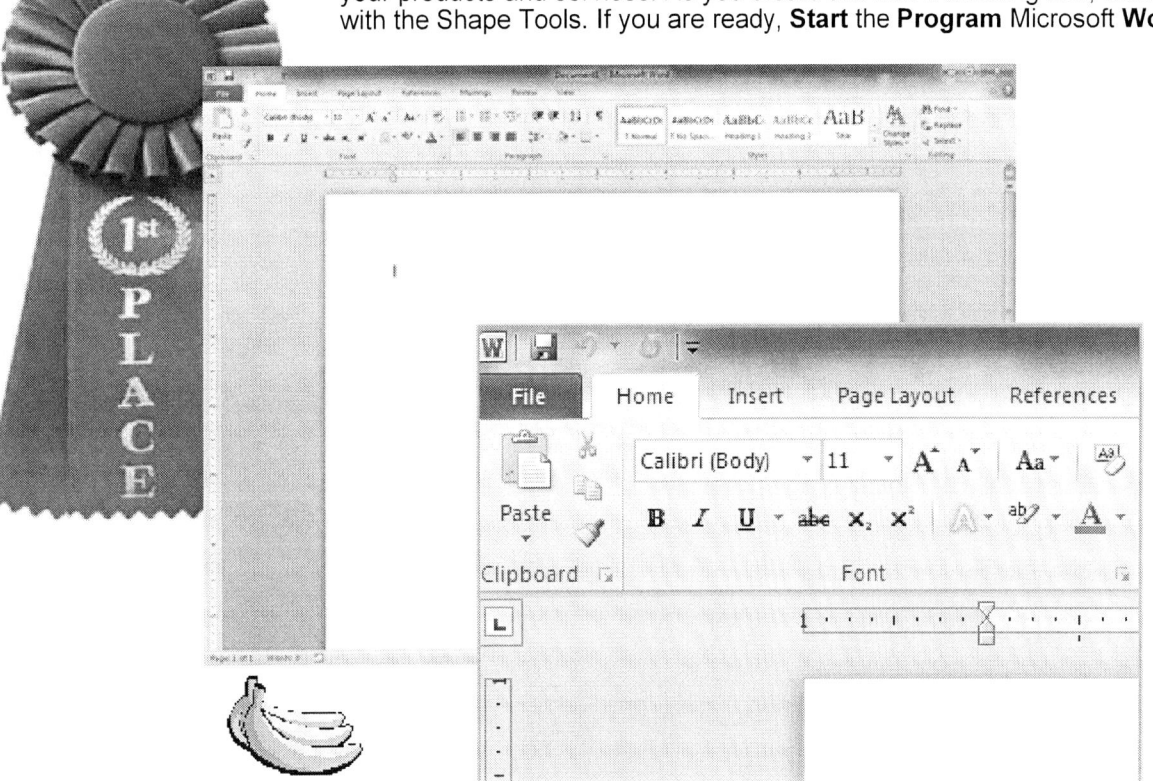

**What do you see from the top of the screen?** Is there a Title Bar that says Microsoft Word? Yes.

Is there a **Home** Ribbon with the **Clipboard, Font and Paragraph** Groups? Yes.

If your screen looks similar to the example on this page, then you are ready to get started.

## Begin with the Text

The five "W's" of good writing are: who, what, when, where, and why. Who are you? What are you saying to me? Why does it matter? All communication and marketing begins with the name.

**1. Enter the name**

**Type**: Charlotte's Website

**Select**: Charlotte's Website.

Go to **Home ->Font.**

Select: Tahoma, 36 pt

**Select:** Charlotte's.

Go to **Home->Font**.

Select: Bold.

Go to **Home->Font->Font Color.**

Select:Blue

**2. Enter the text**

**Type**: The Best in Farm Fresh Food Delivered to Your Door!

**Select** that text.

Go to **Home -> Font.**

Select: Tahoma, 16 pt

Home -> Font

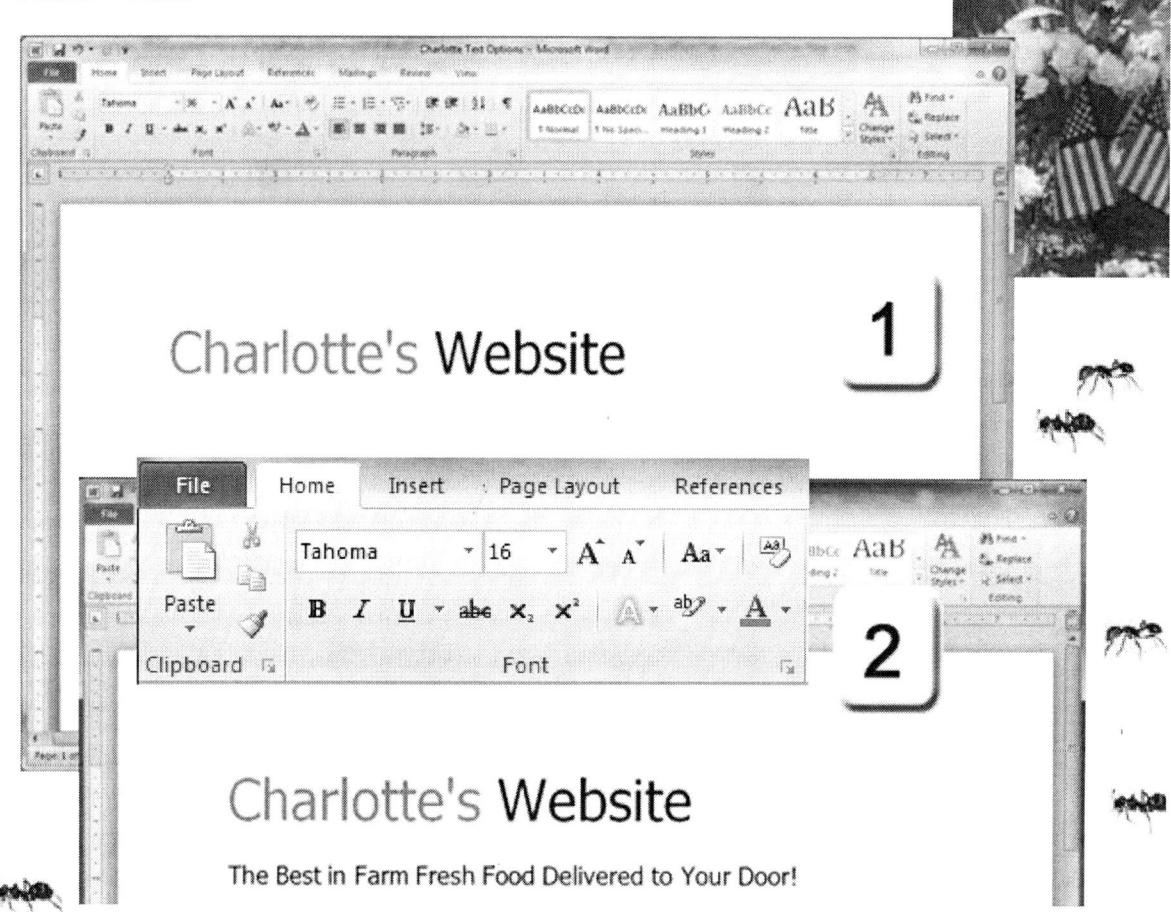

Exam 77-881: Microsoft Word 2010 Core
2. Formatting Content
2-1. Apply font and paragraph attributes

**Insert A Picture**
There are **sample files** that you can use for this flyer. You are also welcome to use your own imagination.

**3. Insert and Format a Picture**
Go to **Insert->Illustrations->Picture.**

Look in the **Documents** folder**.**
**Select** a picture for this flyer.

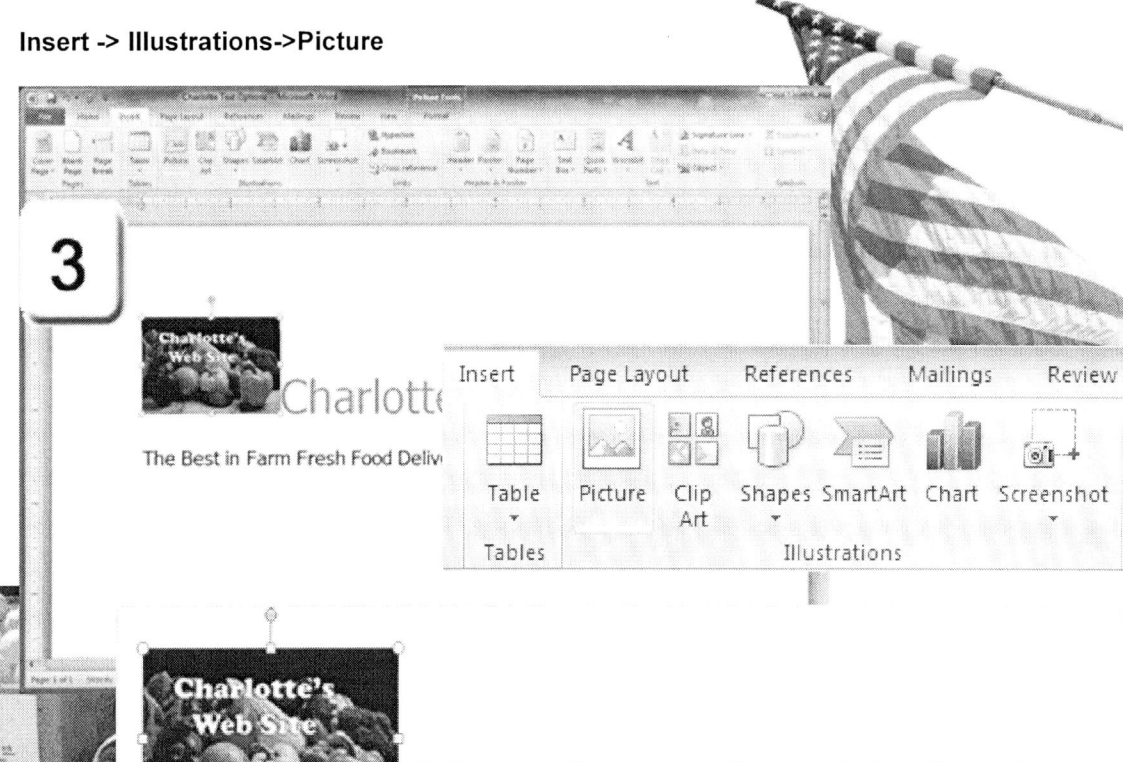

**Charlotte's Website**

The Best in Farm Fresh Food Delivered to Your Door!

Exam 77-881: Microsoft Word 2010 Core
4. Including Illustrations and Graphics in a Document
4-2. Insert and format shapes, WordArt, and SmartArt

## Picture Styles

Microsoft Word 2007 and Word 2010 offer a gallery of **Picture Shapes**, **Borders** and **Effects**. These format options can be found in the **Picture Styles**.

### 4. Format with Picture Styles

Click on the picture to **Select** it.
Go to the **Format** Ribbon.
Choose a **Picture Style**.

**Picture Tools -> Format -> Picture Styles**

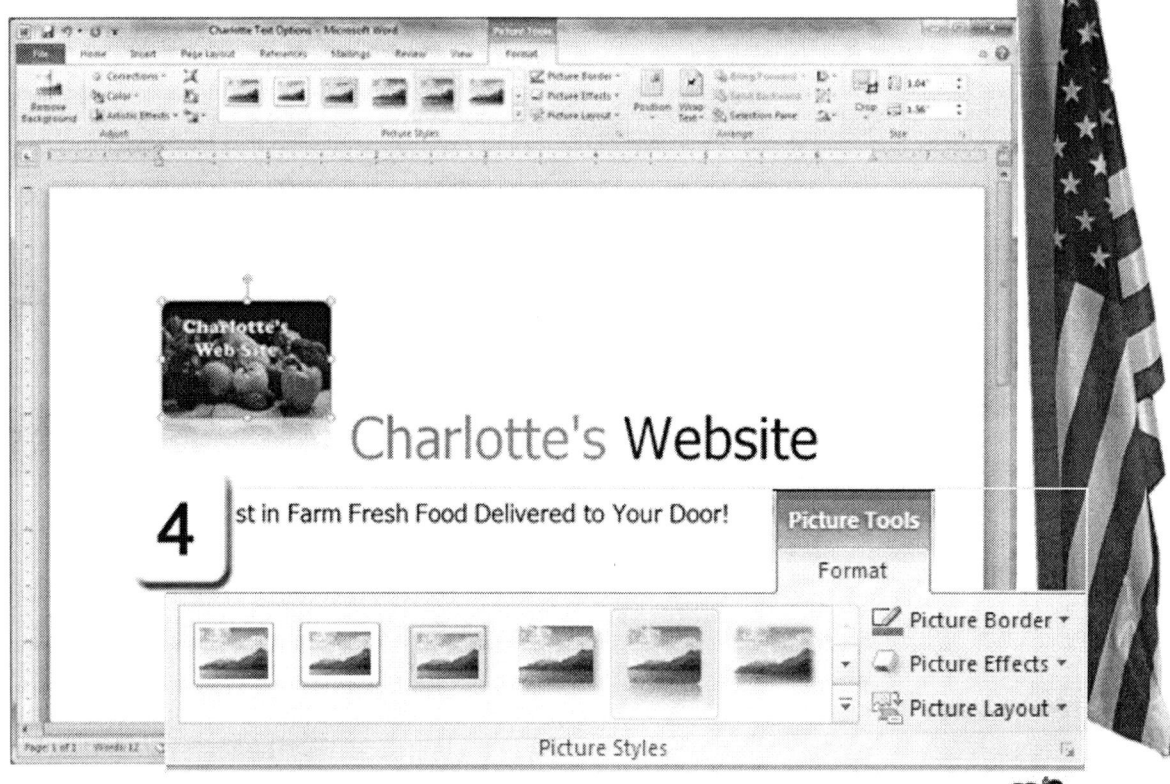

**Memo to Self:** There are small up and down arrows on the right side of the gallery so that you can see more options.

Exam 77-881: Microsoft Word 2010 Core
4. Including Illustrations and Graphics in a Document
4-1. Insert and format Pictures in a document

**Picture Tools -> Format -> Size ->Crop-> Crop to Shape**

## Crop to Shape

**Crop to Shape** takes your pictures and places it inside of a shape. As we saw in the previous section, you can find Crop to Shape in the **Size** group on the right side of the Picture Tools.

**Before You Begin: Add a Picture**

Go to **Insert->Picture**.
Choose a another picture. The example on this page is a flag.

**5.Try it: Crop the Picture Shape**

Click on the picture to select it.
Go to **Picture Tools -> Format.**
Find the **Size** group.
Click on **Crop -> Crop to Shape.**

**What Do You See?** There are basic shapes as well as call outs, math functions (plus or minus) stars, banners and flow chart symbols.

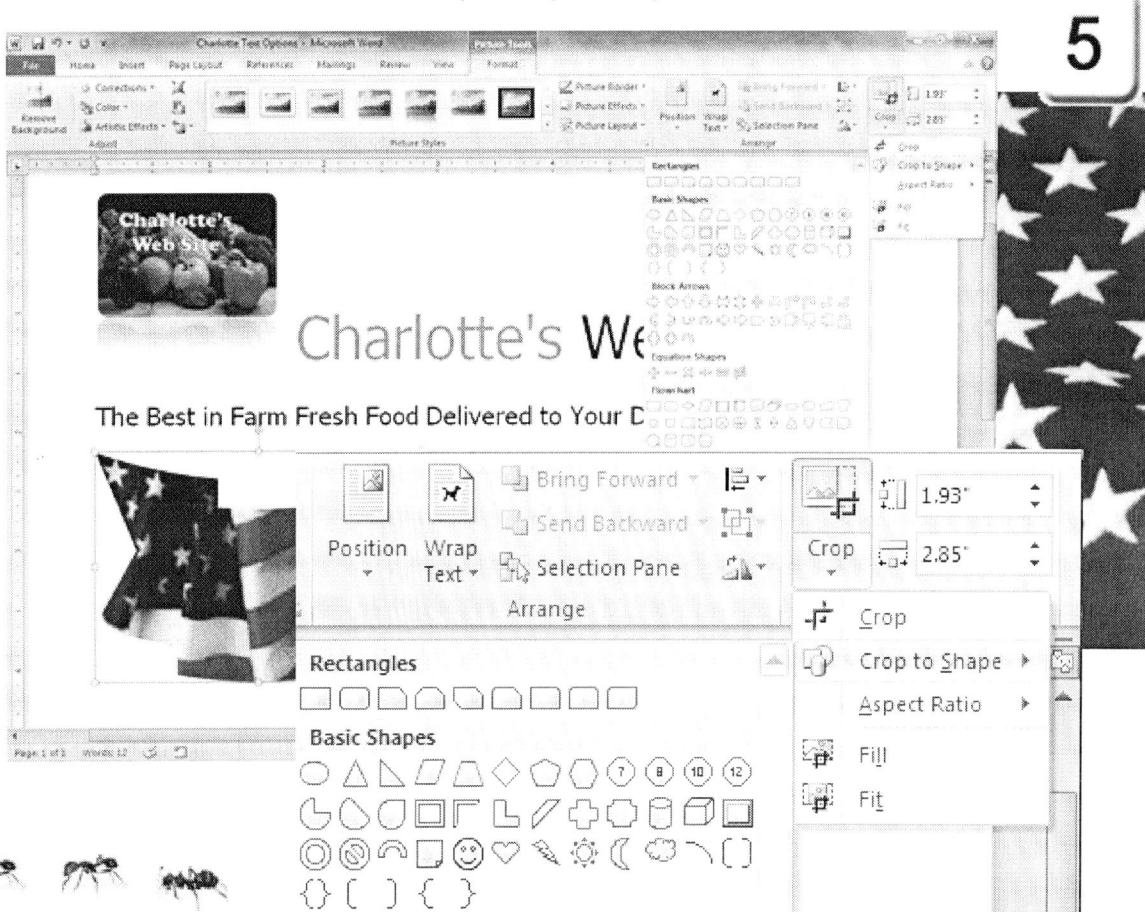

Exam 77-881: Microsoft Word 2010 Core
4. Including Illustrations and Graphics in a Document
4-2. Insert and format shapes, WordArt, and SmartArt: Crop to Shape

**Picture Tools -> Format -> Picture Effects**

## Picture Effects

**Picture Effects** can be very tasty "eye candy." Please, remember your audience. A little bit goes a long way. Too much candy is simply too sweet.

### 6. Format with Picture Effects

Click on the picture to **Select** it.

Go to the **Format** Ribbon.
Choose a **Picture Effect.**

Exam 77-881: Microsoft Word 2010 Core
4. Including Illustrations and Graphics in a Document
4-1. Insert and format Pictures in a document: Picture Effects

## Insert Shapes

A **Shape** is a Textbox with custom formatting. Microsoft PowerPoint uses Textboxes for the headlines and bullet lists on each slide.

Microsoft Word uses Textboxes to put the Mail Merge fields in the right place for a bar code machine to read the envelope correctly.

**1. Try It: Insert Illustrations**
Go to **Insert ->Illustrations.**
Click on **Shapes**.
Choose a **Shape**.

**Draw the Shape**: Hold you cursor on a blank place in your document and drag a small square. You should see a shape that you can select, format and resize.

Keep going, please...

Insert -> Illustrations -> Shapes

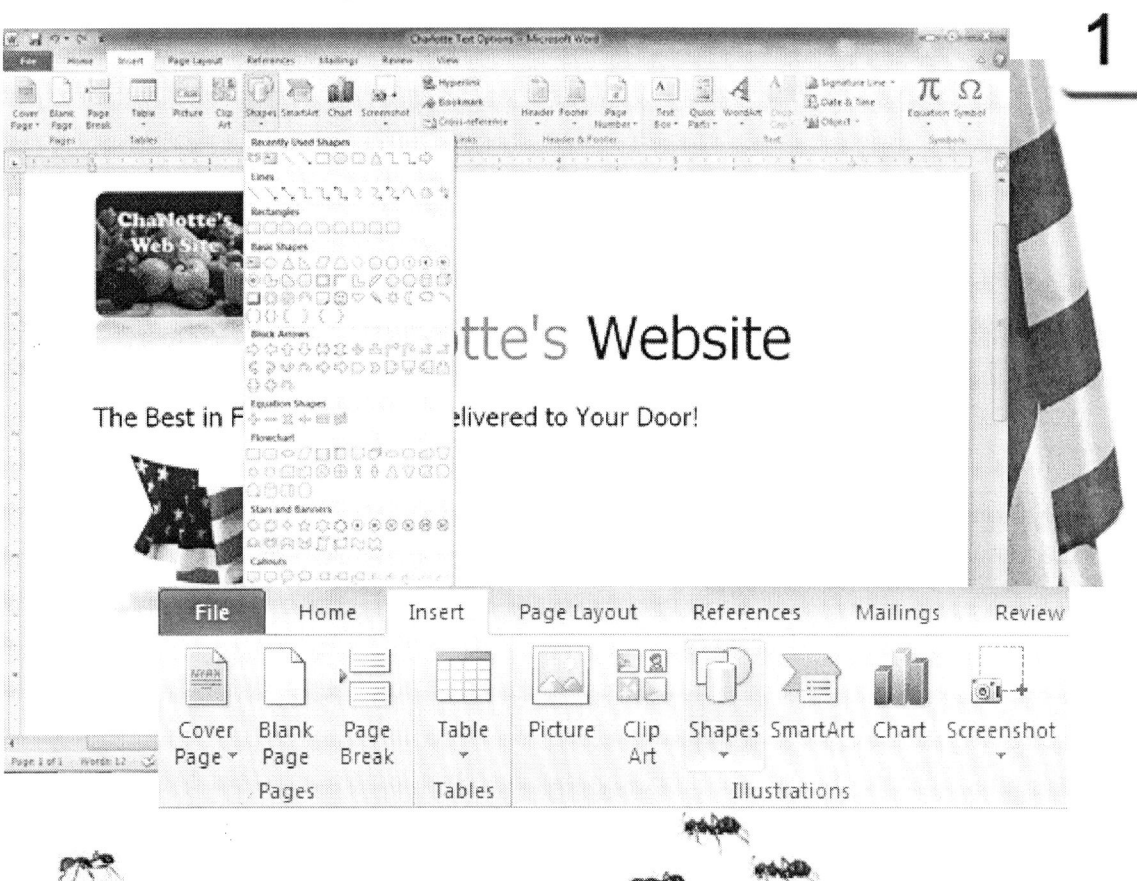

Exam 77-881: Microsoft Word 2010 Core
4. Including Illustrations and Graphics in a Document
4-2. Insert and format shapes, WordArt, and SmartArt

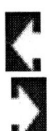

## Format the Shape

When you add a shape to your document you may notice a new ribbon a the top of your screen: the **Drawing Tools.** The Drawing Tools has Insert Shapes, Shape Styles, WordArt, Text, Arrange (layout) and Size.

### 2. Try It: Format the Shape Style

Select the Shape to begin.
Go to **Drawing Tools->Forma**t.
Click on one of the **Shape Styles**.

Keep going...

**Drawing Tools -> Format -> Shape Styles**

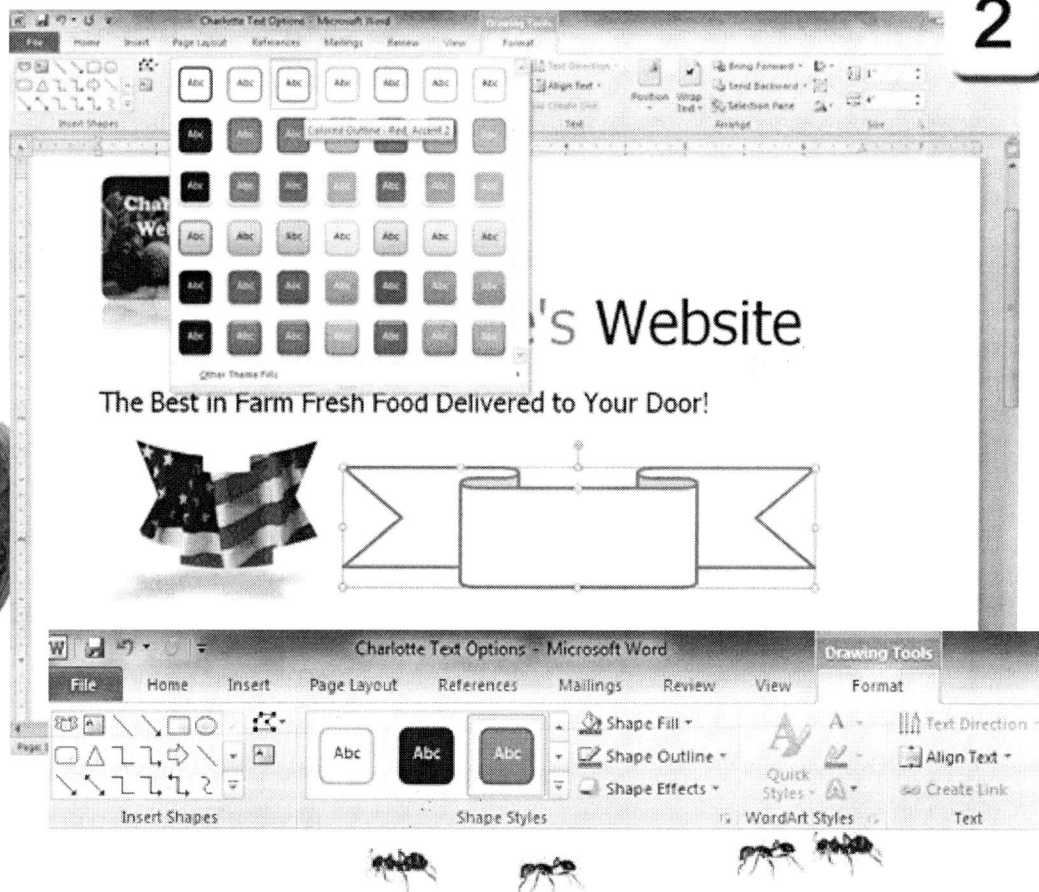

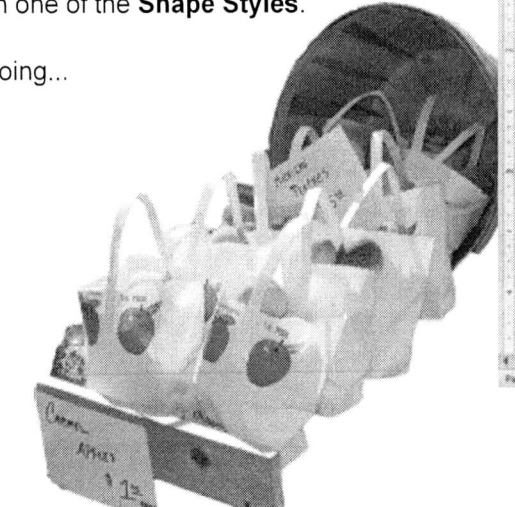

Exam 77-881: Microsoft Word 2010 Core
4. Including Illustrations and Graphics in a Document
4-2. Insert and format shapes, WordArt, and SmartArt: Shape Styles

Drawing Tools -> Format -> Shape Fill

## More Style Options

Look in the **Shape Styles.** You should see the same tools that you can use to format a picture: Fill, Outline and Effects.

### 3. Try It: Format the Shape

Click on the Shape to select it.

Go to **Drawing Tools->Format.** Go to **Shape Fill** and choose a Color or Gradient if you wish.

Keep going...

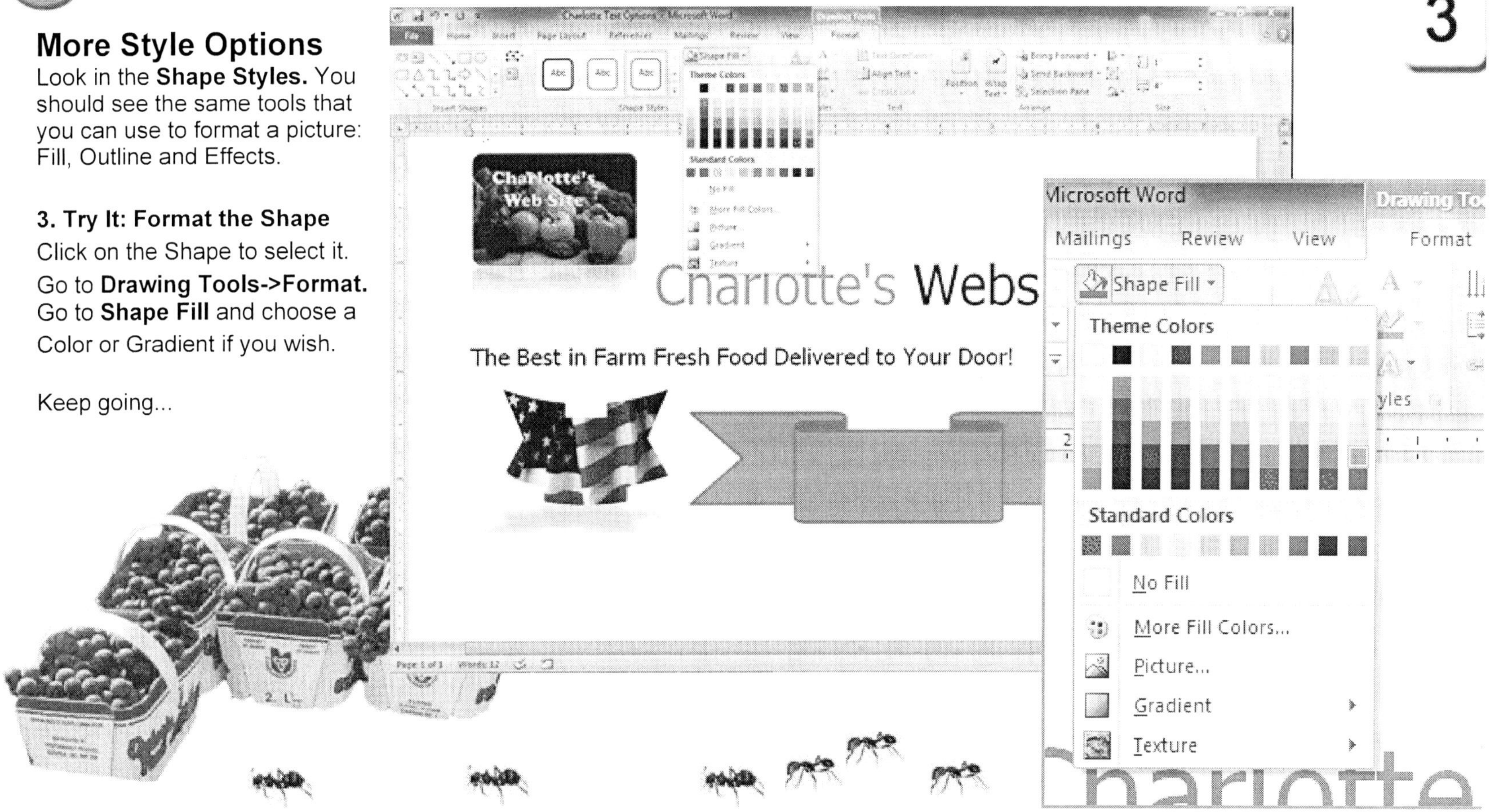

Exam 77-881: Microsoft Word 2010 Core
4. Including Illustrations and Graphics in a Document
4-2. Insert and format shapes, WordArt, and SmartArt: Shape Fill

## Format the Size

Most people resize a picture or a shape by dragging one of the handles. There is another method for sizing an object that is more precise.

Look in the **Drawing Tools** for the **Size** group and you will see that you can edit the numbers.

**4. Try It: Format the Size**
**Select** the Shape.
Go to **Drawing Tools -> Format.**
Go to the **Size** group and edit the height and the width.

Drawing Tools -> Format -> Size

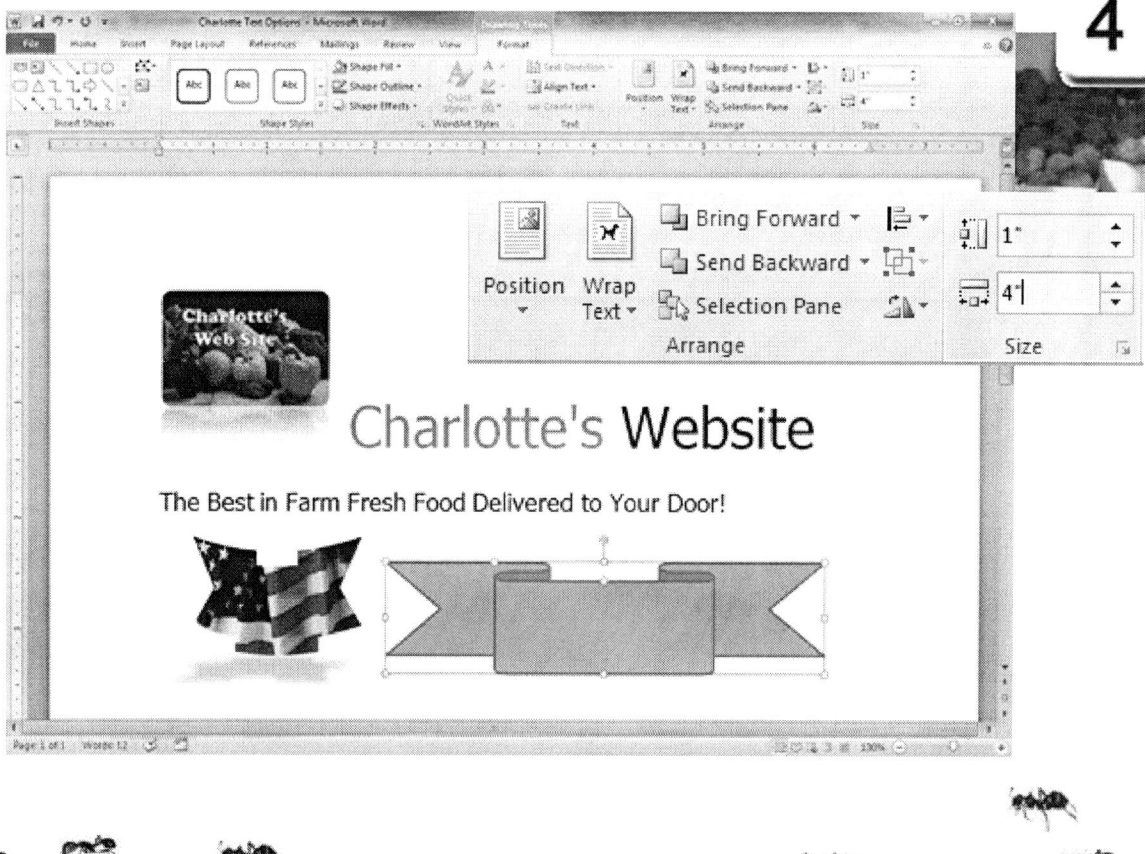

Exam 77-881: Microsoft Word 2010 Core
4. Including Illustrations and Graphics in a Document
4-2. Insert and format shapes, WordArt, and SmartArt: Format the size

Drawing Tools -> Format -> Text

## Add Text to the Shape

You can add **Text** to a Shape if you wish. Here are the steps.

**5. Format the Shape (Add Text)**

Before you begin, please click on the shape to select it. You should see the **Drawing Tools**.

**Right Click** the Shape and you should see a short list of Options. Click **Add Text**.

Type: Fresh is Best!

**Memo to self:** You may also be able to just left-click and just start typing in the shape.

Exam 77-881: Microsoft Word 2010 Core
4. Including Illustrations and Graphics in a Document
4-2. Insert and format shapes, WordArt, and SmartArt: Add Text to a Shape

## Modify the Text

One of the best new formatting tools is the **Text Effects.** In addition to the Shadows, Reflections, Glows and Bevels. you can **Transform** the shape of the Text.

### 6. Try It: Format the Text Effects

**Select** the Text Box.
Go to **Drawing Tools -> Format.**
Go to the **WordArt Styles** group.
Go to **Transform** and choose a Style.

**What Do You See?** Word 2010 will provide a Live Preview as you run your mouse over the options.

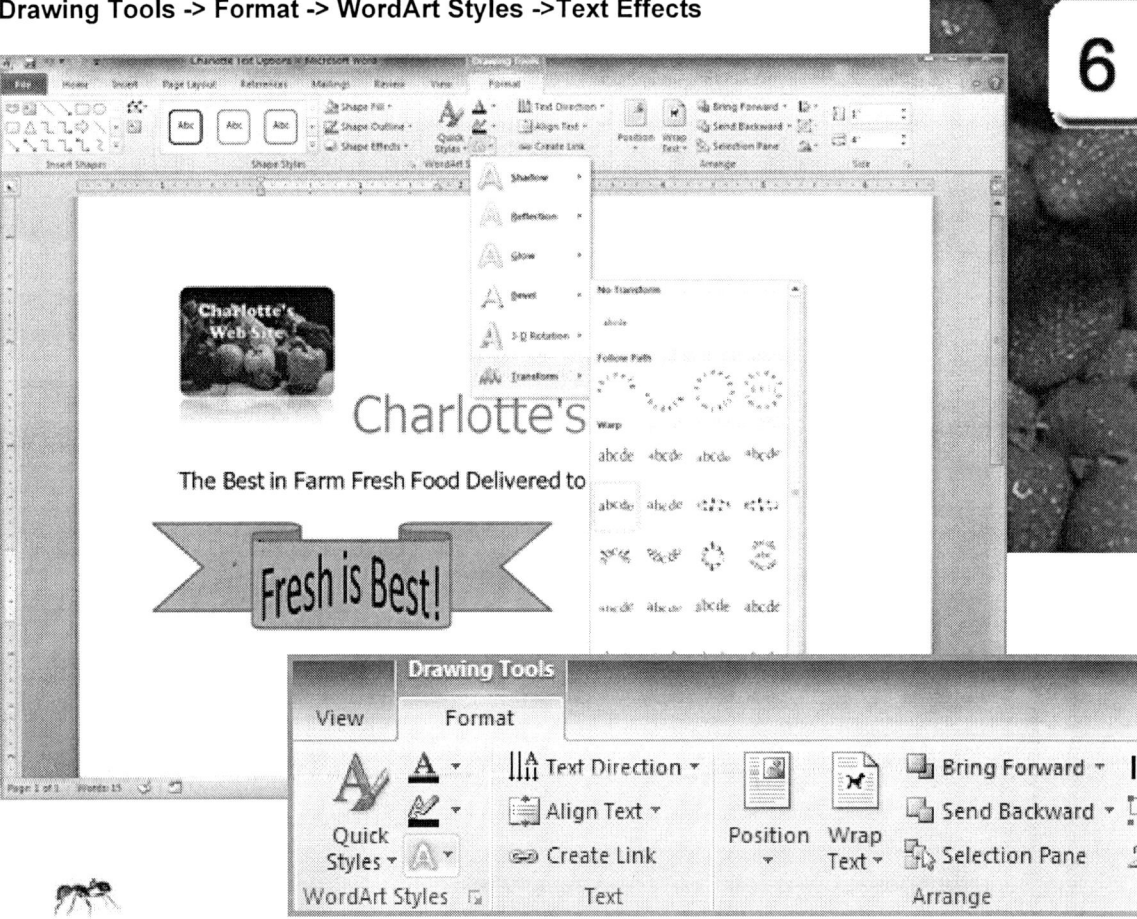

Exam 77-881: Microsoft Word 2010 Core
4. Including Illustrations and Graphics in a Document
4-2. Insert and format shapes, WordArt, and SmartArt: Transform

## Format with Quick Styles

The **Drawing Tools** has an impressive array of **Quick Styles** that you can use to format the Text in this Shape.

**1. Try It: Format the Quick Styles**
**Select** the Text Box.
Select the Text Box.
Go to **Drawing Tools -> Format**.
Go to **WordArt Styles**.
Go to **Quick Styles** and choose one from the library.

**2. What Do You See?** Some of the Quick Style formats are easier to read than others. Keep in mind that the purpose of any eye candy is to draw attention to your message and make it easier to remember.

Well, that was good practice. You do not have to save this document.

The next pages introduce a new, but similar, set of options and Styles.

Drawing Tools -> Format -> WordArt Styles ->Quick Styles

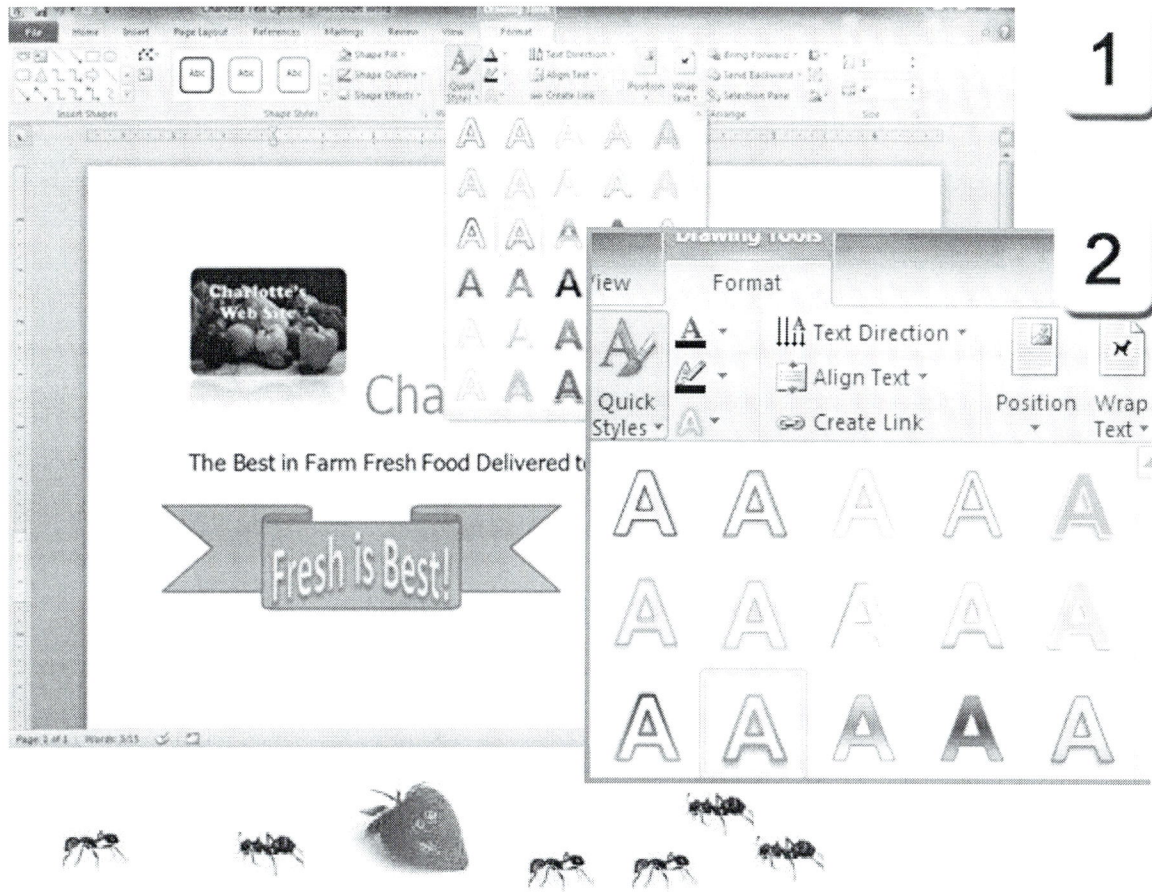

Exam 77-881: Microsoft Word 2010 Core
4. Including Illustrations and Graphics in a Document
4-2. Insert and format shapes, WordArt, and SmartArt: Apply Quick Styles

## Hello SmartArt!

Some **Shapes and Text Boxes** have additional functionality. In fact, these Text Boxes have so many options that Microsoft named them SmartArt.

**SmartArt** creates graphics based on your text. An Organization Chart is one example of SmartArt that automatically adjusts the layout if you add a new employee.

**Before You Begin**
**Save** and close your work.
Go to **File ->New -> Blank Page**.

**Try This: Insert SmartArt**
1. Go to **Insert ->Illustrations->SmartArt**.
Keep going...

**Insert ->Illustrations->SmartArt**

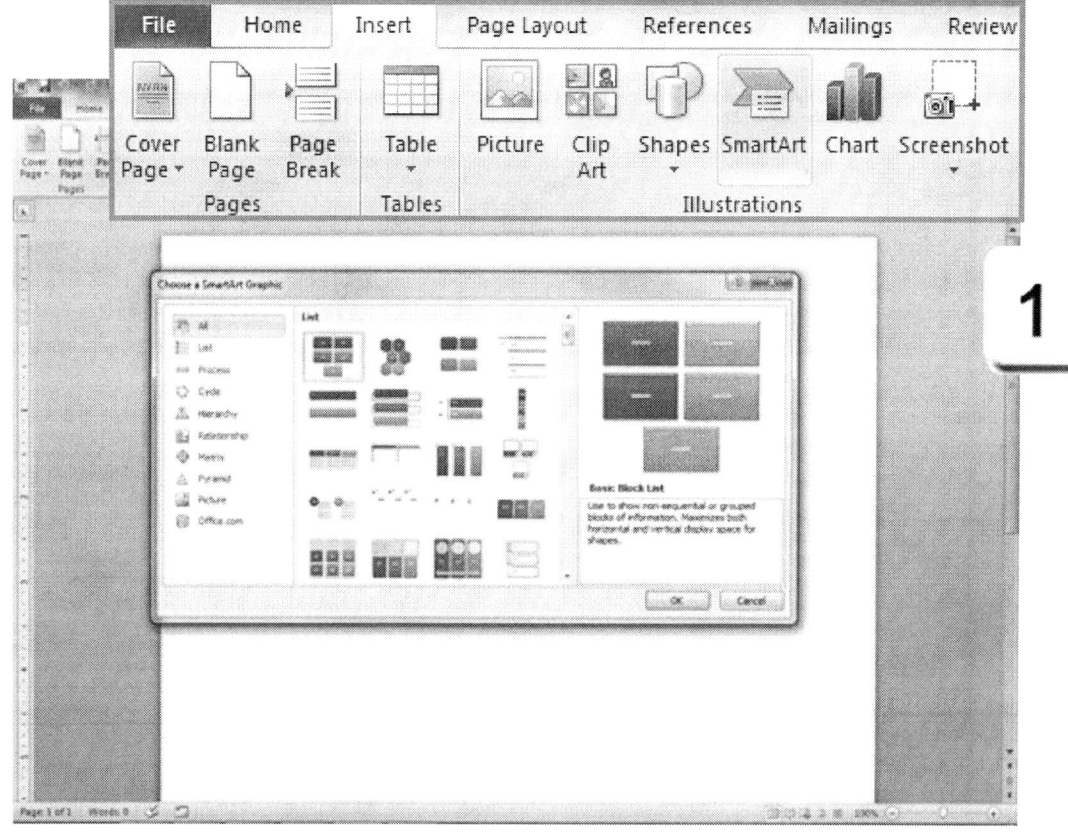

Exam 77-881: Microsoft Word 2010 Core
4. Including Illustrations and Graphics in a Document
4-2. Insert and format shapes, WordArt, and SmartArt

# SmartArt Graphics

**Choose a SmartArt Graphic**

The SmartArt library includes:
List
Process
Cycle
Hierarchy
Relationship
Matrix
Pyramid
Office.com

As you click on each option, you should see a sample of the chart, as well as a short description of how you might find this image useful.

**2. Select: Hierarchy**.

**3. What Do You See?** There will be a new SmartArt graphic.

Keep going...

Insert ->Illustrations->SmartArt ->Hierarchy

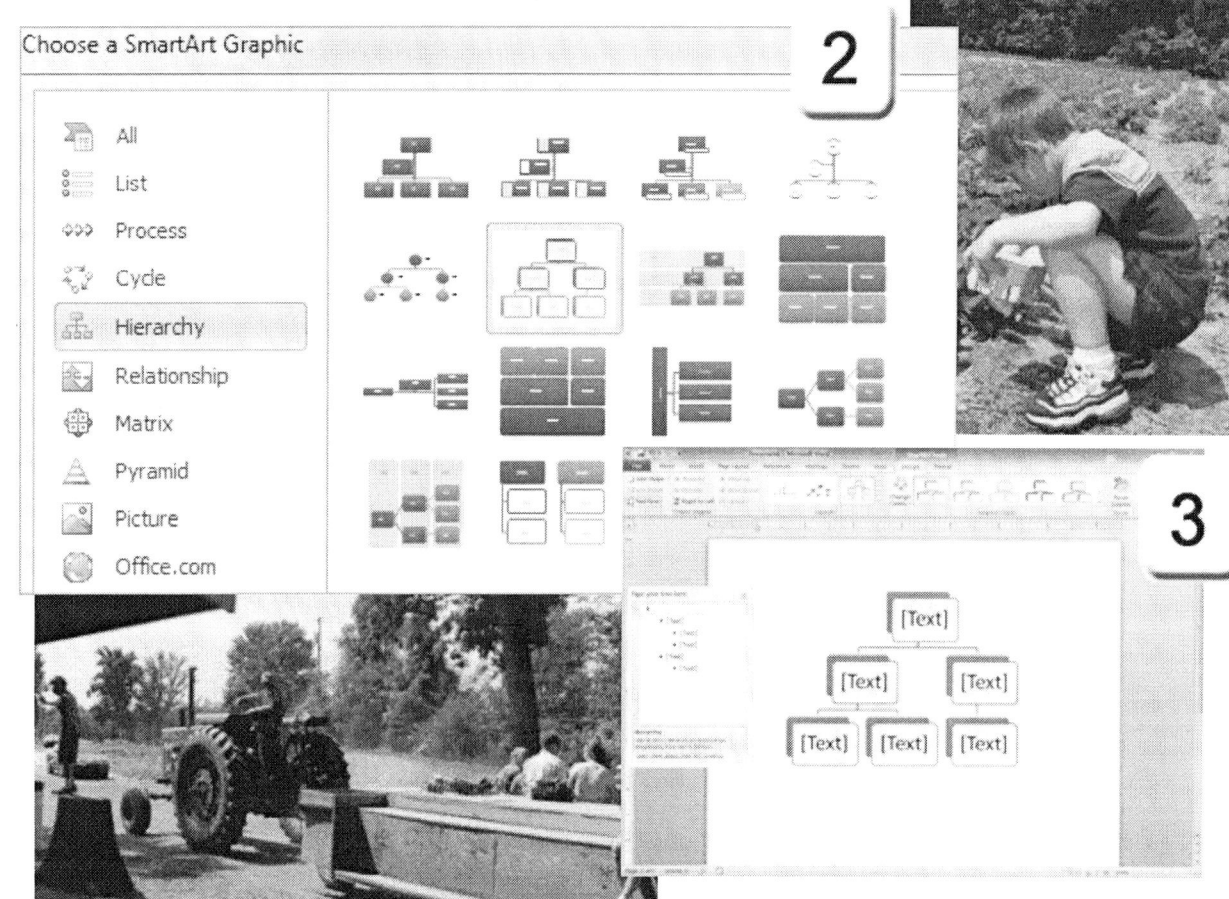

Exam 77-881: Microsoft Word 2010 Core
4. Including Illustrations and Graphics in a Document
4-2. Insert and format shapes, WordArt, and SmartArt

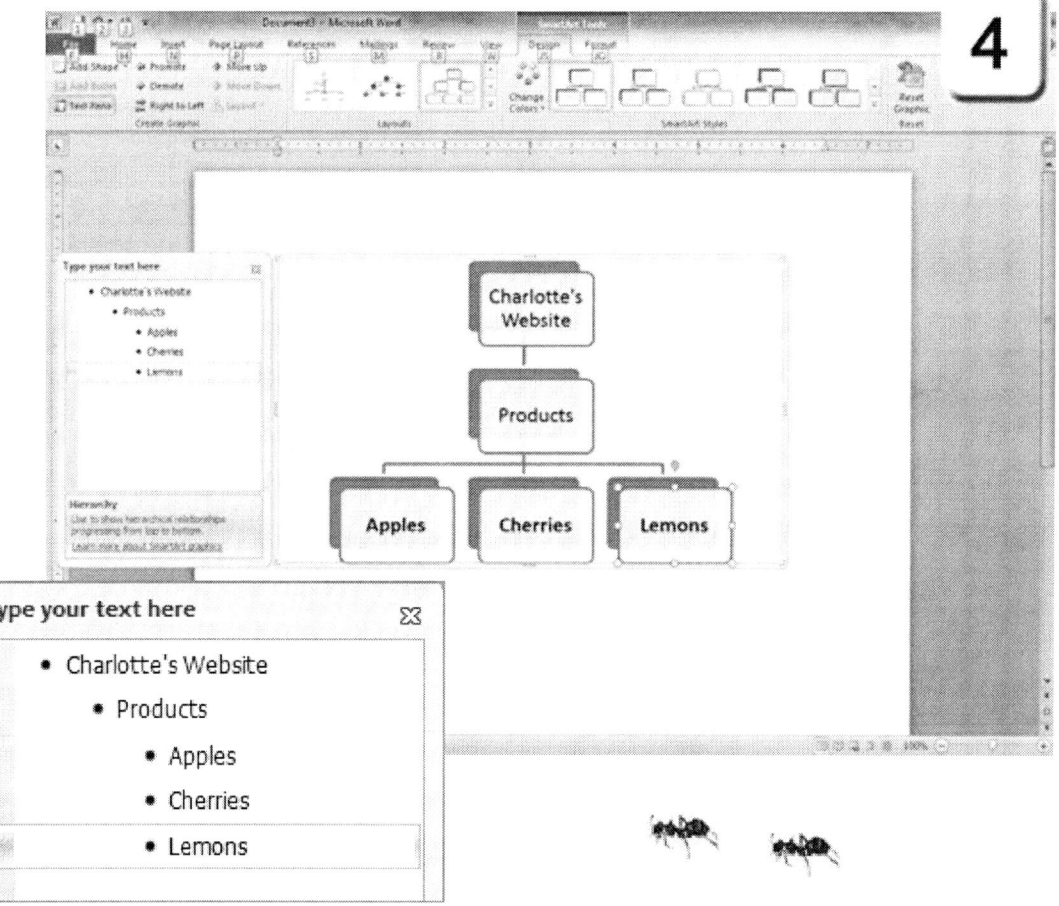

**Insert ->Illustrations->SmartArt**

## Edit the SmartArt

**What Do You See?** There are two parts to the SmartArt graphic: the Text Box. and the Diagram. Whatever you type in the Text Box will be displayed in the Diagram.

**4. Try This: Enter Sample Text**
Go to the **Text Box.**
**Type:** Charlotte's Website.
On the second line type: Products.

**Please add the following:**
Apples
Cherries
Lemons

Keep going...

Exam 77-881: Microsoft Word 2010 Core
4. Including Illustrations and Graphics in a Document
4-2. Insert and format shapes, WordArt, and SmartArt

## SmartArt Tools

The **SmartArt Tools** are similar to the Text Box options. You can use the **Design** Ribbon to edit and improve your chart. The Design tools include options for changing the Layout, Color, Style, Fill, Shape and Outline.

**5. Try It: Use SmartArt Styles**

Click on the SmartArt diagram.

Go to **SmartArt Tools ->Design.**
Select: **SmartArt Styles.**

**What Do You See?** The **Quick Styles** offer a wonderful array of "eye-candy." The Computer Mama enjoys the **Polished** effect.

**Memo To Self:** It's called eye-candy because it looks so sweet and sticky, like a tasty confection.

**SmartArt Tools ->Design ->SmartArt Styles**

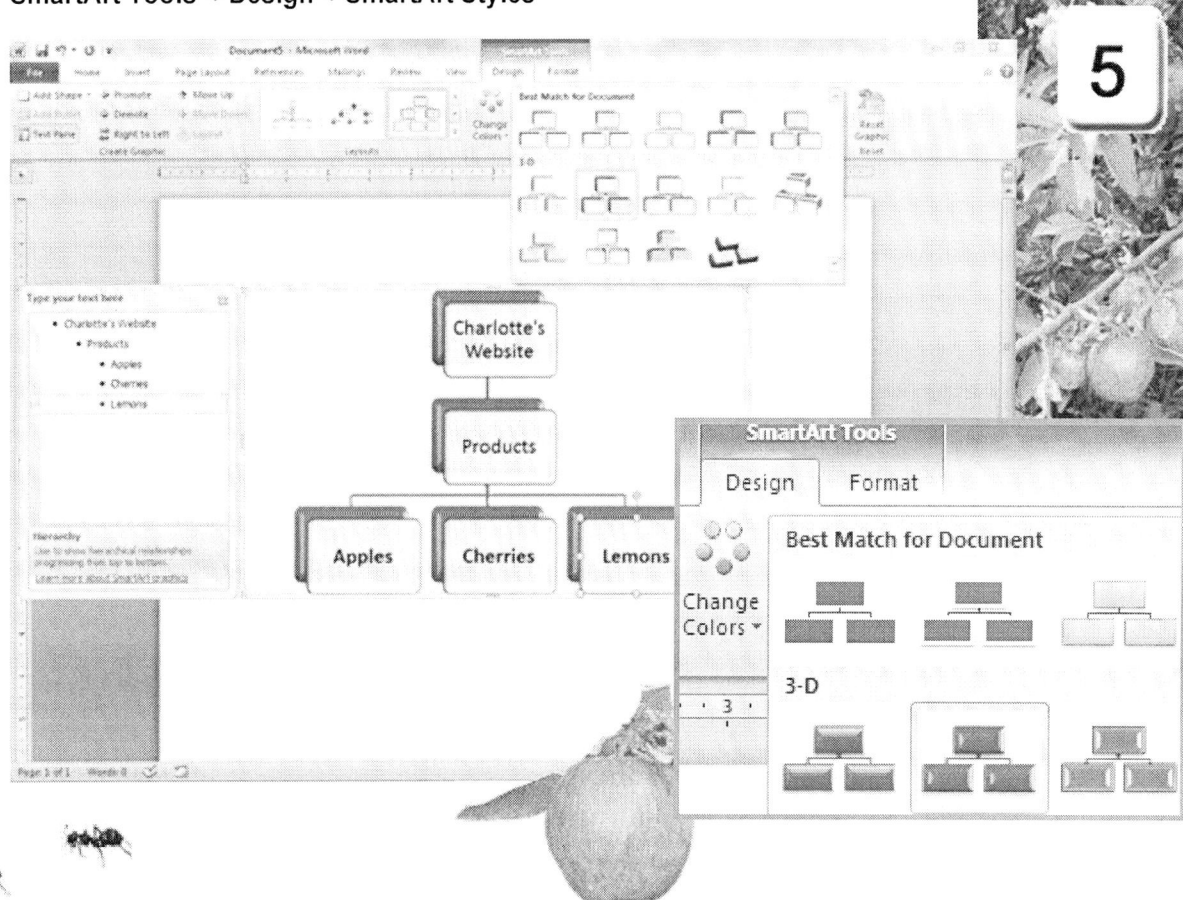

Exam 77-881: Microsoft Word 2010 Core
4. Including Illustrations and Graphics in a Document
4-2. Insert and format shapes, WordArt, and SmartArt: Apply Quick Styles

## Change the Colors

You can use color to format your SmartArt: color is a very powerful method to focus and teach.

**6. Try This: Change the Colors**
Click on the SmartArt diagram.
Go to **SmartArt Tools ->Design**.
Select: **Change Colors**.

**What Do You See?** The **Style** gallery includes several different formats. As you run your mouse over the examples, Microsoft Word 2010's **Live Preview** will display these colors on your diagram.

**SmartArt Tools -> Design -> SmartArt Styles-> Change Colors**

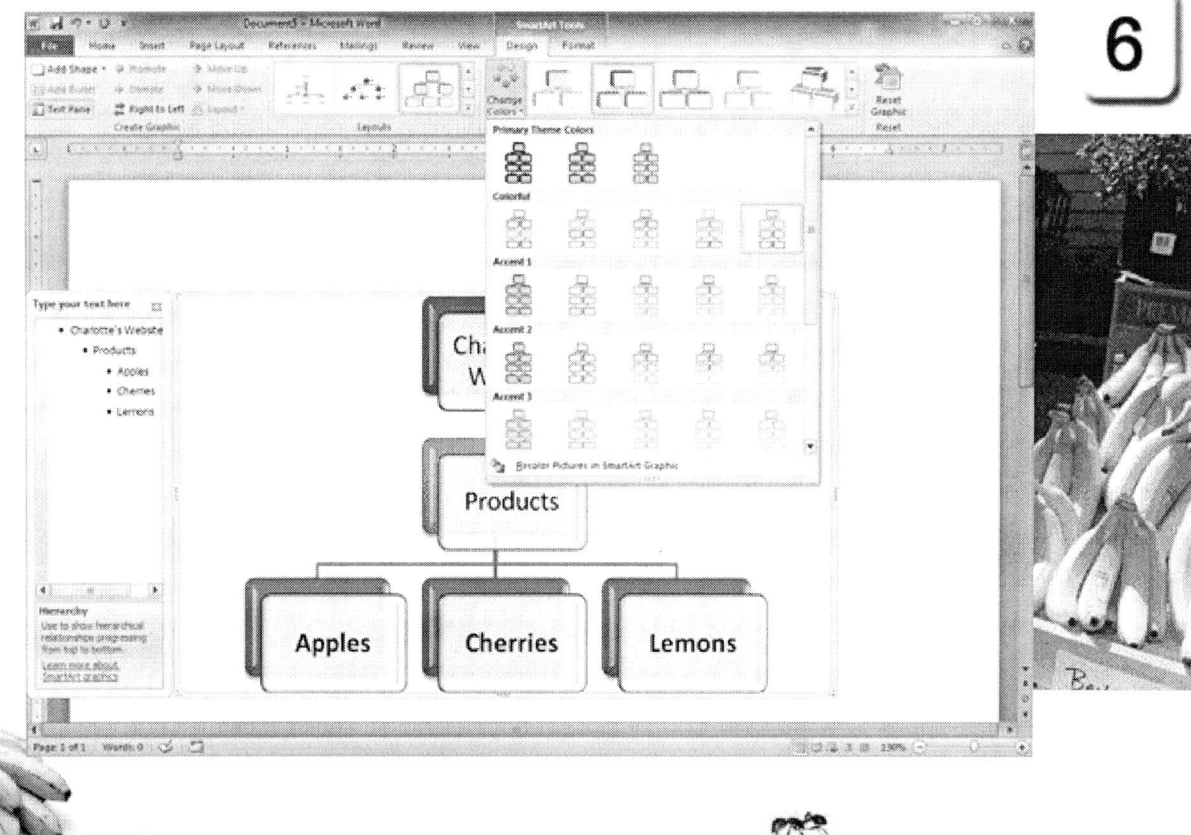

6

Exam 77-881: Microsoft Word 2010 Core
4. Including Illustrations and Graphics in a Document
4-2. Insert and format shapes, WordArt, and SmartArt: Change Colors

Insert ->Illustrations->SmartArt

## How Smart Is It?

The **SmartArt** can dynamically adjust to match your text. Say you wanted to add another product to this sample diagram. Here are the steps you would take. Watch what happens. ;-)

**1. Try This: Edit the Text**

**Select** the SmartArt diagram.

**2. Place** your cursor after the word, Lemons and hit the Enter key on your keyboard to create a new, blank line.

**Type**: Bananas.

**3. What Do You See?** The diagram should automatically update to include your new item.

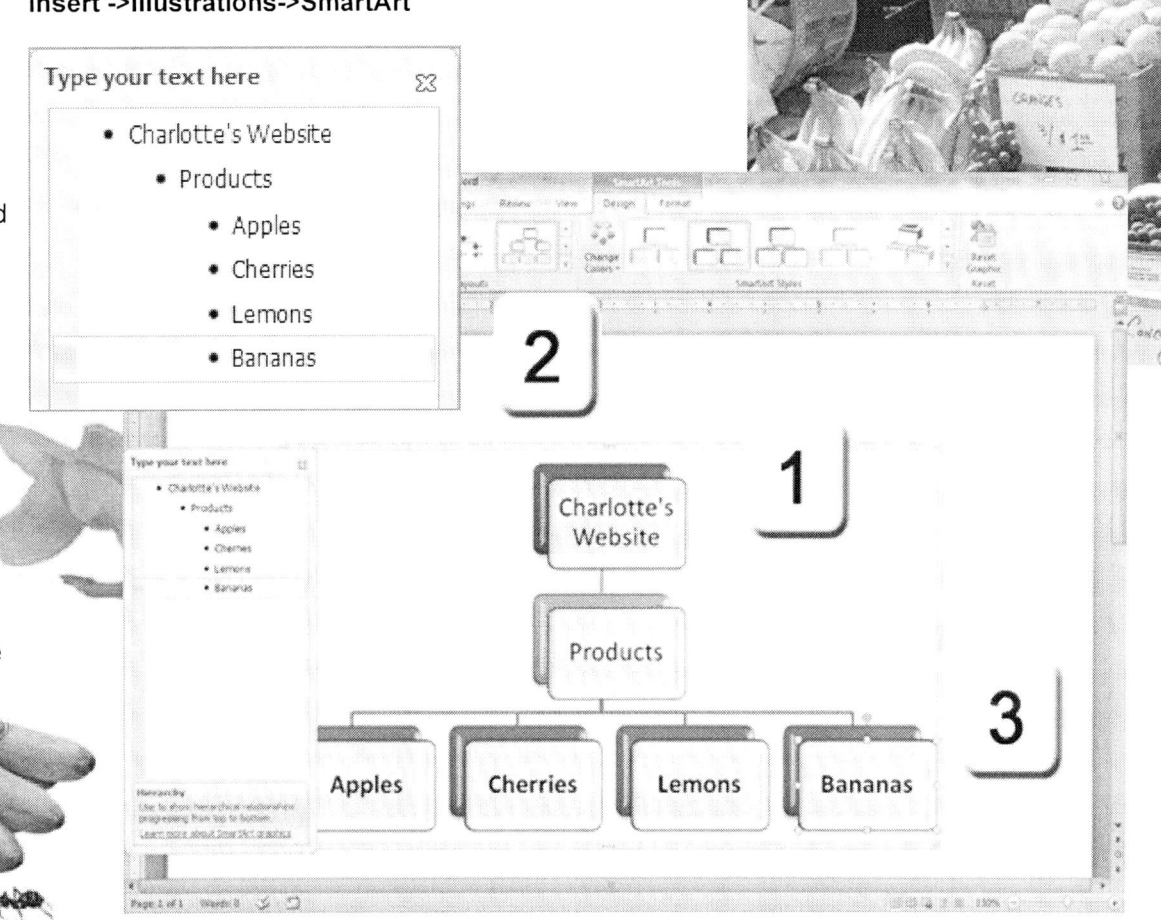

Exam 77-881: Microsoft Word 2010 Core
4. Including Illustrations and Graphics in a Document
4-2. Insert and format shapes, WordArt, and SmartArt

## SmartArt Tools

The **SmartArt Tools** offer two ribbons: **Design** and **Format**. Let's review the **Design** options.

**Before You Begin:** Select the SmartArt. The **SmartArt Tools** should be available.

### 1. Try It: SmartArt Design
Go to **SmartArt Tools ->Design**. Go to **Create Graphic**.

**What Do You See?** You can use the Graphic options to:
Add a Shape
Add a Bullet
Make the Text Pane visible

Keep going...

**SmartArt Tools -> Design -> Create Graphic**

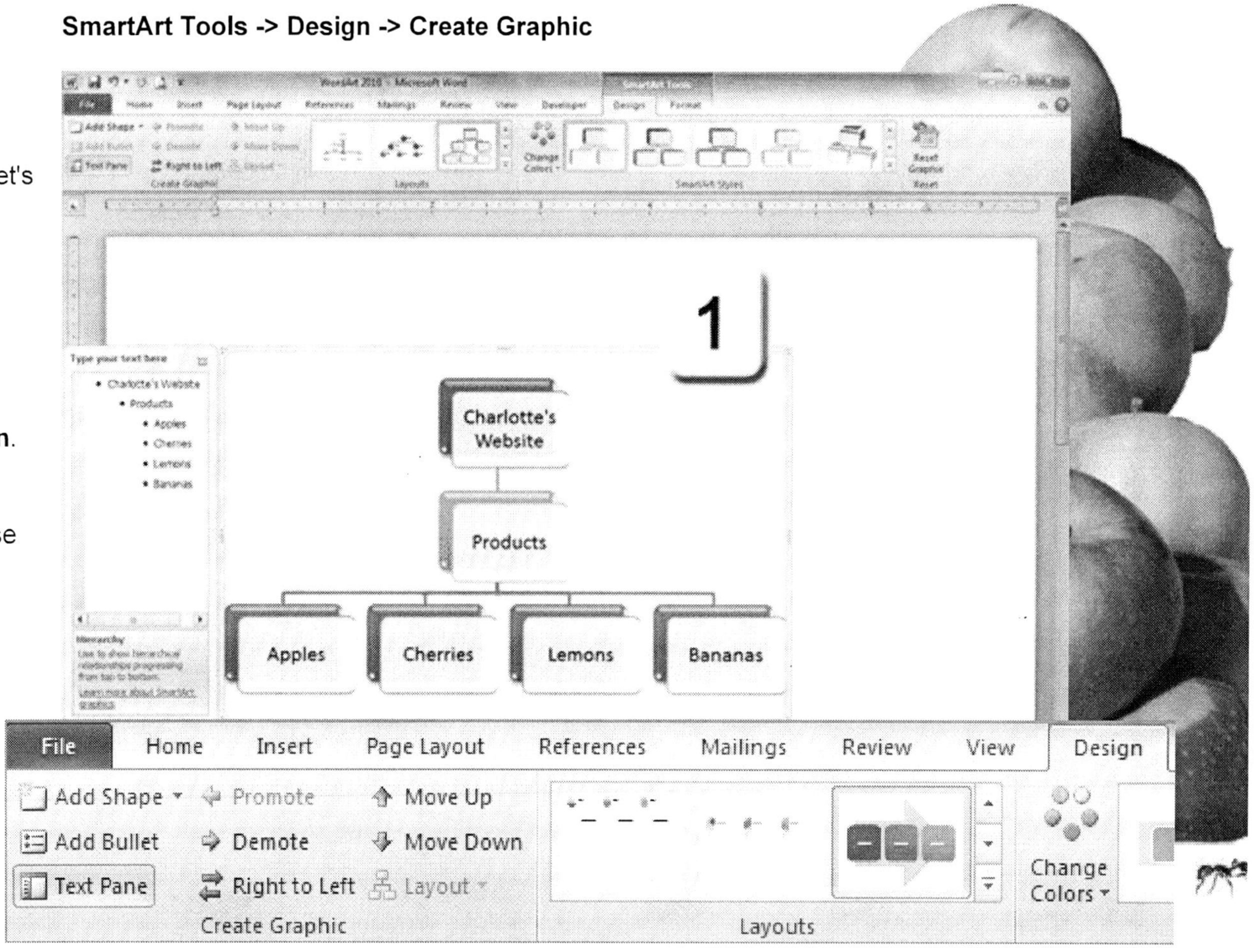

Exam 77-881: Microsoft Word 2010 Core
4. Including Illustrations and Graphics in a Document
4-2. Insert and format shapes, WordArt, and SmartArt: Design Tools

## View the Text Pane

You can Show or Hide the **Text Pane** if you wish. The Text Pane is the data outline to the left of the SmartArt diagram.

**2. Try This, Too: View the Text Pane**

Click on the SmartArt diagram.

Go to **SmartArt Tools ->Design**.
Select: **Text Pane**.

**What Do You See?** The **Text Pane** can be displayed or hidden.

**What Else Do You See?** If you look on the left side of the SmartArt Diagram, there is a small set of arrows that you can use to Show or Hide the Text Pane as well.

Keep going...

**SmartArt Tools -> Design -> Text Pane**

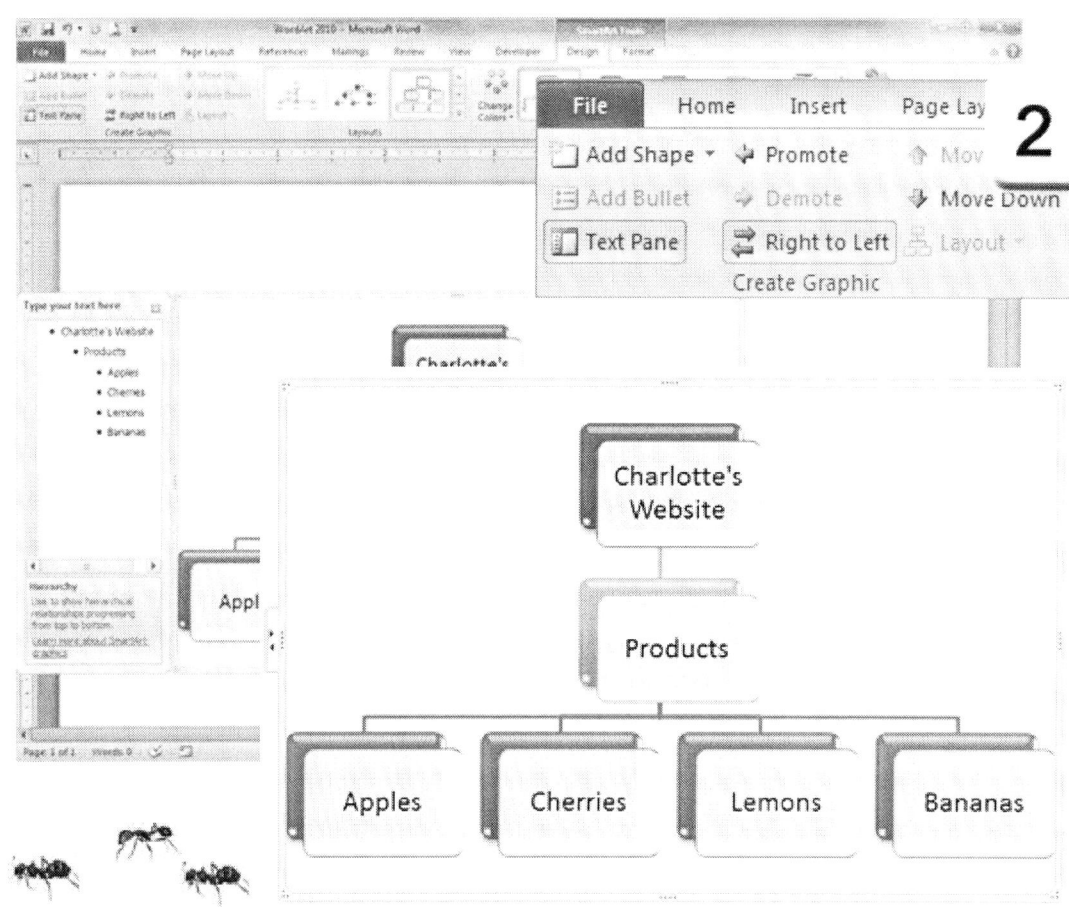

Exam 77-881: Microsoft Word 2010 Core
4. Including Illustrations and Graphics in a Document
4-2. Insert and format shapes, WordArt, and SmartArt: Text Pane

## Edit the Layout

The **Create Graphic Tools** help you arrange the SmartArt Layout. **Promote** and **Demote** change the level in the hierarchy. **Right to Left** changes the sort order on the level that you select.

**Before You Begin**: Select the SmartArt. The **SmartArt Tools** should be available. Click on any shape in the bottom level in the SmartArt diagram.

**1. Try It: Switch Right to Left**
Go to **SmartArt Tools ->Design**.
Go to **Create Graphic**.
Click on **Right to Left**.

**2. What Do You See?** When you choose **Right to Left** the Shapes will be displayed in Reverse order from the way they are listed in the Text Pane.

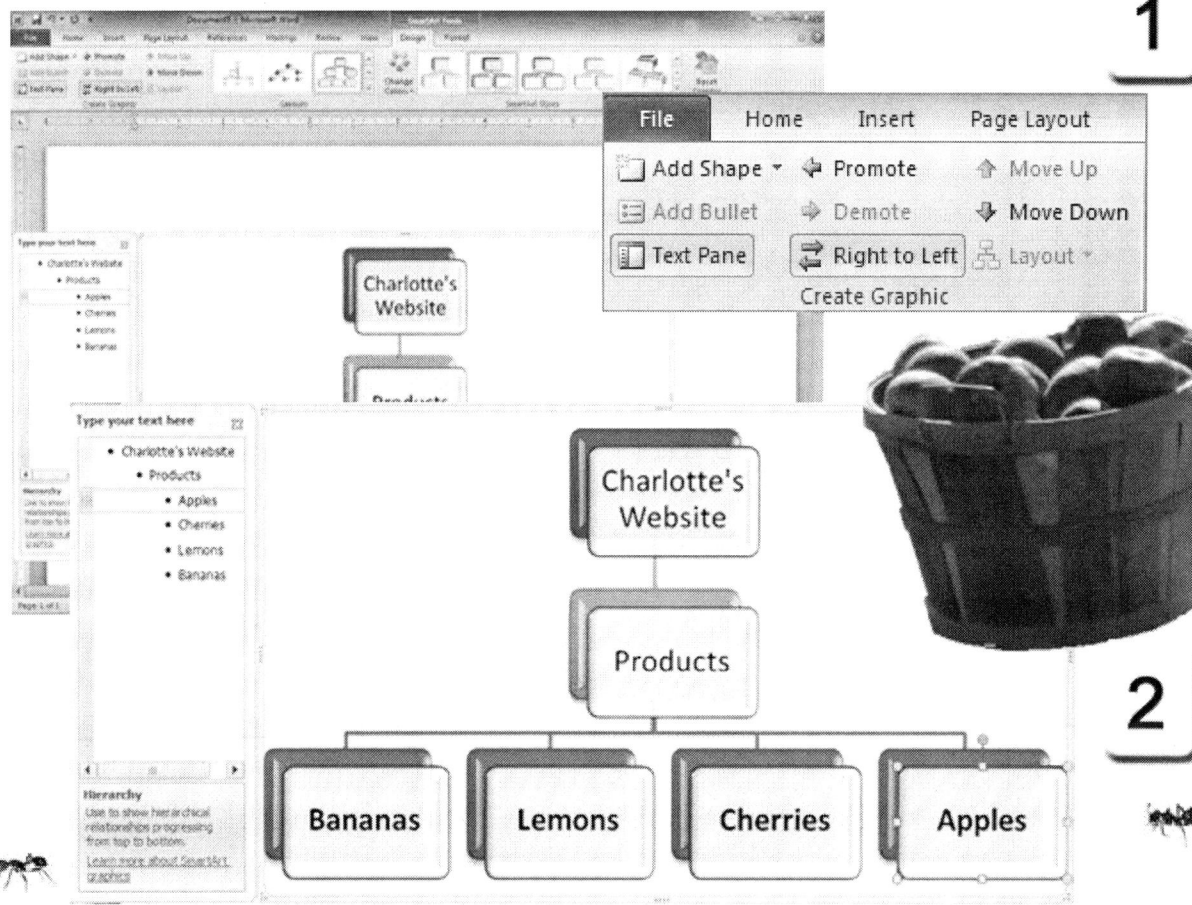

Exam 77-881: Microsoft Word 2010 Core
4. Including Illustrations and Graphics in a Document
4-2. Insert and format shapes, WordArt, and SmartArt: Right to Left

## Add a Shape

More **SmartArt Tools**. Here are the steps to add a new shape to the SmartArt diagram.

**Before You Begin:** Select the SmartArt. The **SmartArt Tools** should be available. Click on the top shape in the SmartArt.

**1. Try It: Add A Shape**
Go to **SmartArt Tools ->Design.**
Go to **Create Graphic.**
Go to **Add Shape.**

**2. What Do You See?** When you choose **Add Shape Below** a new shape will be added to the SmartArt below the shape you selected. A new bullet will be added to the **Text Pane** as well.

SmartArt Tools -> Design -> Create Graphic ->Add Shape

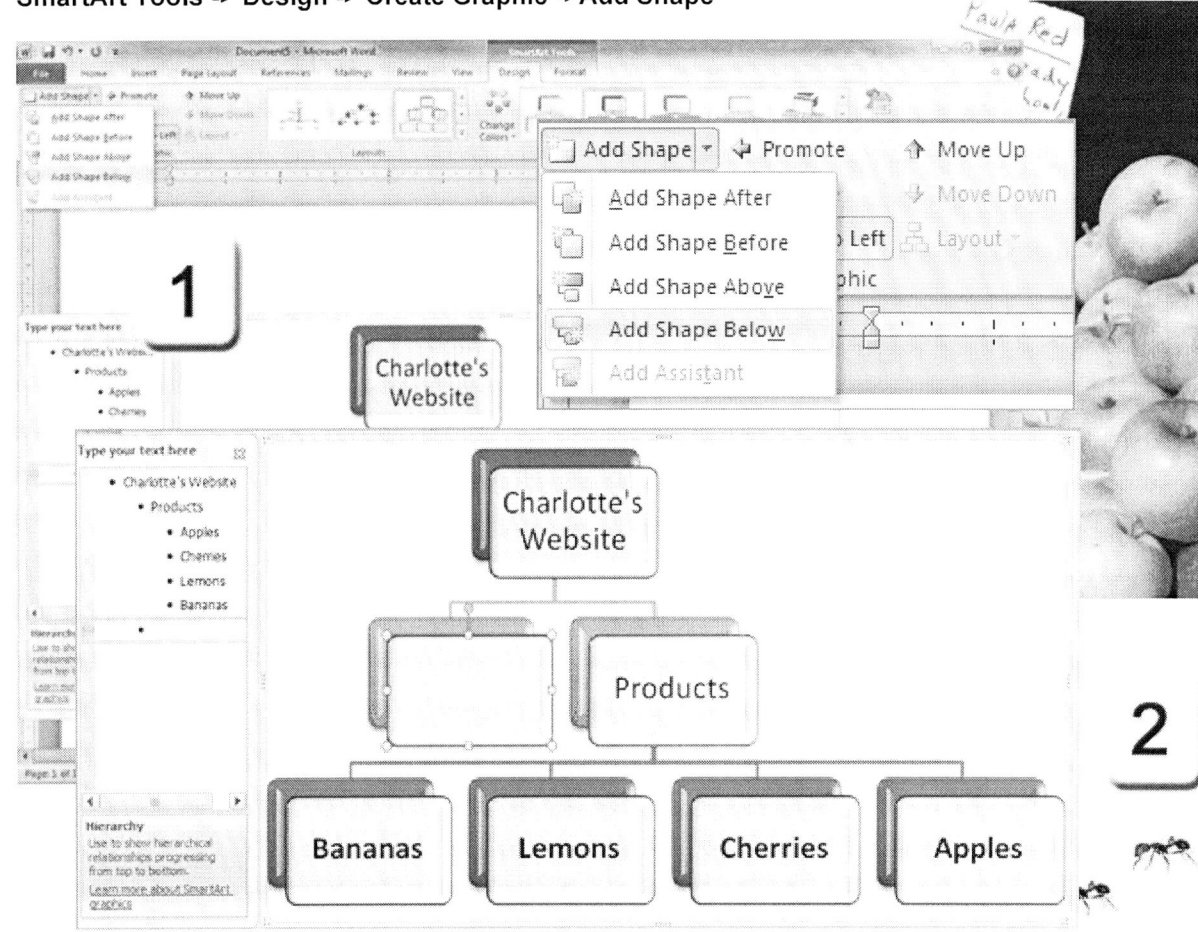

Exam 77-881: Microsoft Word 2010 Core
4. Including Illustrations and Graphics in a Document
4-2. Insert and format shapes, WordArt, and SmartArt: Add Shape

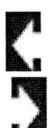

## Format the SmartArt

**SmartArt has Shapes.** You can use the **Format** tools to focus on one particular Shape. The **Format** ribbon offers many of the same options as the Drawing or Shape ribbon.

**1. Try It: Change the Shape**

**Select** one shape in the SmartArt. Go to **SmartArt Tools ->Format.** Go to **Shape ->Change Shape.**

**2. What Do You See?** You can choose a different shape from the list.

In this example, the Shape has two part: a glassy shape on top of a colored one. You need to select and format each part separately.

Very good. You can close this document without saving it.

SmartArt Tools -> Format -> Shape -> Change Shape

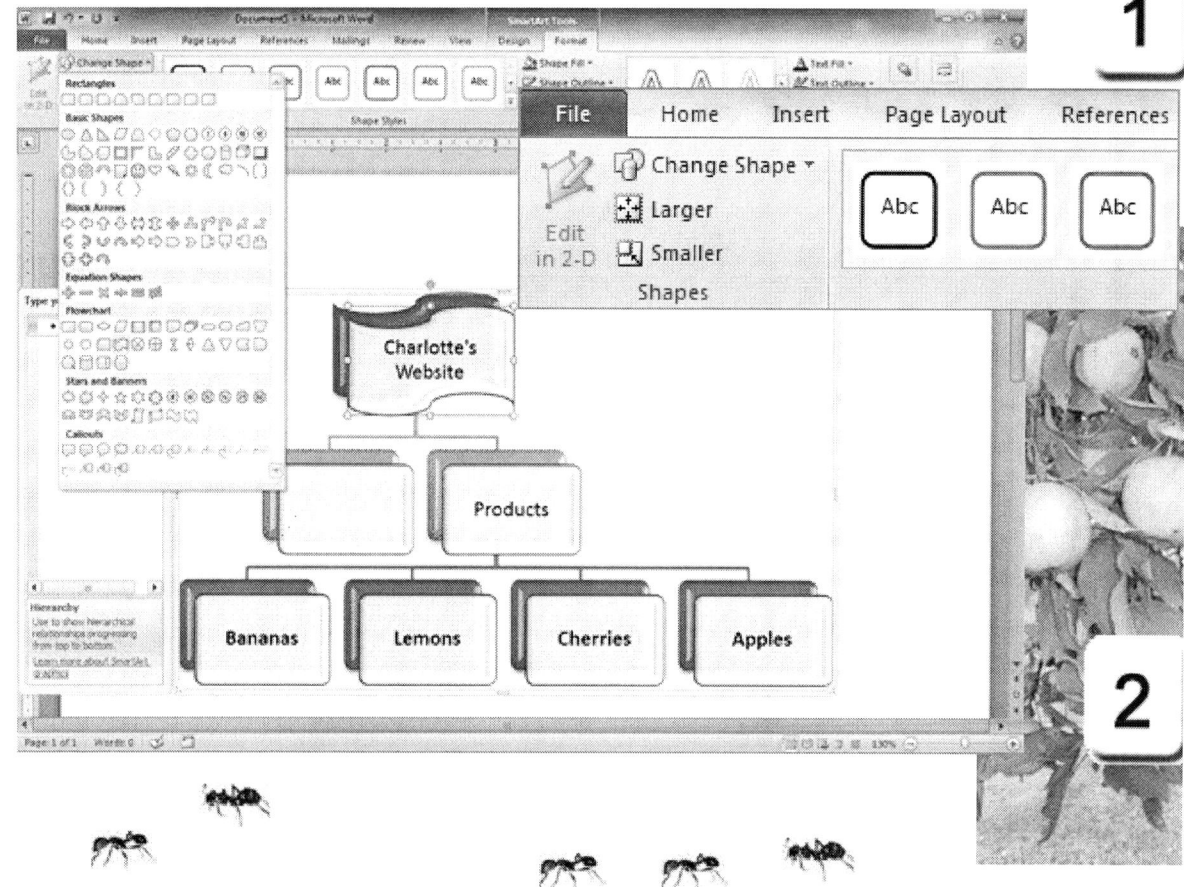

Exam 77-881: Microsoft Word 2010 Core
4. Including Illustrations and Graphics in a Document
4-2. Insert and format shapes, WordArt, and SmartArt: Change Shape

# WYSIWYG

**WYSIWYG** was Geek Speak for What You See Is What You Get. Page Layout and Print Preview were new options at the time of Windows 95.

**Visualization** is a fundamental concept in computers. Computers, especially the Microsoft Office 2010 programs, are visual.

The previous pages demonstrated how to create Shapes and Graphics that tell a story or teach a message. The next pages look at how you can change the **View** in Word.

**Insert -> Illustrations**

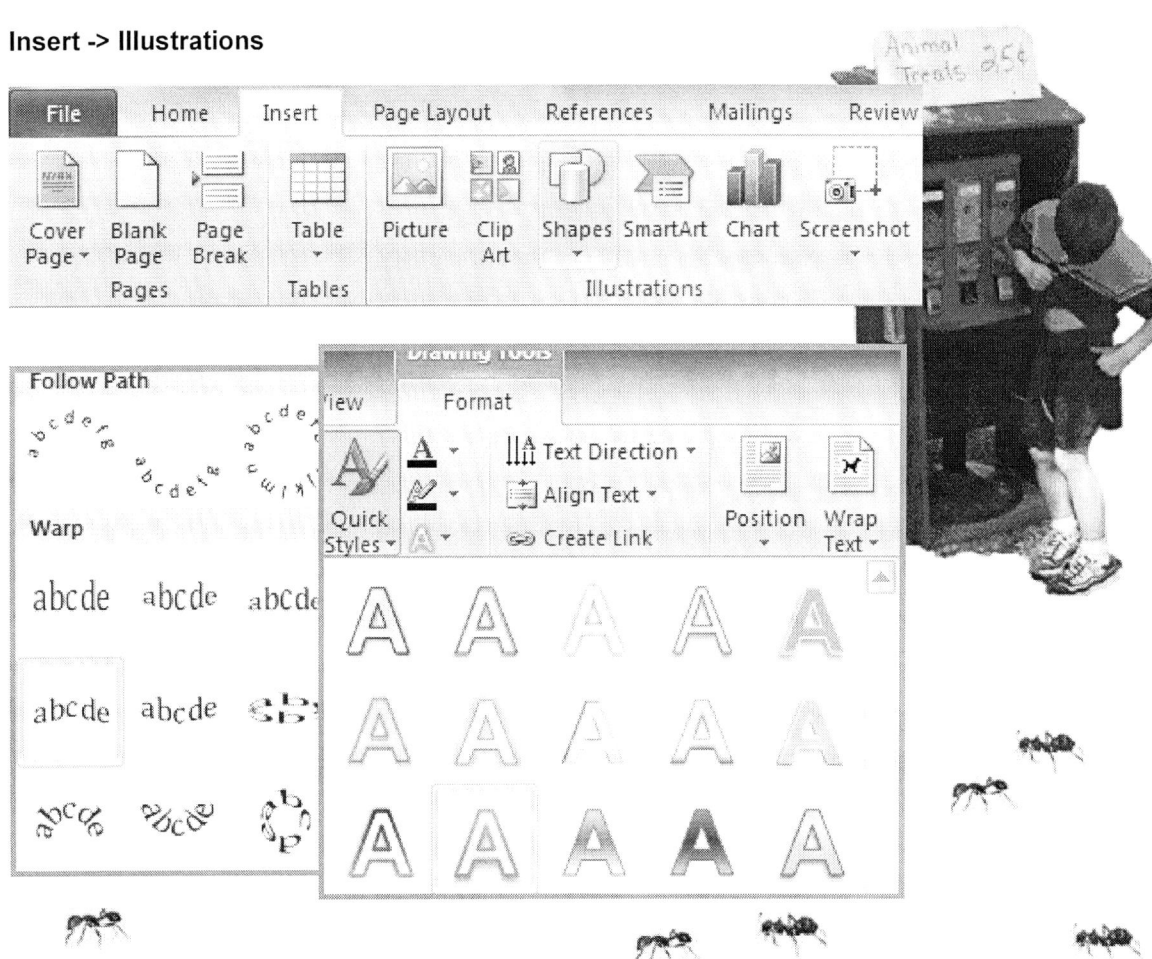

Exam 77-881: Microsoft Word 2010 Core
4. Including Illustrations and Graphics in a Document
4-2. Insert and format shapes, WordArt, and SmartArt

## Document Views

The **Document Views** lets you choose which view works best with your work. Most people edit their documents in the **Print Layout**: WYSIWYG. There are several other views that can be useful.

### 1. Try It: Change the View

Before you begin: you can open a couple of sample documents if you wish. The example on this page has TWO pages, which are shown side by side.

Go to the **Full Screen Reading View**.
**2. What Do You See?** The document is displayed in a very simple window.

There are no tool bars or ribbons.

Keep going...

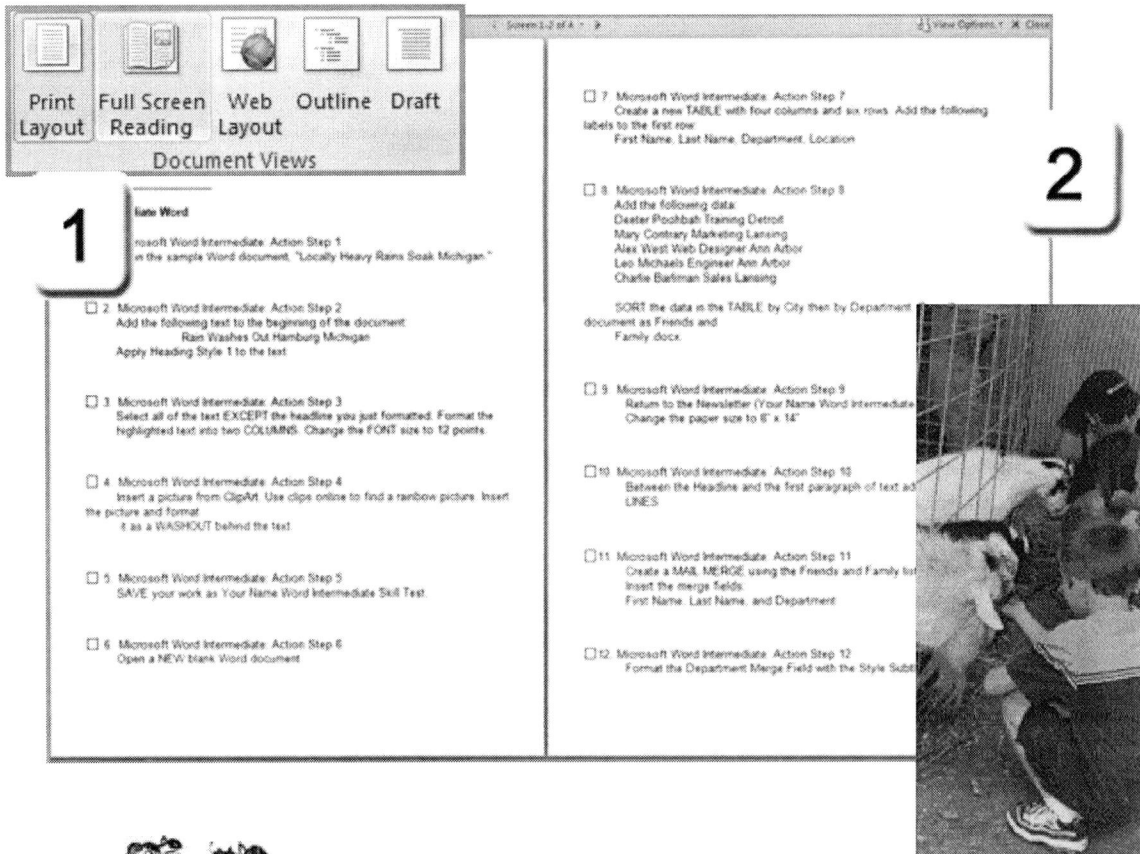

Exam 77-881: Microsoft Word 2010 Core
1. Sharing and Maintaining Documents
1.1 Apply different views to a document: Document Views

View -> Document Views ->Full Screen Reading

## Reading Views

The **Full Screen Reading View** offers **Tools** that help you Research, Highlight Text and even increase the Text Size.

**3. Try It: Review the Tools**

Go to the **Full Screen Reading View**.
Find the **Research** Tool.

**4. Try It: Change the View Options**

Go to the **Full Screen Reading View**.
Select **Increase Text Size**

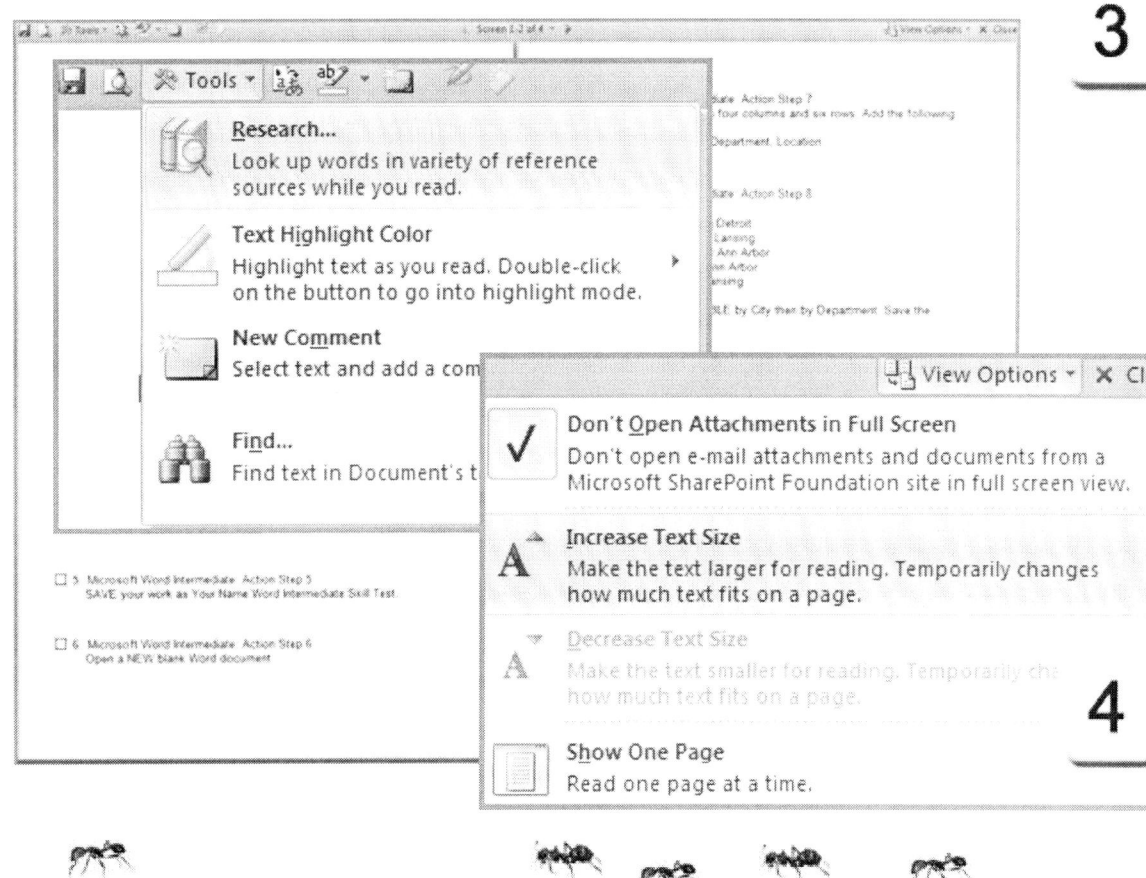

Exam 77-881: Microsoft Word 2010 Core
1. Sharing and Maintaining Documents
1.1 Apply different views to a document: Reading View

## Change the View

There are two ways you can **Zoom** into your work: the **View** Ribbon and the **Zoom Slider**.

The **Zoom Slider** is in the lower right corner of your Word 2010 document. You can drag the slider or use the plus and minus buttons if you wish. The same options are available in the **Zoom** window.

**Try This: Change the Zoom**
Go to **View ->Zoom**.

**Memo to self:** Make it big enough for the old Computer Mama to read, OK?

### View -> Zoom

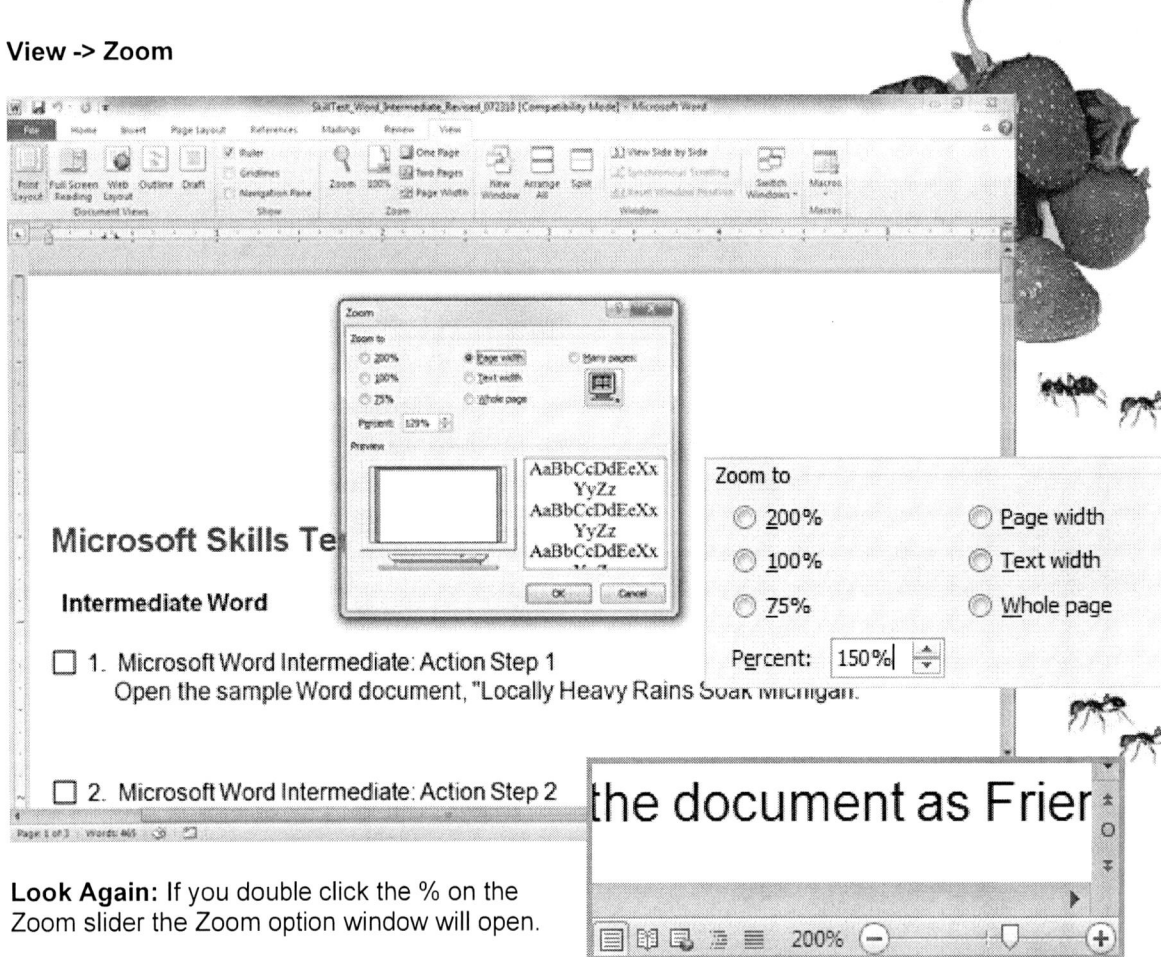

**Look Again:** If you double click the % on the Zoom slider the Zoom option window will open.

Exam 77-881: Microsoft Word 2010 Core
1. Sharing and Maintaining Documents
1.1 Apply different views to a document: Zoom

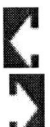

View -> Window -> Split Screen

## Split Screen

Say you had a long document with many pages that you are working on. You can **Split Screen** to see two pages at the same time.

**1. Try It: Spilt the Screen**
Go to **View ->Zoom.**
Select **Split Screen.**

**2. What Do You See?** You should see a line following your cursor. When you click your cursor about halfway down the screen, Microsoft Word will display your document in two windows.

Each window can be scrolled and viewed separately.

**Remove the Split** When you are done editing this mighty document, you can go back to the **View** Ribbon and **Remove the Split**.

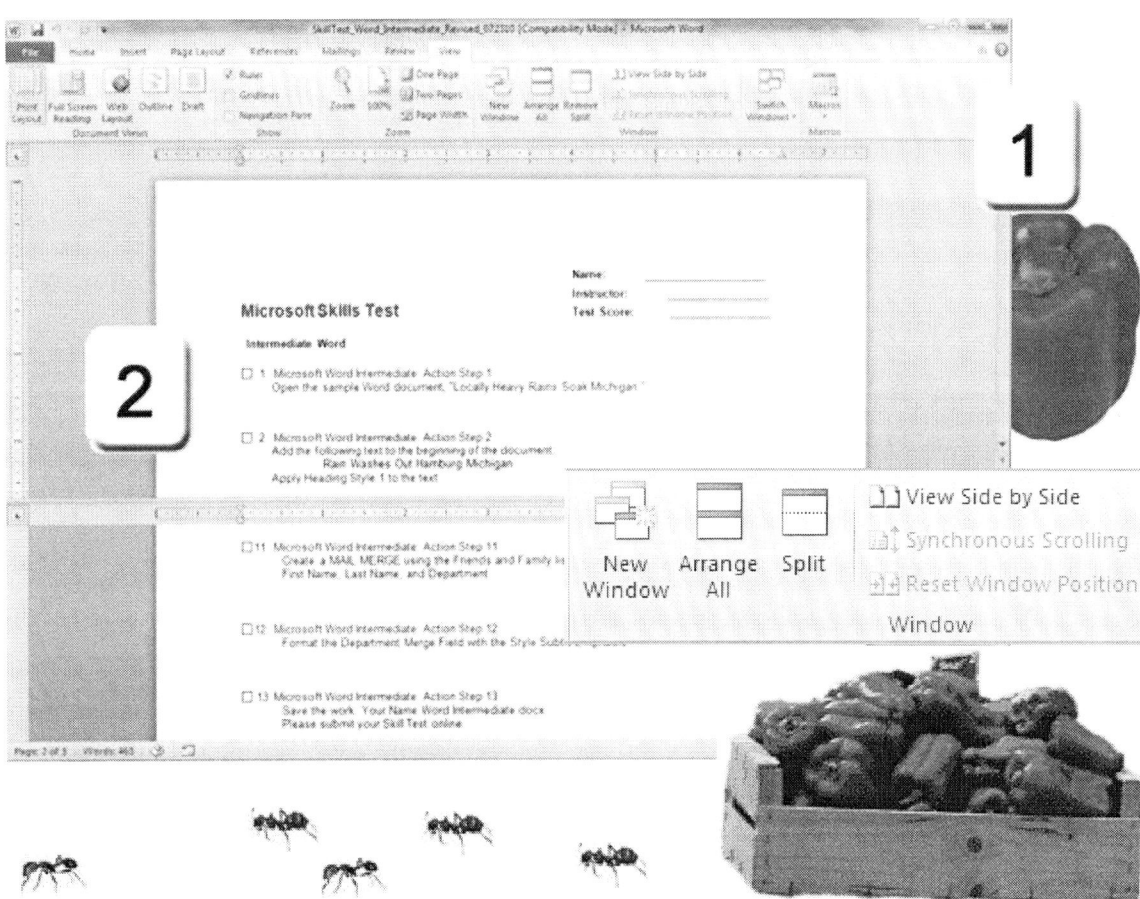

Exam 77-881: Microsoft Word 2010 Core
1. Sharing and Maintaining Documents
1.1 Apply different views to a document: Split Screen

## Side By Side

OK, say you wanted to compare two different documents side by side. This example begins by having two sample documents open, please.

**1. Try It: View Side by Side**
Go to **View -> Window**.
Select **View Side by Side**.

**2. What Do You See?** Two documents that you had opened should be displayed side by side in two different windows. By default, both windows have the same **View** (Zoom) as well as **Synchronized Scrolling**. You can change those options if you wish.

When you are done comparing these files side by side, you can click on **Reset Window Position** to return to a full screen view.

**View -> Window -> View Side by Side**

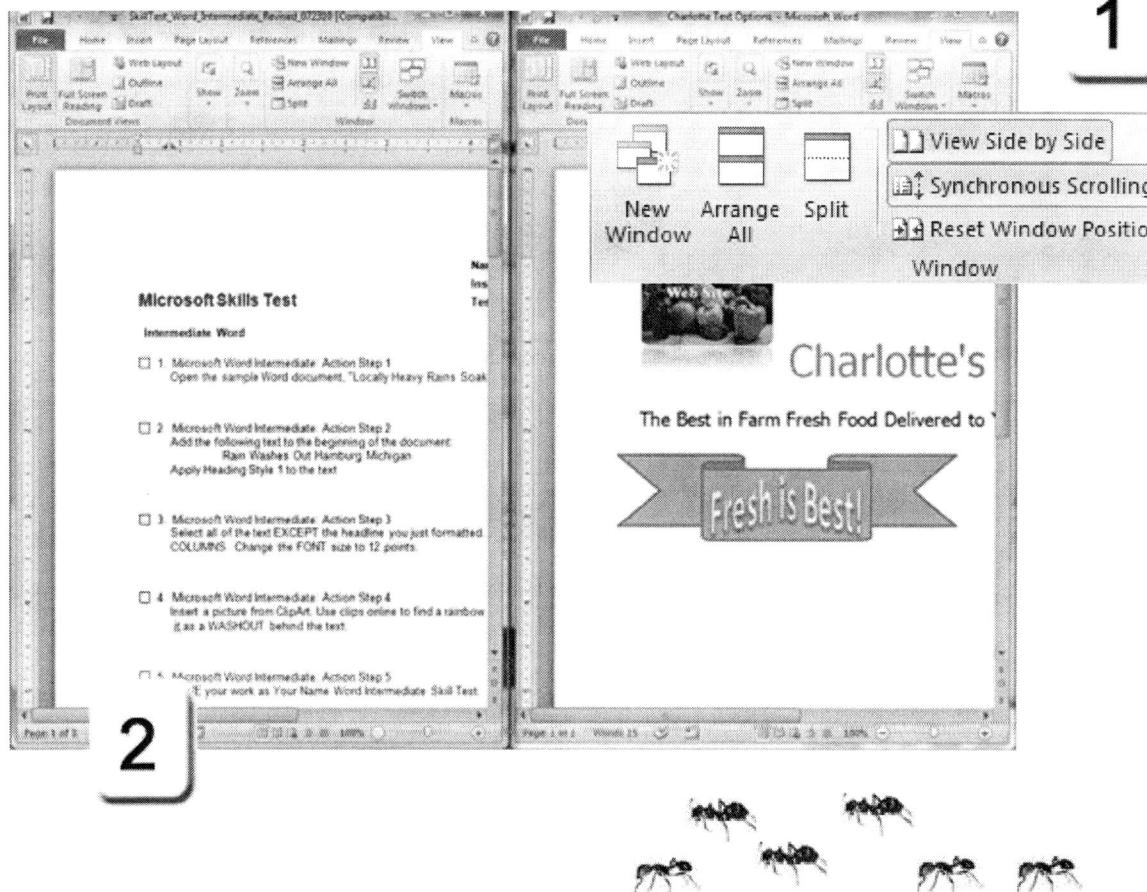

Exam 77-881: Microsoft Word 2010 Core
1. Sharing and Maintaining Documents
1.1 Apply different views to a document: Side by Side

## Arrange All

Say you had three (3) documents open at once (multi-tasking!). You can set up Word to display three windows, one on top of another, if you wish.

**1. Try This, Too: Arrange All**
Go to **View -> Window.**
Select **Arrange All.**

**2. What Do You See?** Three documents will open in three windows. Each document can be scrolled and viewed independently.

Very good.

View -> Window -> Arrange All

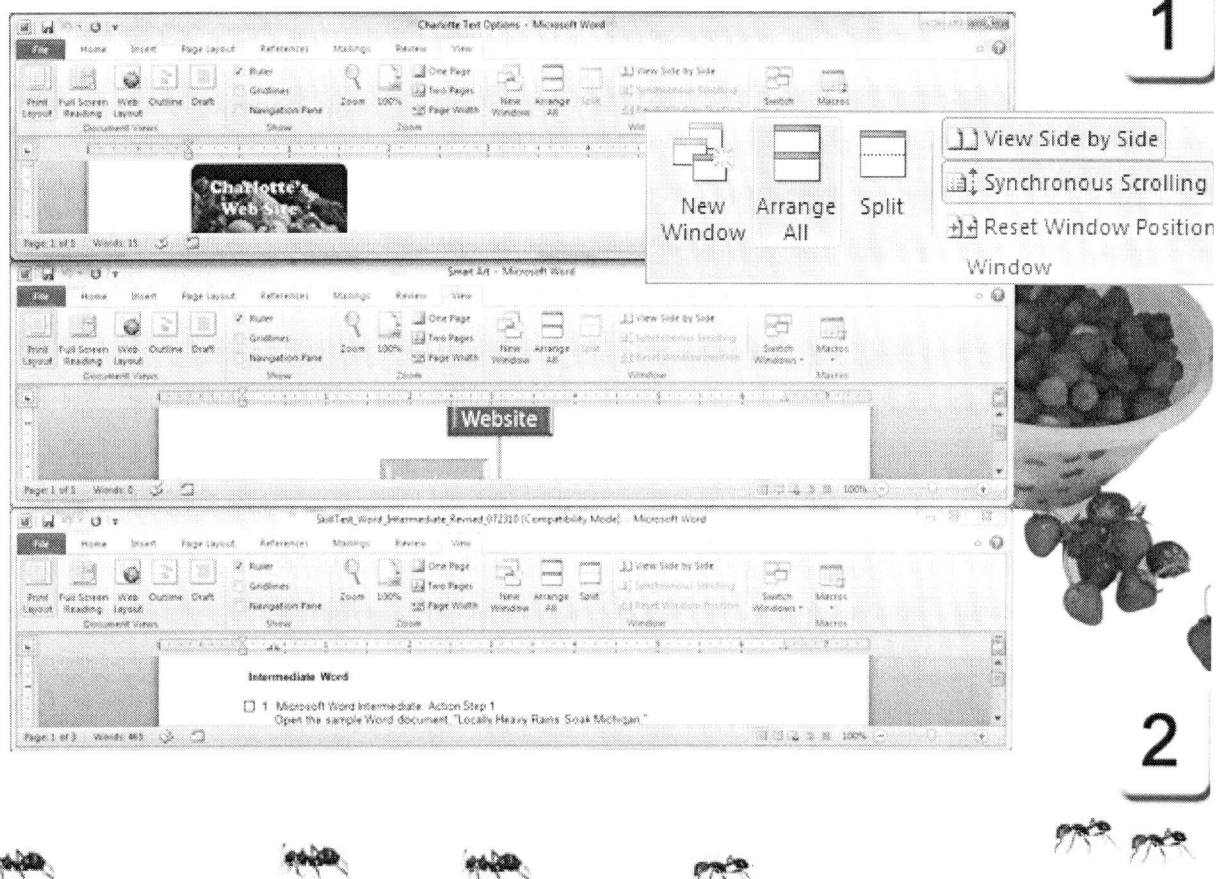

Exam 77-881: Microsoft Word 2010 Core
1. Sharing and Maintaining Documents
1.1 Apply different views to a document: Arrange All

## New Window

There is another option that you can use to edit your documents: you can create a COPY of your document in a **New Window**. That way, you can have page 2 and maybe page 23 open at the same time.

**1. Try This: Open in a New Window**
Say you opened a file called Mydoc..
Go to **View->New Window**.

**2. What Do You See?** Another copy of the MyDoc file will open in a new window. The title of the second document would say MyDoc:2, indicating that it the second window.

**View -> Window -> New Window**

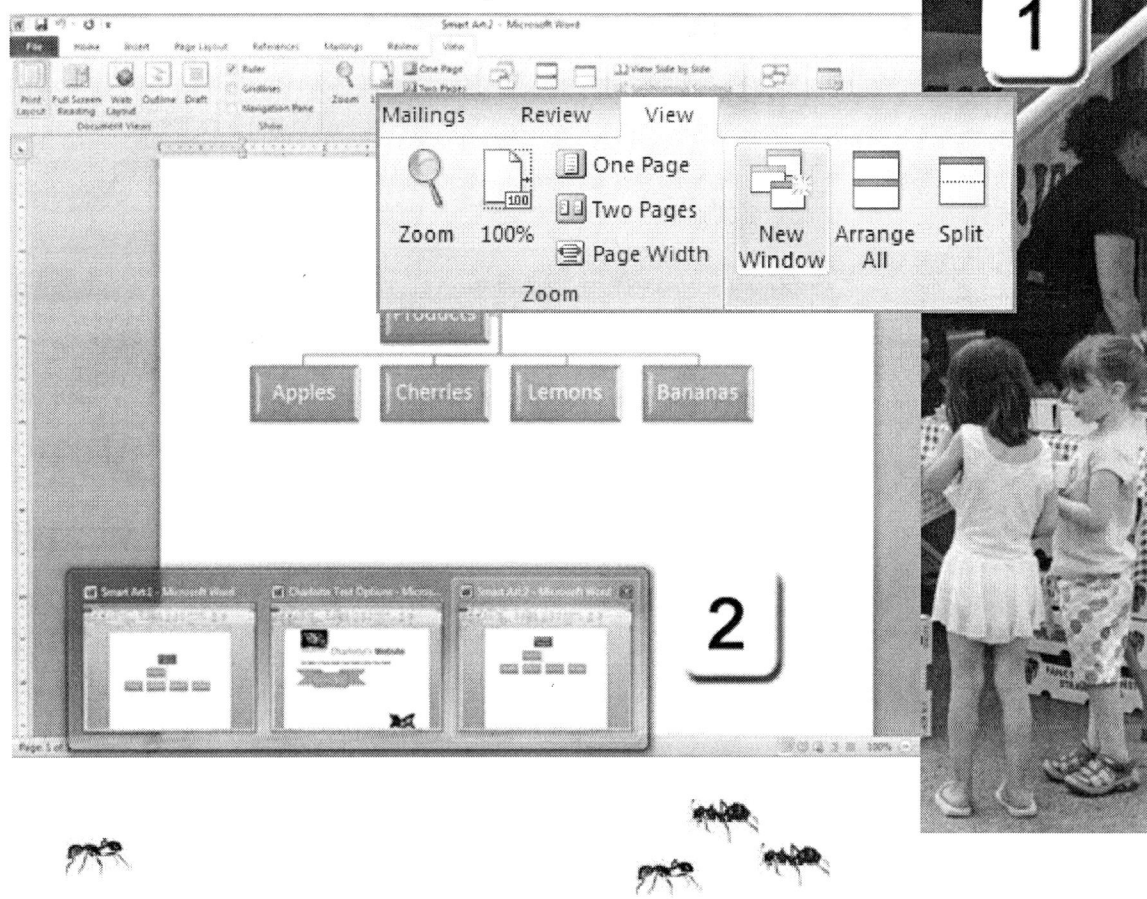

Exam 77-881: Microsoft Word 2010 Core
1. Sharing and Maintaining Documents
1.1 Apply different views to a document: New Window

## Switch Windows

**Switch Windows** allows you to choose which document you would like to work on. In this example, there are four documents open in Word.

**1. Try It: Switch Windows**
Before you begin, please open three or four different documents in Microsoft Word 2010.

Go to **View -> Window.**
**Click on Switch Window.**

**2. What Do You See?** All of the open documents are listed under Switch Windows. The one you are currently working on has a check mark.

View -> Window -> Switch Window

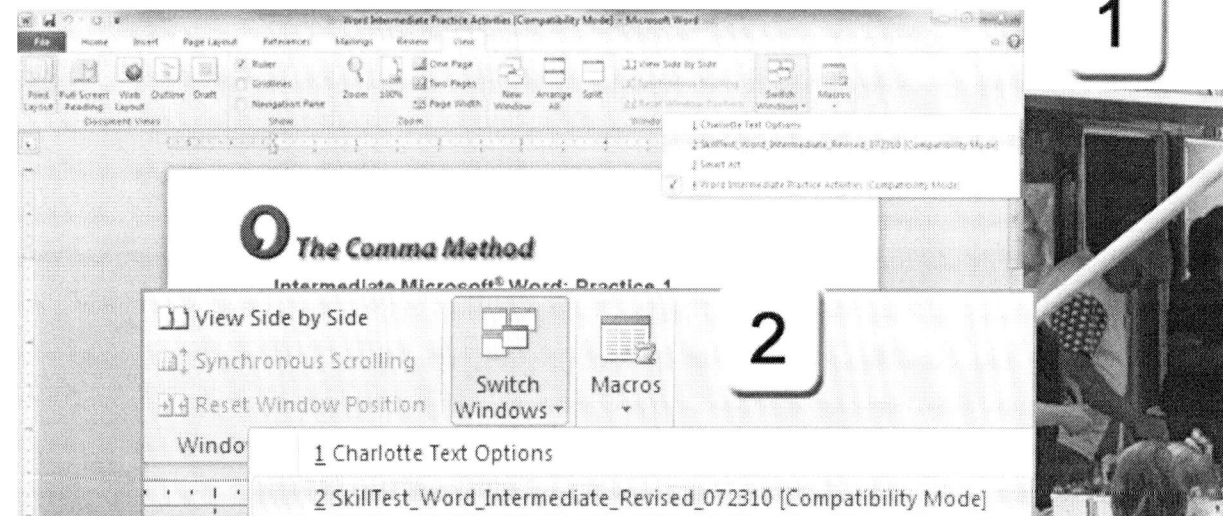

Exam 77-881: Microsoft Word 2010 Core
1. Sharing and Maintaining Documents
1.1 Apply different views to a document: Switch Windows

## Summary

The purpose of this lesson was to learn and practice the formatting options for Pictures, Shapes and SmartArt.

**WYSIWYG: What You See Is What You Get...no surprises.** Each of the **Illustrations**, as well as the various **View** options give you a Live Preview. You can see how it looks on screen a well as on the page.

Well, you done good.
You get two cookies.

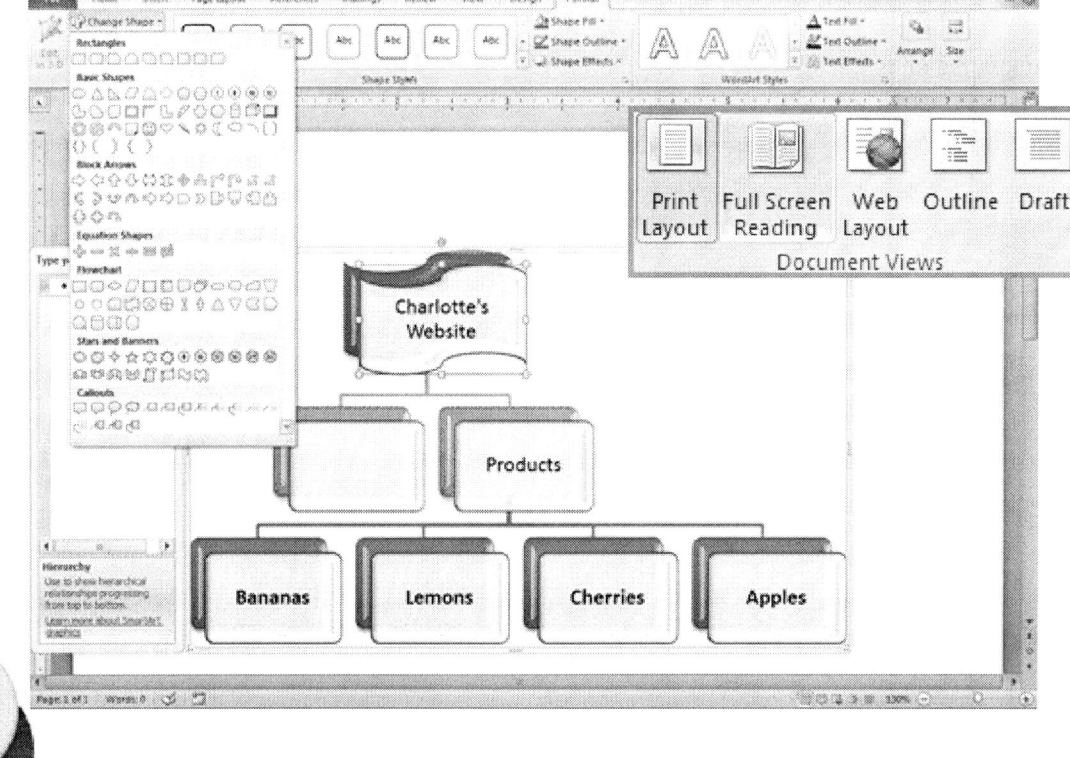

# Practice Activities

## Lesson: First Prize

**Before You Begin:** Start Microsoft Word 2010. You should see a new, blank document.

**Try This: Do the following steps**

1. Insert SmartArt.
2. Choose a SmartArt Graphic: Cycle. Choose the Basic or Block Cycle
3. Add the following text:
Design new products
Make new products
Survey the customers
Make recommendations
Make improvements

4. Apply a SmartArt Style.
5. Change the colors.
6. Select the shape: Design New Products. Change the Shape into a star.
7. Save this document as Your Name Practice 5.

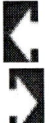

# Test Yourself

1. Which are true about Shapes in Word? (Select all correct answers)
a. The Shapes command is on the Insert Ribbon
b. Shapes are text boxes with special formatting
c. You can put text in a Shape
d. You can resize a Shape like a picture
Tip: Beginning Word, page 127

3. Live Preview allows you to see changes without applying them to the selected item.
a. TRUE
b. FALSE
Tip: Beginning Word, page 132

4. Which command allows you to compare two documents at the same time?
a. Split Screen
b. Side by Side
c. Reading Mode
Tip: Beginning Word, page 150

5. The Arrange All button will place all open Microsoft Word documents so the windows are one on top of the other.
a. TRUE
b. FALSE
Tip: Beginning Word, page 151

6. Where is the Crop to Shape command?
a. Picture Tools Ribbon-> Arrange Group
b. Insert Ribbon-> Picture group
c. Picture Tools Ribbon-> Size group
Tip: Beginning Word, page 125

7. Which of the following have Quick Styles? (Select all correct answers)
a. Shapes
b. SmartArt
c. Pictures
d. WordArt
e. Text
Tip: Beginning Word, page 145

8. Which of the following commands is found in the Insert ->Illustrations group?
a. Table
b. Picture
c. ClipArt
d. Shape
e. SmartArt
Tip: Beginning Word, page 145

9. SmartArt automatically adjusts to fit the text.
a. True
b. False
Tip: Beginning Word, page 139

10. Which of the following can be formatted on SmartArt?
(Select all correct answers)
a. Color
b. Style
c. Fill
D. Shape
E. Outline
Tip: Beginning Word, page 137, 138

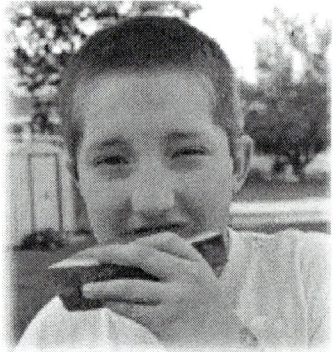

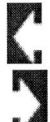

**Word 2010: Graphics and Quick Parts**

# First Impressions

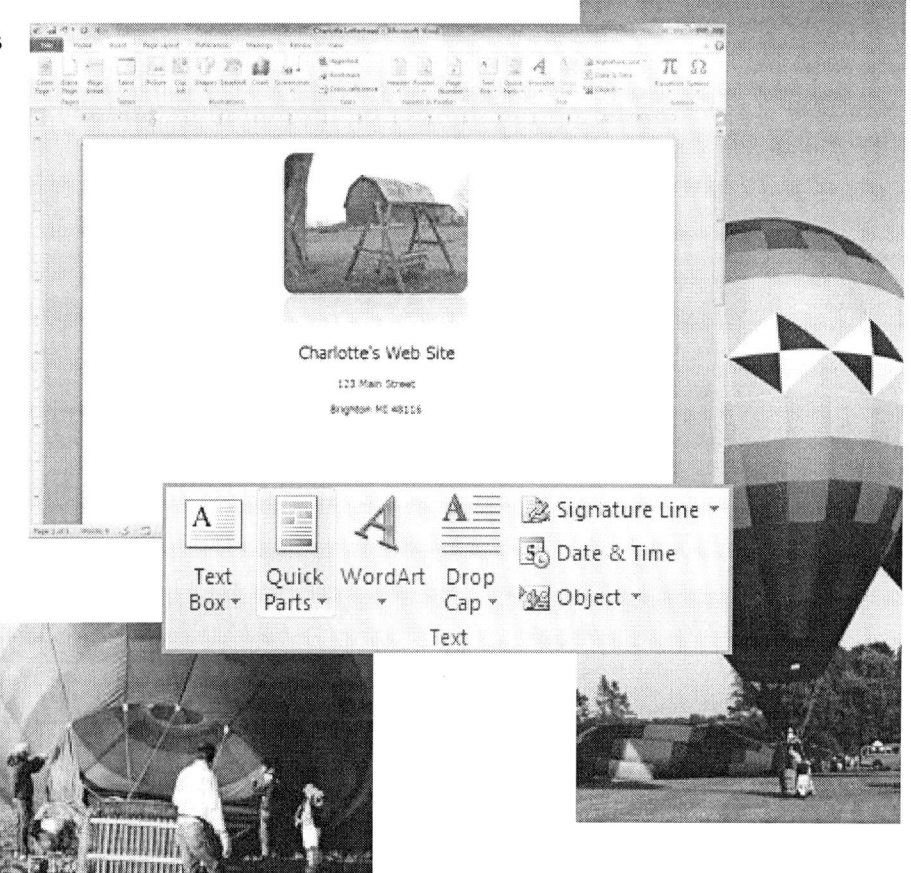

## Beginning Word

**In this lesson, you will learn how to:**

1. Use the Insert Date and Time options

2. Insert a Text Box

3. Format a Text Box including Shape, Quick Styles, Effects and

Text Direction

4. Create linked Text Boxes

5. Use Quick Parts

6. Create new Quick Parts

© 2010 Comma Productions

 # Lesson 7: First Impressions

## 1. Readings
Read Lesson 7 in the Beginning Word guide, page 157-190.

## Project
Custom stationery using a template, Graphics, and Quick Parts.

## Downloads
Charlottes Letterhead

Graphic files used in the lesson:
Logo, Farm, FarmersMarket1, FarmersMarket2, Michigan-Balloonfest-22 Michigan-Balloonfest-29

## 2. Practice
Complete the Practice Activity for this lesson, page 189.

## 3. Assessment
Review the Test questions, page 190.

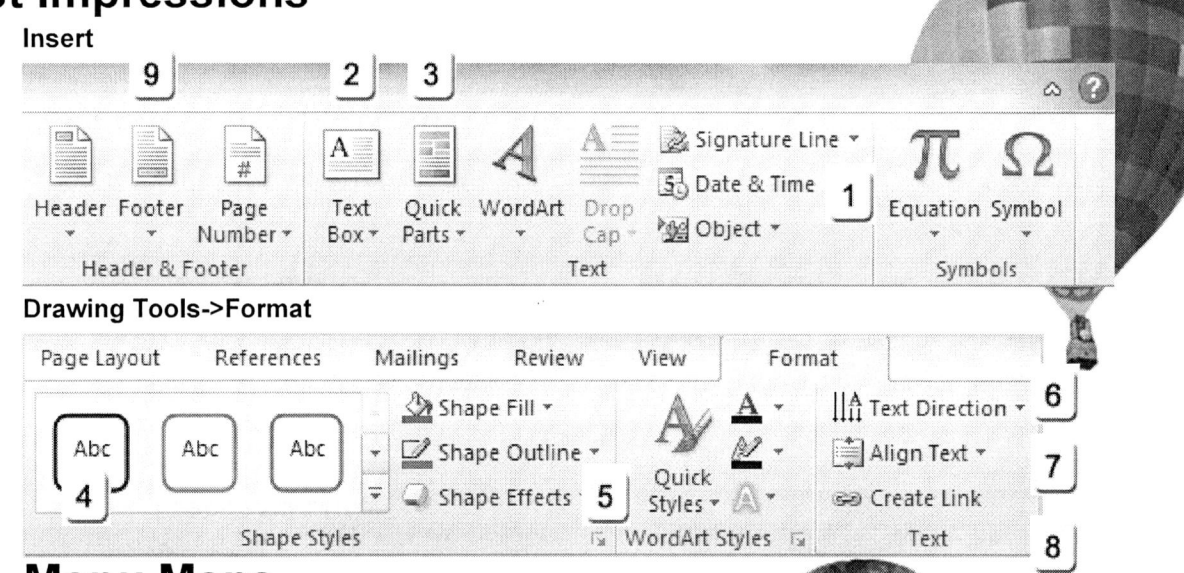

**Insert**

**Drawing Tools->Format**

## Menu Maps
This lesson shows options on the **Insert** and **Drawing Tools**.
1. Insert-> Date and Time, page 167
2. Insert-> Text Box, page 168
3. Insert-> Quick Parts, page 169
4. Drawing Tools-> Format -> Shape Styles, page 171
5. Drawing Tools-> Format -> Shape Effects, page 172
6. Drawing Tools-> Format -> Text Direction, page 175
7. Drawing Tools-> Format -> Text Alignment, page 176
8. Drawing Tools-> Format -> Create Link, page 177
9. Insert ->Footer, page 185

# Create Business Stationery

You can use the formatting options in Microsoft Word 2010 to create professional business stationery. Image is very important in business. Many firms invest a lot of time and talent into their letterhead. The logo and type setting on business stationery is sometimes called the Corporate Stripe. Formatting helps your company documentation look consistent. It also identifies a corporate brand. Please **Start** the **Program Microsoft Word**.

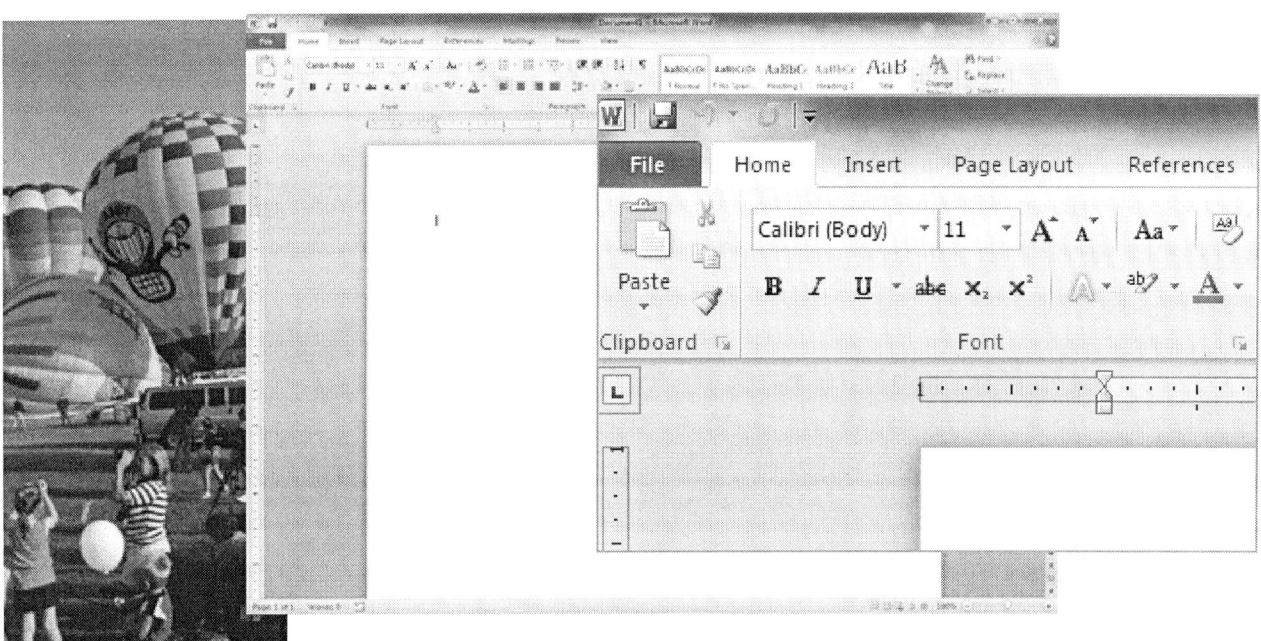

What do you see, from the top of the screen? Is there a **Title Bar** that says Microsoft Word? Yes.

Is there a **Home** Ribbon with the **Clipboard, Font and Paragraph** Groups? Yes.

If your screen looks similar to the example on this page, then you are ready to get started.

## Begin the Document

Begin with a blank document. You can practice with the company name and logo pictured on these pages, or create your own if you wish.

### 1. Type the name and address

Please type:

Charlotte's Web Site
123 Main Street
Brighton MI 48116.

### 2. Select the text

Nothing happens in a computer until you select it, first.

**Memo to Self:** Try selecting the type backwards. For some reason, it has always been easier in Windows to highlight backwards.

Home -> Font

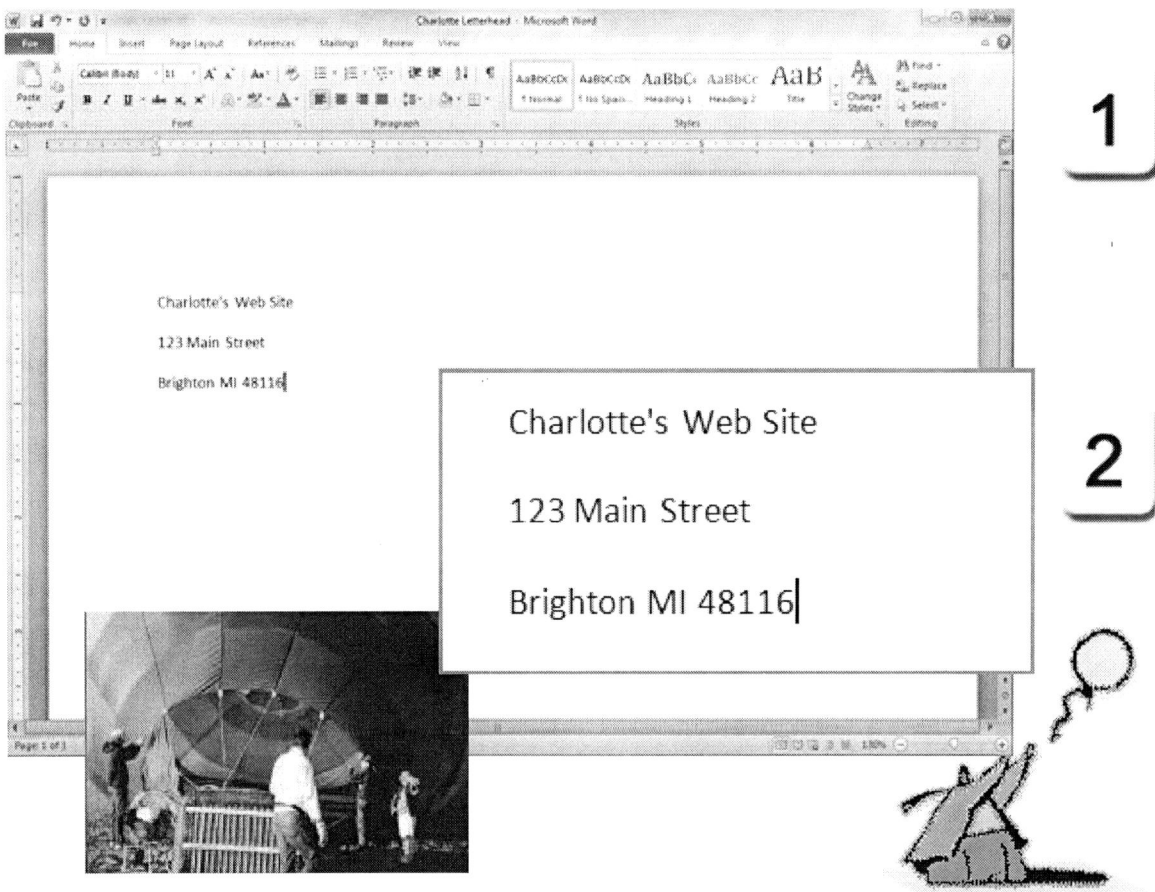

## Format the Type

Calibri is the default type face—or font—for Microsoft Word 2007 and Word 2010. In marketing, the company name and address should be special. It is supposed to call attention to itself. The name can be differentiated with big, bold type.

### 3. Select a Different Font

Select the name and address.
Go to **Home->Font**
Please select Tahoma from the list. It is a simple, elegant font.

### 4. Center the Paragraph

Select the name and address
Go to **Home ->Paragraph**
Click on the **Center** button.

Keep going...

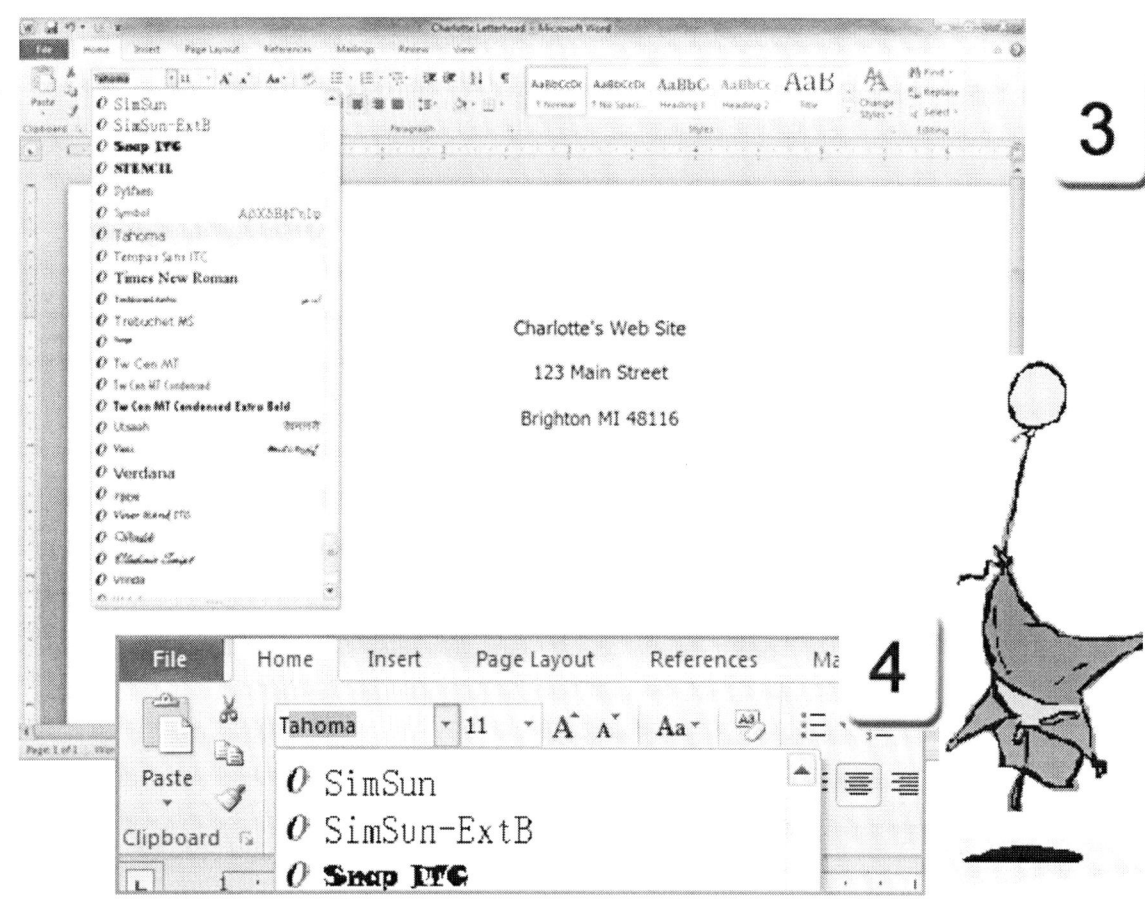

**Exam 77-881: Microsoft Word 2010 Core**
**2. Formatting Content**
**2-1. Apply font and paragraph attributes**

**5. Emphasize the Name**
**Select** Charlotte's Website
**Change the size** of the business
name by clicking on the down
arrow to the right of the "11."
**Choose** "18" from the list.

Now, the company name is
bigger and bolder than the
address.

Keep going...

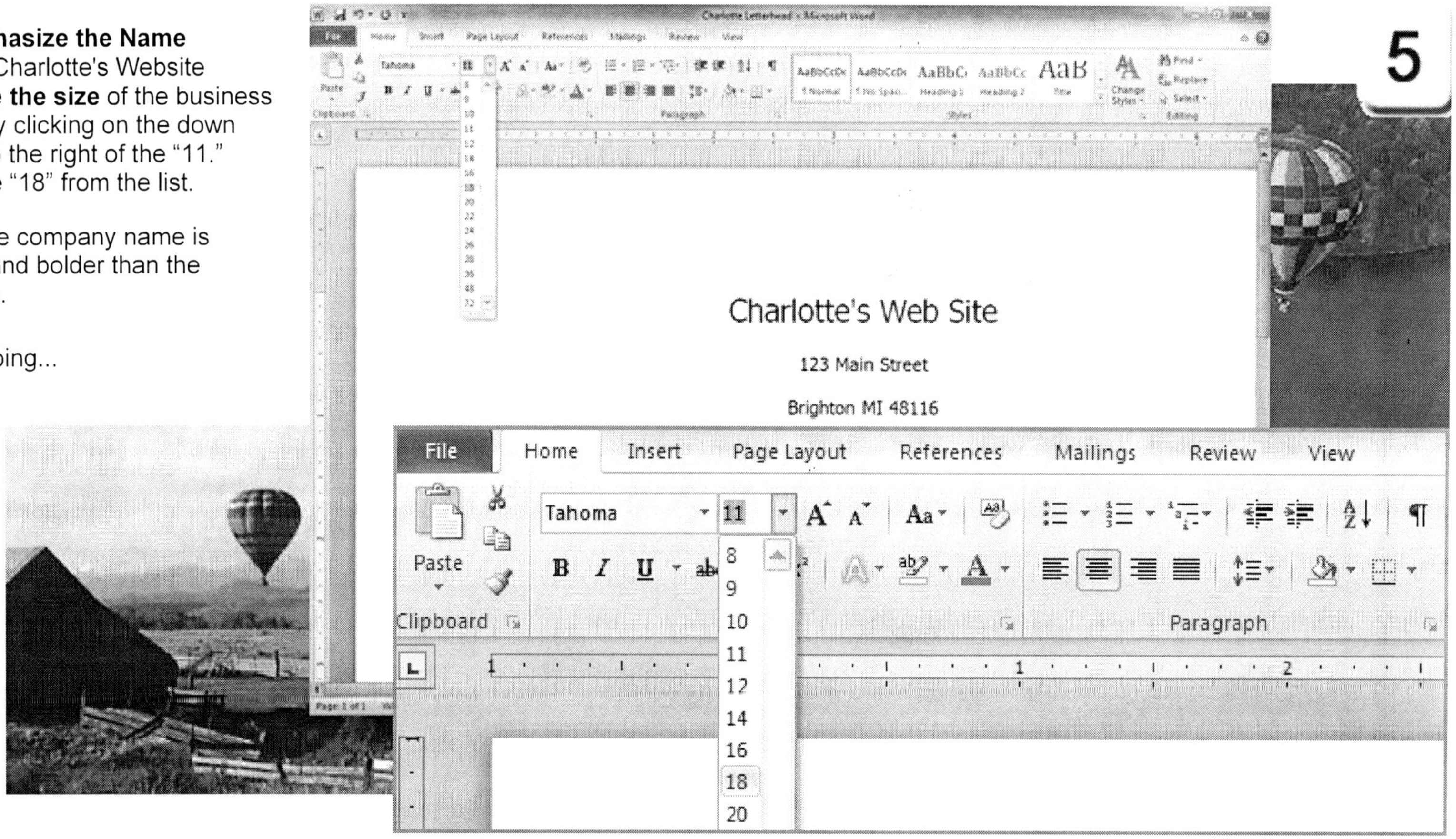

Charlotte's Web Site

123 Main Street

Brighton MI 48116

**Exam 77-881: Microsoft Word 2010 Core**
**2. Formatting Content**
**2-1. Apply font and paragraph attributes**

## Add a Company Logo

A logo is a picture or graphic that identifies your team . It is important not only for sales, but for your own team experience: A logo says, "We belong."

There are some **sample files** that you can copy to your **Documents** folder, or you can use your own graphics.

### 6. Insert a Picture

Go to the **Insert** Ribbon.
Click on **Picture**.

You will be asked to locate your pictures. The next steps show you how to find the files in the **Documents** folder.

Insert -> Picture -> From File

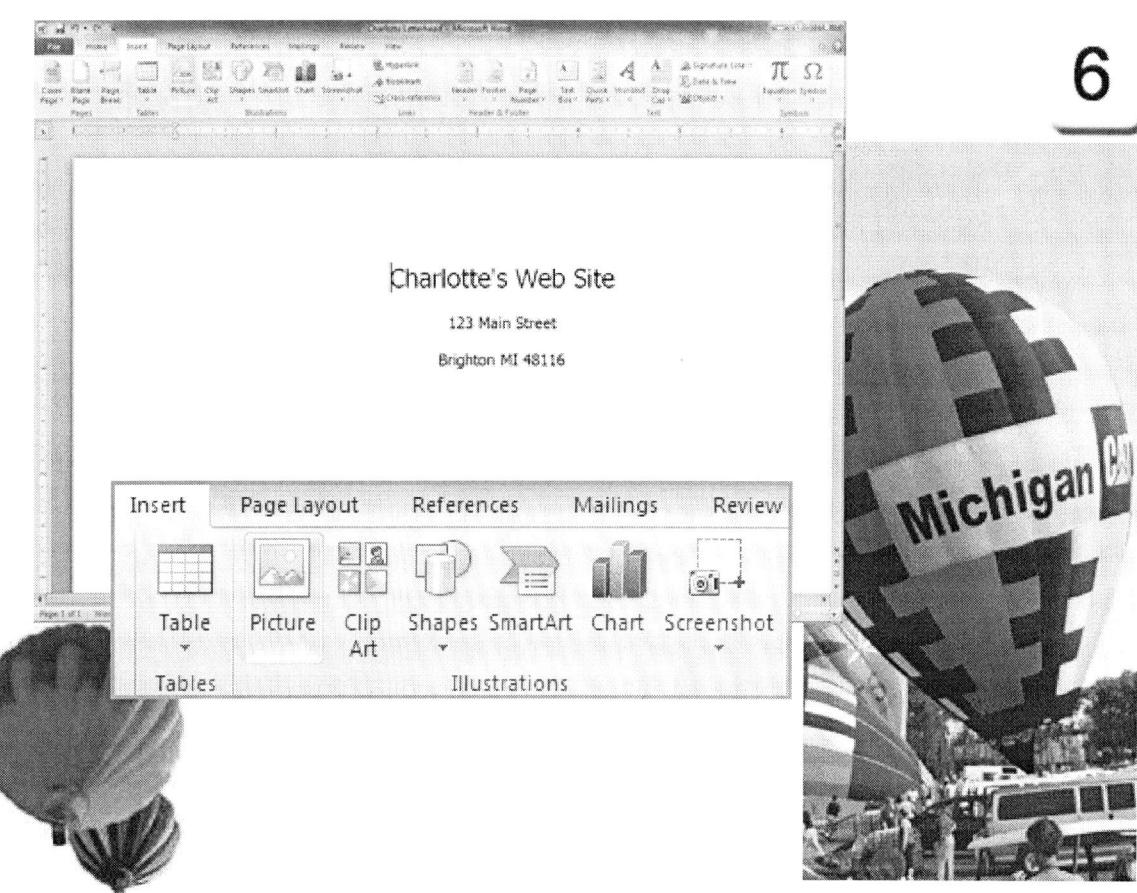

6

Exam 77-881: Microsoft Word 2010 Core
4. Including Illustrations and Graphics in a Document
4-1. Insert and format Pictures in a document

## Find a Picture

By default, your **Documents, Music Pictures and Videos** can be found in your **Libraries**. Some cameras download your pictures to their own folders. This lesson assumes that you saved some sample pictures to the Pictures folder.

**7. Locate and Select a Picture**
Look in the **Pictures** folder

Double click one of the sample pictures to insert into your document.

You can also select the picture and then click on the **Insert** button in the lower right hand corner.

**Insert -> Picture -> From File**

Farm1

Exam 77-881: Microsoft Word 2010 Core
4. Including Illustrations and Graphics in a Document
4-1. Insert and format Pictures in a document

## Format the Picture

The picture was inserted into the document as **In Line With Text**. This is the default setting for how pictures interact with text.

In effect, the picture is anchored to the line, same as any word. The picture will be easier to work with if you change the **Text Wrapping.**

**Tight** means that the text will flow, or wrap, around the picture. This makes it easy to move the picture like a sticky-note.

### 8. Change the Text Wrap to Top and Bottom

Click once on the picture to select it

Go to the **Format** Ribbon

Find **Arrange ->Wrap Text**

Select **Top and Bottom.**

Go ahead: format the Picture Style and add a shadow or a reflection.

**Picture Tools -> Format ->Arrange ->Wrap Text**

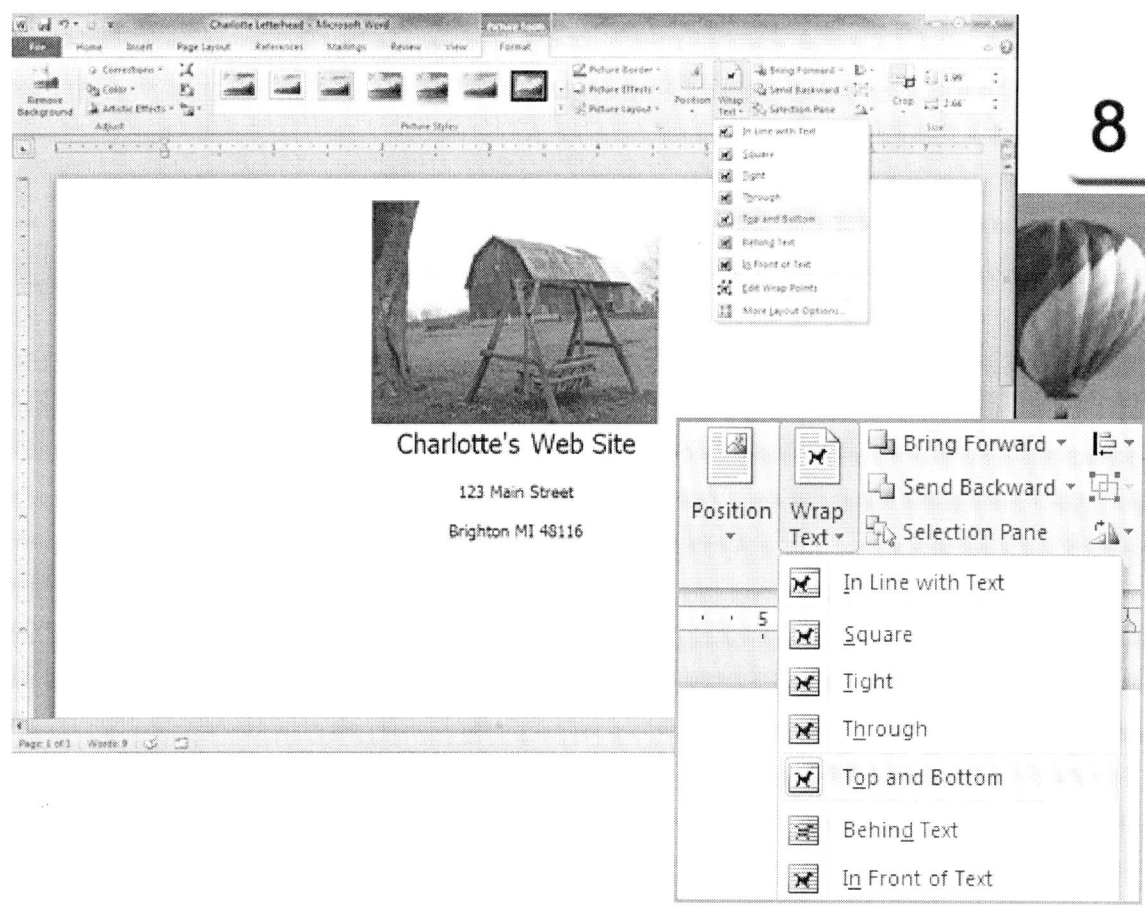

Exam 77-881: Microsoft Word 2010 Core
4. Including Illustrations and Graphics in a Document
4-1. Insert and format Pictures in a document: Wrap Text

## Create a Sample Letter

Please type a sample business letter. Before you begin look again: where is your cursor? If your cursor is still CENTERED, please go to **Home-> Paragraph** and align the text LEFT.

**Suggested text:**
Dear Sir,

Thank you for your recent order from Charlotte's Website.

Sincerely...

**Do This: Save your Letter**
Go to **File -> Save**.
File Name: Charlotte's Letterhead.

**File -> Save**

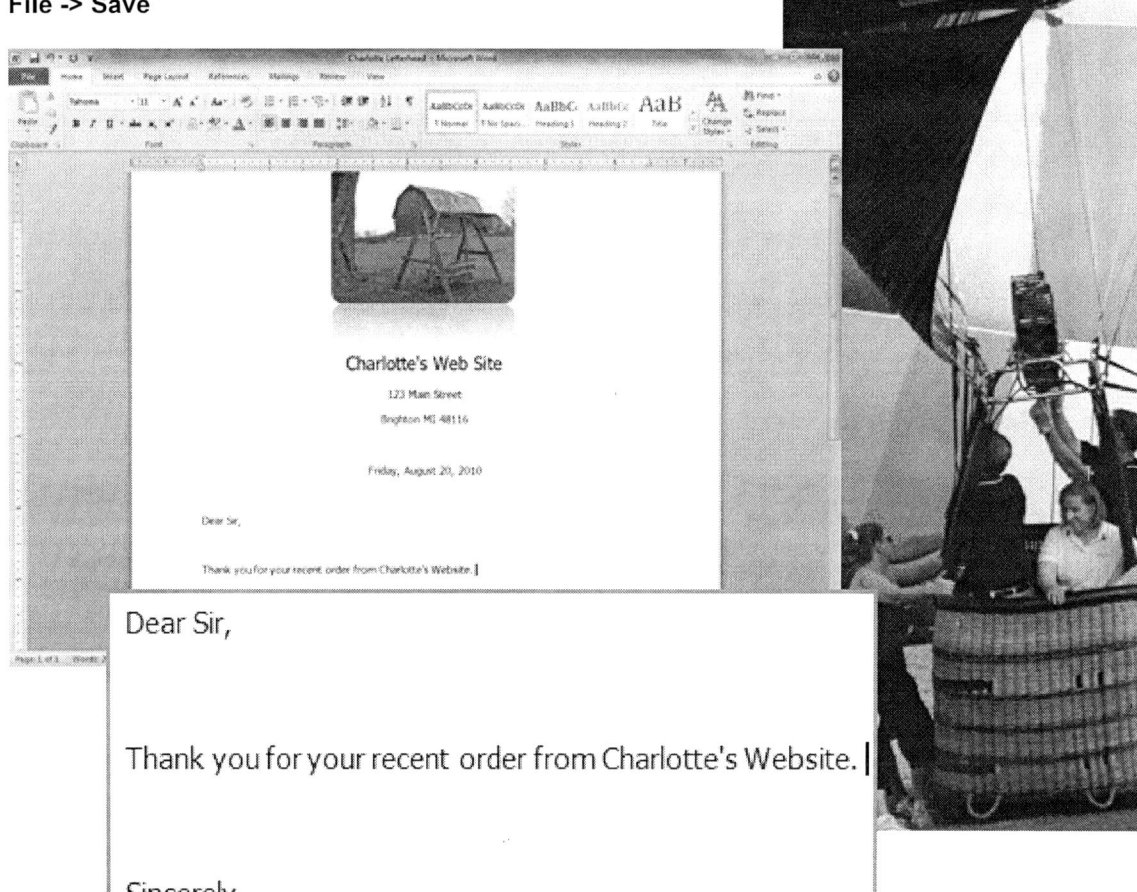

Dear Sir,

Thank you for your recent order from Charlotte's Website. |

Sincerely,

## Insert Text

Microsoft Word 2010 has **Text Boxes, Quick Parts and Building Blocks** that help you compose a professional letter. These steps show how to **Insert** the **Date and Time.**

**Before You Begin**
Place your cursor after the zip code and press **Enter** a couple of times to create a few blank lines. Notice that the cursor may still be centered. The Date/Time pictured on this page is centered as well.

**9. Insert the Date and Time**
Go to **Insert ->Date & Time.**
Select a **LONG** date format.

A **LONG** date format spells out the month, day and year. **(MM/DD/YYYY)**. Some countries write the date as day, month, year. (DD/M/YY). Using this format could minimize the confusion with the Short date format that uses only numbers.

Insert ->Date & Time

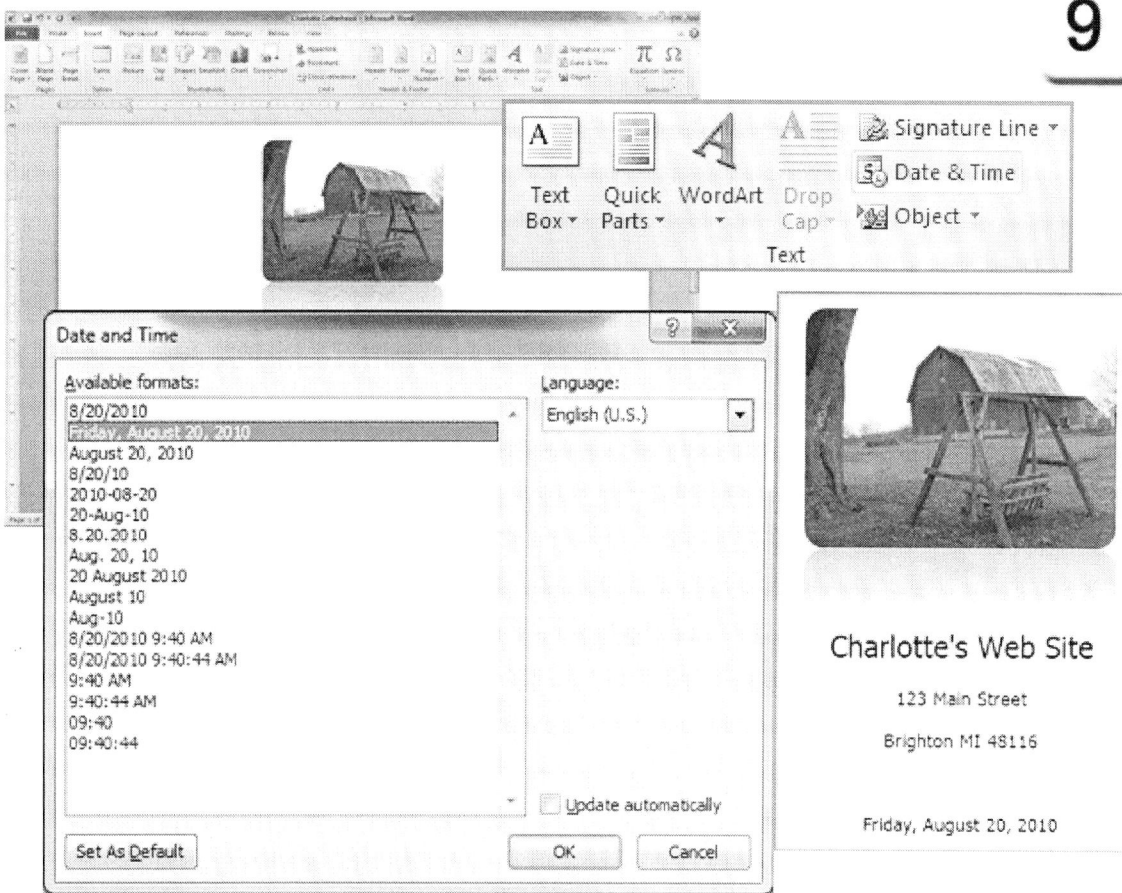

9

Charlotte's Web Site

123 Main Street

Brighton MI 48116

Friday, August 20, 2010

Exam 77-881: Microsoft Word 2010 Core
3. Applying Page Layout and Reusable Content
3-3. Construct content in a document by using the Quick Parts tool

# Insert a Text Box

A **Text Box** is a convenient way to add quotes, bling, and other marketing elements to your flyer.

## 1. Try This: Insert a Text Box

Go to **Insert ->Text Box.**
Please use the small down arrow to see the **Built-In** boxes.
**Select** Alphabet Sidebar.

## 2. What Do You See?
A new Text Box, a formatted **Sidebar** will be placed into your document.

Keep going...

**Insert -> Text Box -> Alphabet Sidebar**

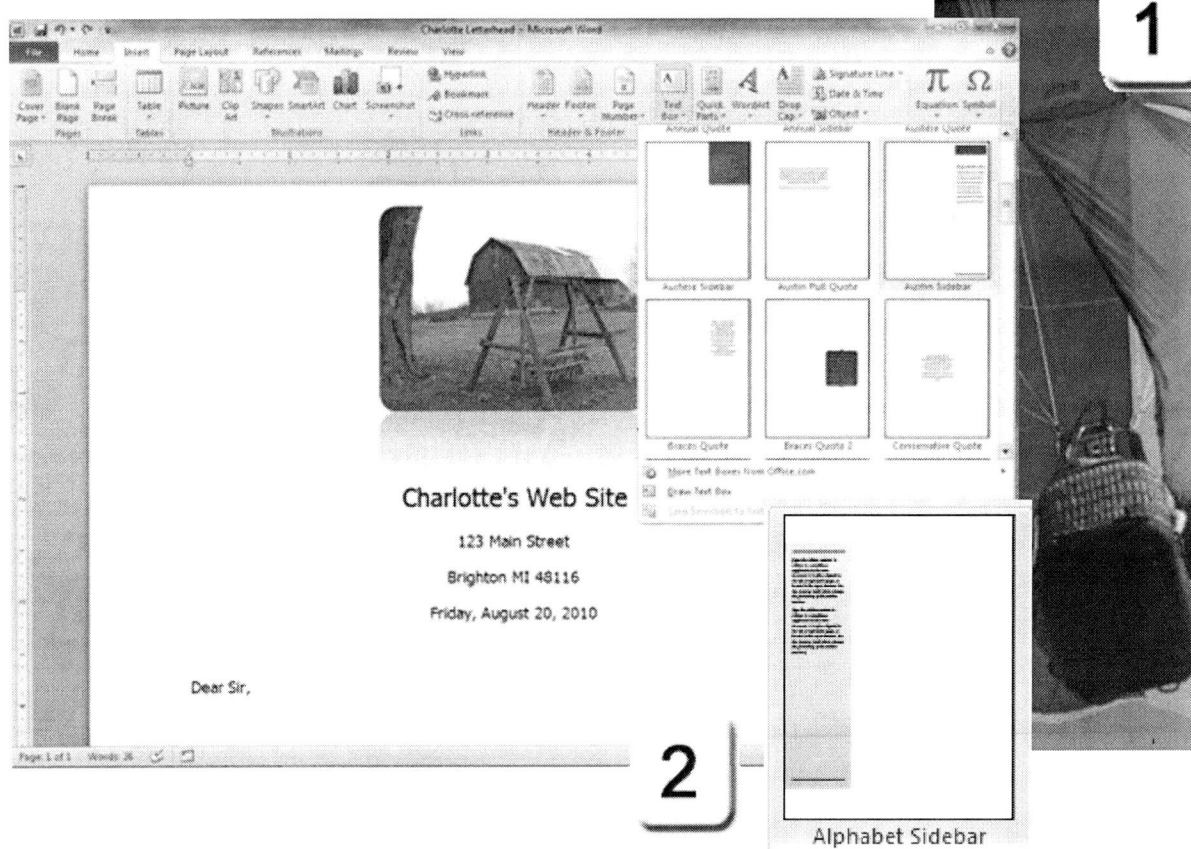

Exam 77-881: Microsoft Word 2010 Core
4. Including Illustrations and Graphics in a Document
4-4. Apply and manipulate text boxes

## The Quick Parts Sidebar

A **Sidebar** is a column of additional information on the left or right of a document. One example of a side bar would be a formal letter that lists the executives and director's names.

Another way you can use the Sidebar is to list the products or services that the company does.

### 3. Try This, Edit the Side Bar
Add the following sample text:
Fresh Fruits
Apples
Avocados
Kiwis
Pears

Fresh Vegetables
Chives
Tomatoes

You can format the sample text bold if you wish. Save your changes.

**Insert -> Text Box -> Alphabet Sidebar**

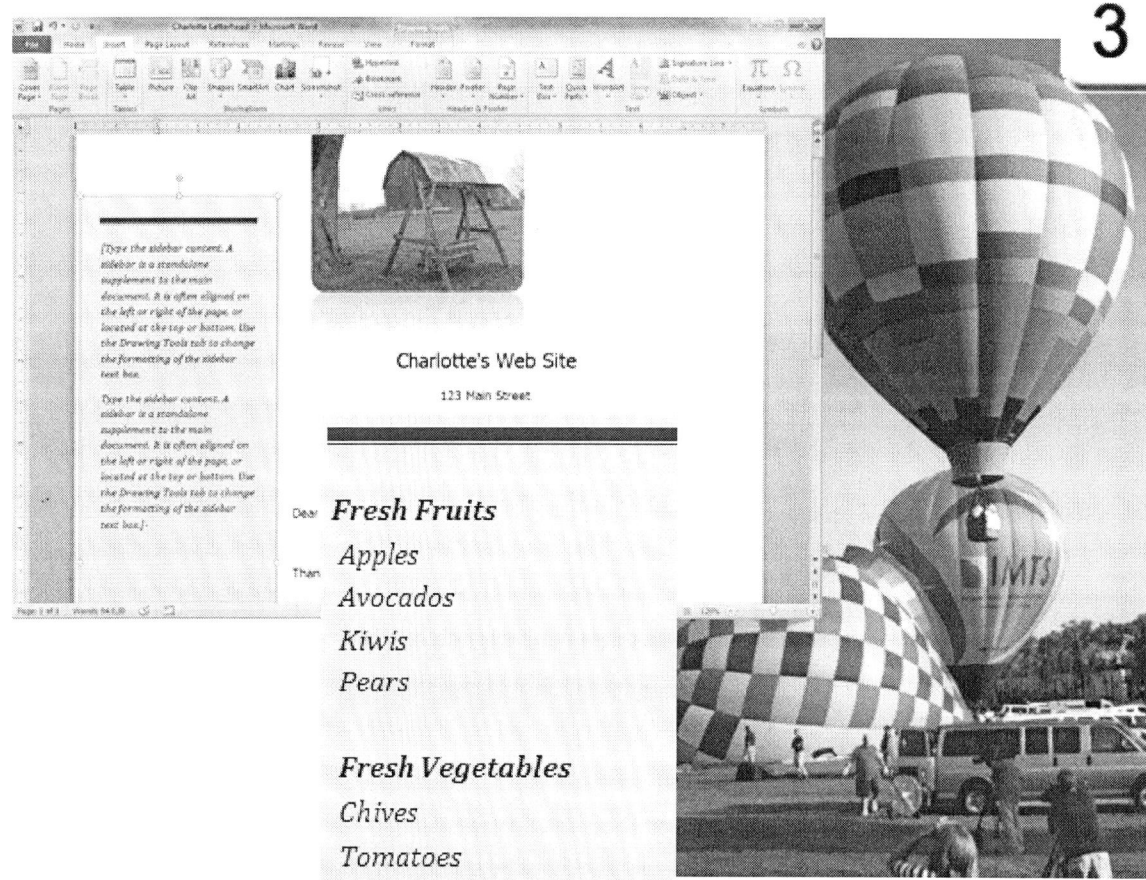

Exam 77-881: Microsoft Word 2010 Core
3. Applying Page Layout and Reusable Content
3-3. Construct content in a document by using the Quick Parts tool

**Drawing Tools ->Insert Shapes ->Change Shape**

## Textbox Formatting

**Stating the Obvious: A Text Box is a Shape...with Text.** When you select a Text Box, you should see the **Drawing Tools** at the top of the screen.

Text Boxes, like Shapes and Pictures in the previous lesson, can be formatted.

**1. Try This. Format the Shape**
Click on the Text Box to select it.

**2. Change the Shape**
Go to **Drawing Tools ->Insert Shapes**.
Click on **Change Shape**.
You can choose any **Shape** from the Library.

Keep going...

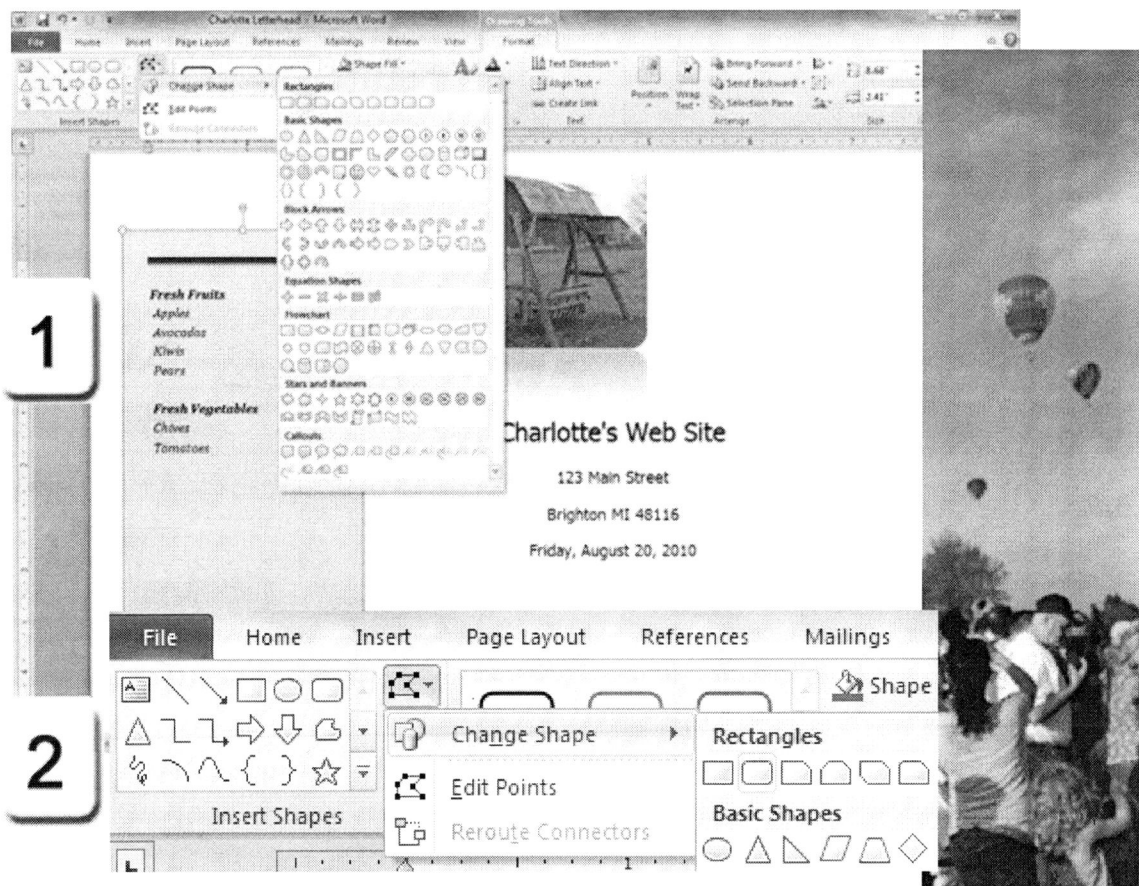

Exam 77-881: Microsoft Word 2010 Core
4. Including Illustrations and Graphics in a Document
4-4. Apply and manipulate text boxes: Change Shape

## Quick Style Formatting

Say you wanted to format the **Outline** and the **Fill** of the Text Box. You can modify both with **Shape Styles**.

**1. Try This. Format the Shape Styles**
Click on the Text Box to select it.

**2. Choose a Style**
Go to **Drawing Tools ->Format.**
Go to **Shape Styles.**
You can choose any **Shape Style** from the Library.

**What Do You See?** Some of the Shape Styles have white borders, other have thin colored outlines. There are jellies and candies as well.

**Who Is Your Audience?** I have always associated shiny, raised bevel formatting with buttons on a screen, rather than a Side Bar on business letterhead.

**Drawing Tools ->Format ->Shape Styles**

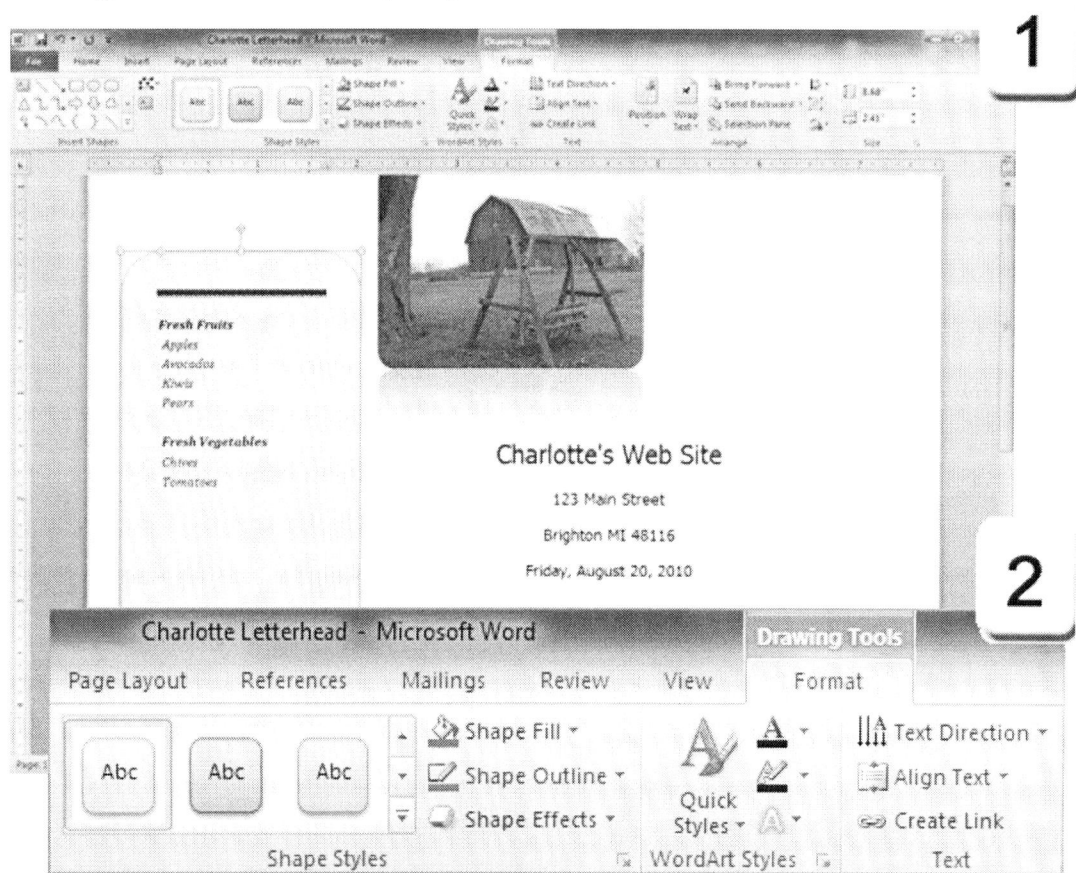

Exam 77-881: Microsoft Word 2010 Core
4. Including Illustrations and Graphics in a Document
4-4. Apply and manipulate text boxes: Apply Quick Styles

## Shape Effects

Look to the right of the **Shape Styles**. There are three formatting options you can use: **Shape Fill**, **Shape Outline** and **Shape Effects**. Shape Effects include shadows, reflections and glowing edges and 3-D rotation.

**1. Try This. Format the Shape Effects**
Click on the Text Box to select it.

**2. Choose a Shape Effect**
Go to **Drawing Tools ->Format.**
Click on **Shape Effects.**
Go to Shadow. You can choose any **Shadow Style** from the Library.

**What Do You See?** The shadows can be **Outer** (on the outside of the border) or **Inner** (on the inside.)

You can also choose a shadow with a **Perspective**, as if the light was shining from one corner or the other.

**Drawing Tools ->Format ->Shape Effects ->Shadows**

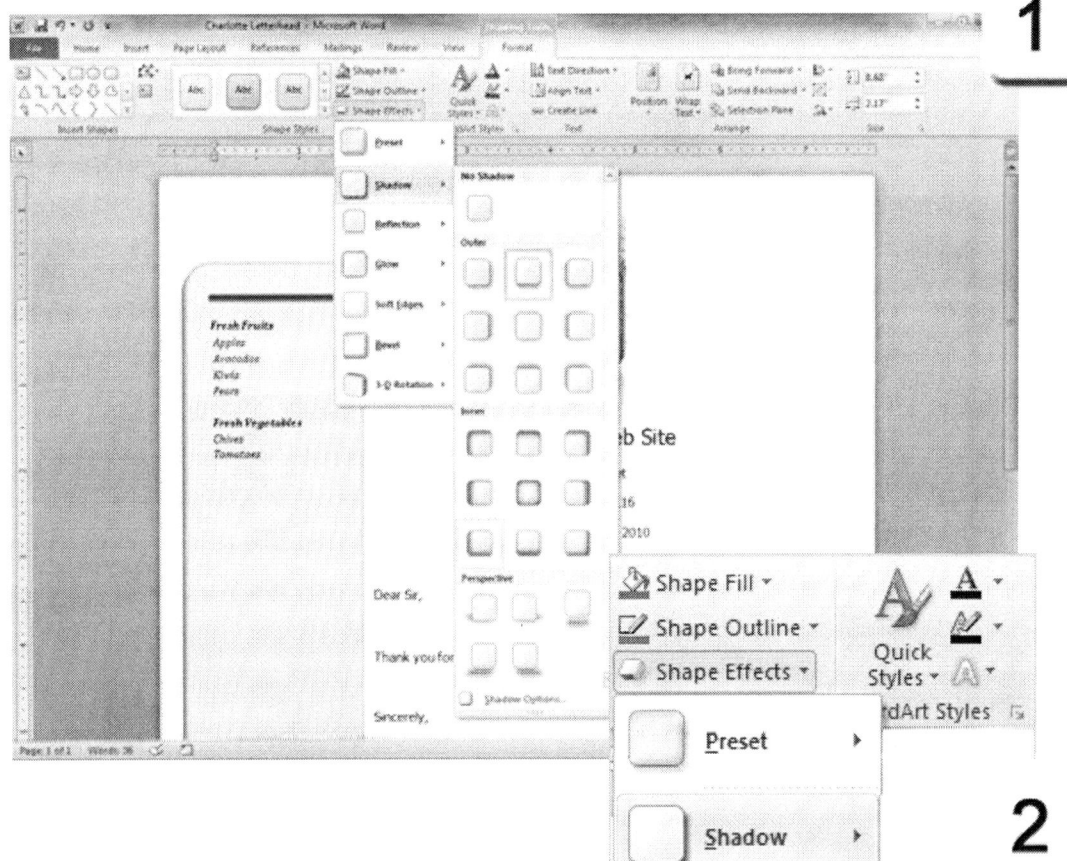

Exam 77-881: Microsoft Word 2010 Core
4. Including Illustrations and Graphics in a Document
4-4. Apply and manipulate text boxes: Shape Effects

## Formatting Text

There are three Text options in the **Drawing Tools**: Text Direction, Align Text and Text Link.

These examples will be be demonstrated with a new, simple Text Box.

**1. Try This. Create a New Text Box**
Go to **Insert->Text Box**.

**2. Choose a Text Box**
Click on Simple Text Box.

Keep going...

**Insert -> Text Box -> Simple Text Box**

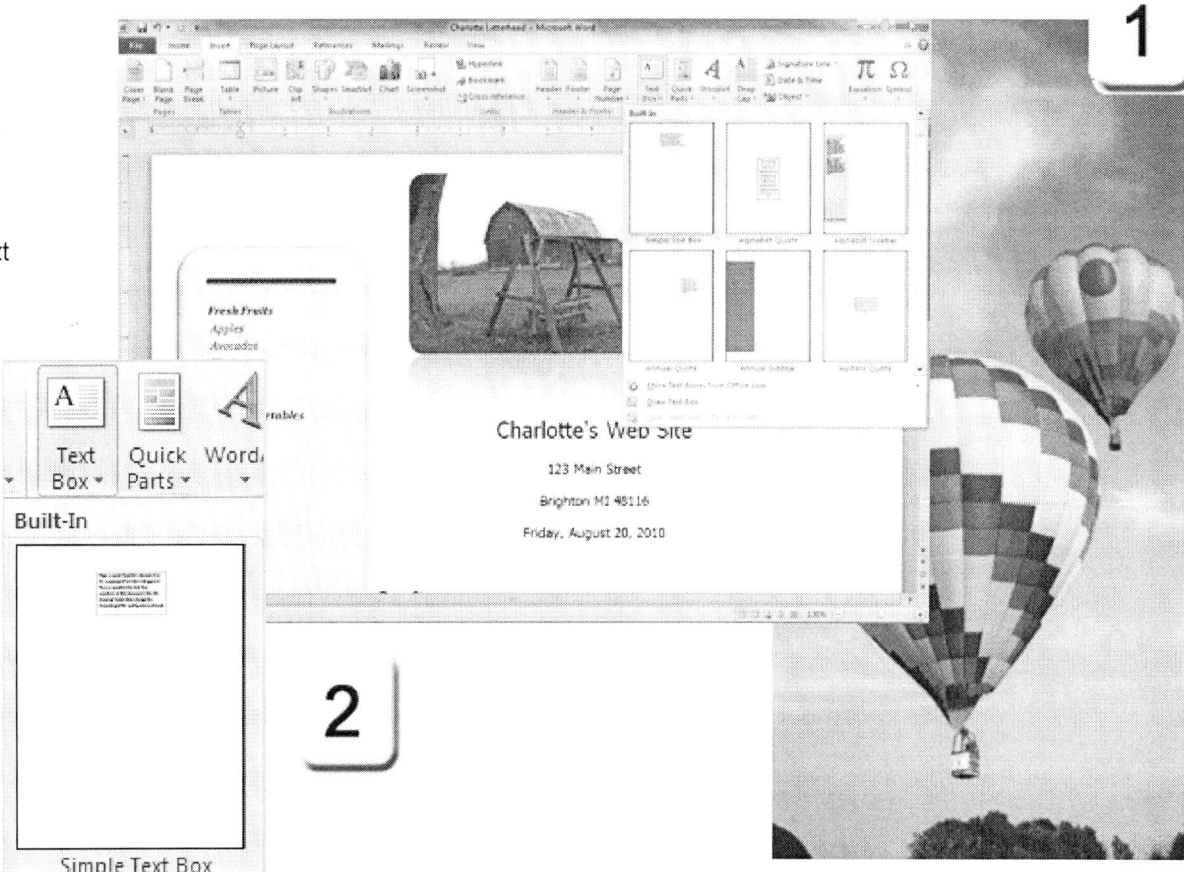

Exam 77-881: Microsoft Word 2010 Core
4. Including Illustrations and Graphics in a Document
4-4. Apply and manipulate text boxes

## Edit the Text Box

**What Do You See?** There should be a new **Text Box** on your page. The Text Box has sample text in it (maybe it's supposed to be helpful hints).

Please edit this text.

### 3. Edit the Text Box

**Select** the Text Box.
Where is your cursor? Is it in the sample text highlighted blue?

**Type**: From the farm to your table: that's fresh!

Keep going...

**Drawing Tools -> Format -> Text**

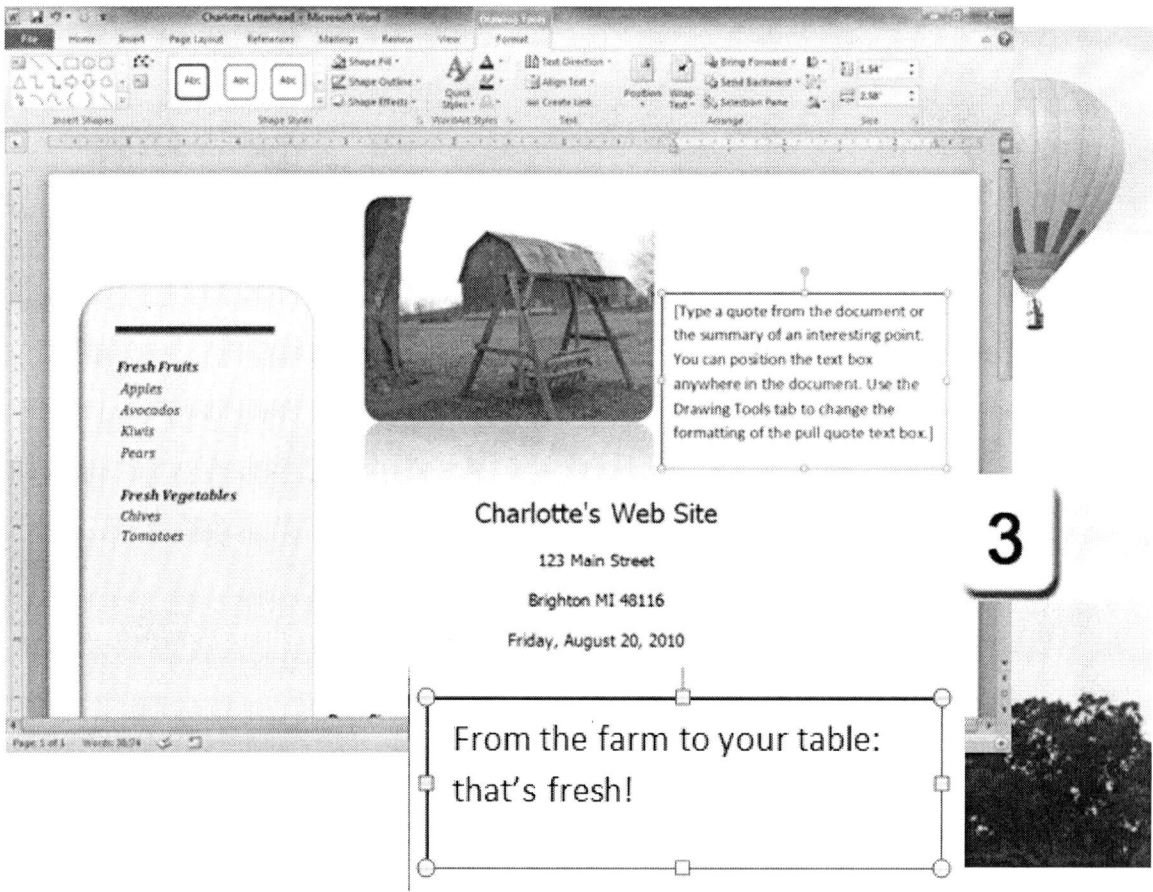

Exam 77-881: Microsoft Word 2010 Core
4. Including Illustrations and Graphics in a Document
4-4. Apply and manipulate text boxes

## Format the Text Direction

The **Text Direction** rotates the Text Box and the Text with it. Here are the options.

**Horizontal** is the default direction.

**Rotate all text 90'** is used for book spines so that you can read the title when the book is laying face up on the desk.

**Rotate all text 270'** is used for Sidebars and marketing.

**1. Try It: Format the Text Direction**
**Select** the Text Box.

**2.** Go to **Drawing Tools -> Format.**
Click on **Text Direction.**
Choose **Rotate all text 270'**

**3. What Do You See?** Both the Text Box and the Text in it are rotated. Can you edit the text after it is rotated?

**Drawing Tools -> Format -> Text Direction**

Exam 77-881: Microsoft Word 2010 Core
4. Including Illustrations and Graphics in a Document
4-4. Apply and manipulate text boxes: Format Text Direction

## Format the Text Alignment

**Align Text** places the text at the top, middle or bottom of a Text Box.

**Before You Begin**: This example works best if you resize the Text Box a little taller so that you see the difference between Top, Middle and Bottom. The Text in this example is Horizontal, not rotated.

**1. Try It: Format the Text Alignment**
Select the Text Box. Use the handles to resize the Text Box a little taller.

**2. Format the Text Alignment**

Go to **Drawing Tools -> Format.**
Click on **Align Text.**

**3. What Do You See?**
The Text in the Text Box should be placed at the top, middle or bottom of the Text Box...there's no surprises here.

**Drawing Tools -> Format -> Align Text**

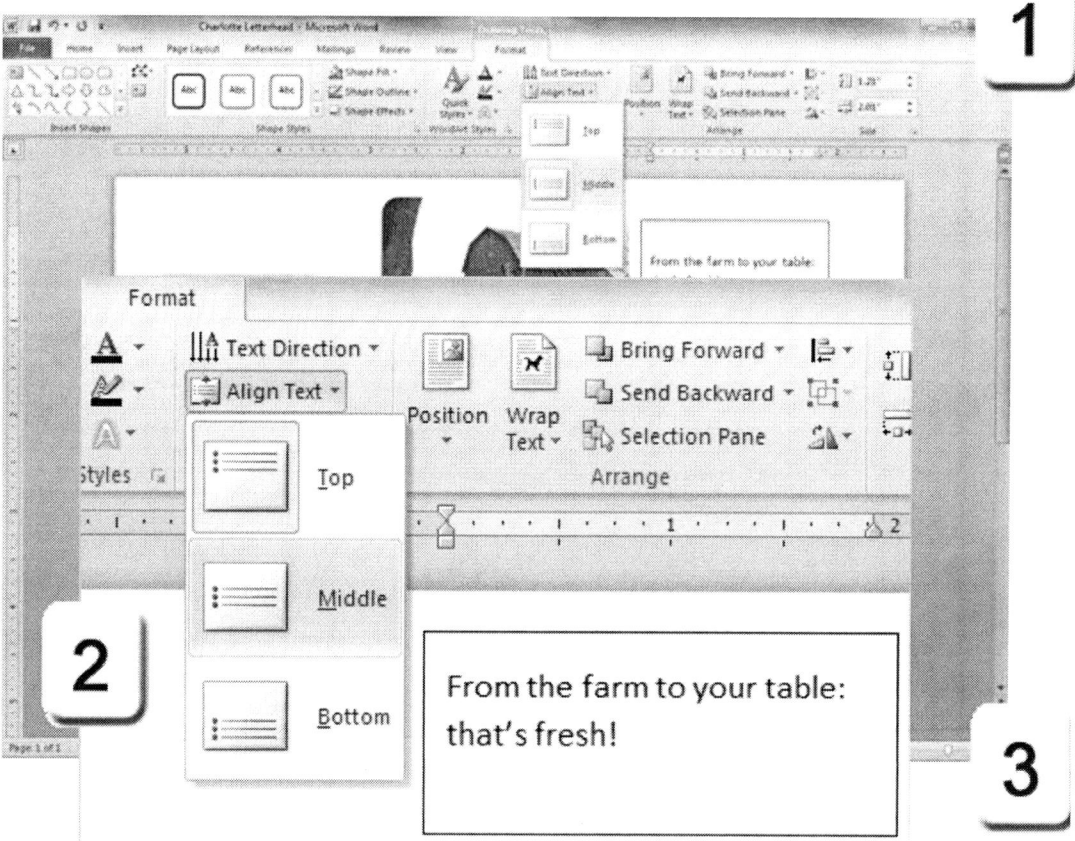

Exam 77-881: Microsoft Word 2010 Core
4. Including Illustrations and Graphics in a Document
4-4. Apply and manipulate text boxes: Align Text

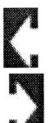

HOME

Take Three

**Insert -> Text Box**

## Create Linked Text Boxes

**Linked Text Boxes** are used to connect two Text Boxes together. Say you have a lot of information in the first Text Box. If you link two Text Boxes, then the extra type from the first one will "spill into" the second Text Box.

**Try This: Enter More Sample Text**
**Before you begin:** Open a new, blank document and add a new, simple Text Box.
**Select** the Text Box.

**Type**: The tomatoes are hand picked from the vines as the dew dries in the morning sun.

The corn squeaks when it is shucked of its fragrant green husks.

The smell of Thanksgiving rises from the garden when you brush against the Mother of Thyme.

**Try This, Too: Format the Text**
Select the word: tomatoes.
Go to **Home ->Font.**
Can you make just one word big, bold and red and another big, bold and green? Yes. ;-)

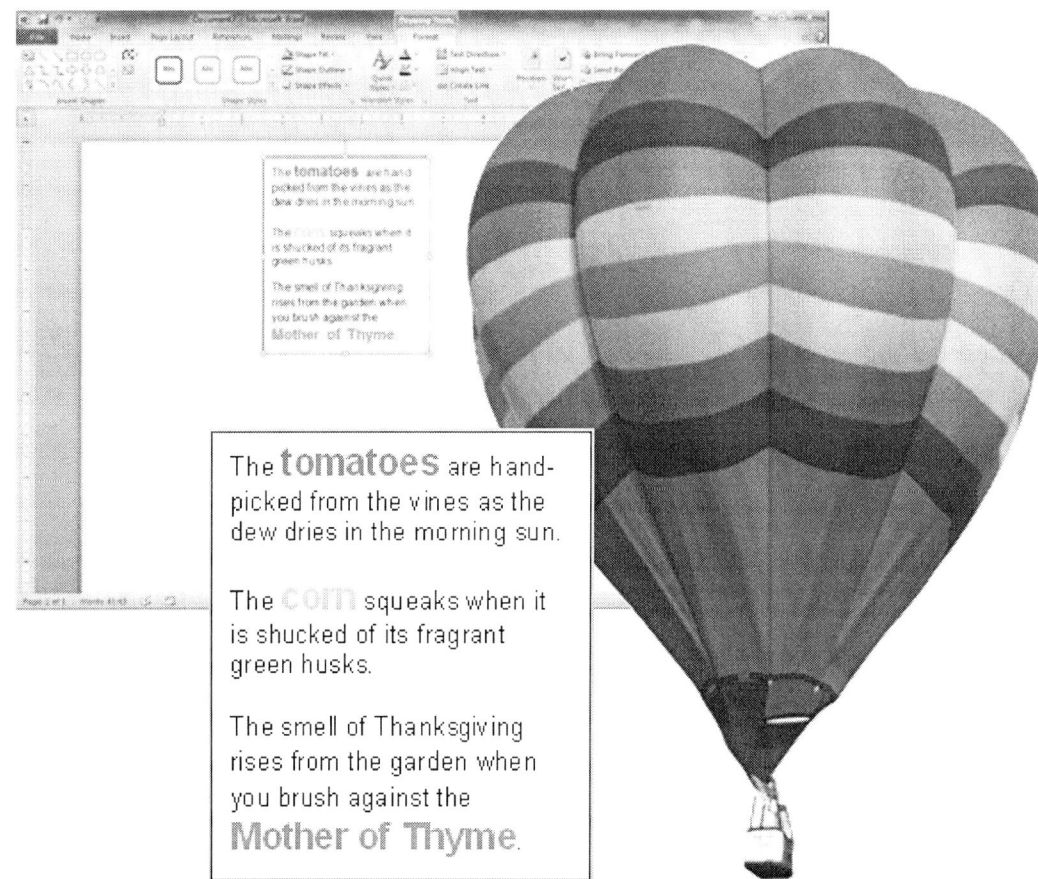

The **tomatoes** are hand-picked from the vines as the dew dries in the morning sun.

The corn squeaks when it is shucked of its fragrant green husks.

The smell of Thanksgiving rises from the garden when you brush against the
Mother of Thyme.

Exam 77-881: Microsoft Word 2010 Core
4. Including Illustrations and Graphics in a Document
4-4. Apply and manipulate text boxes: Create linked text boxes

**Insert -> Text Box -> Simple Text Box**

# Link Two Text Boxes

You can **Link** two **Text Boxes** together.

We just setup a simple Text Box in the previous pages. Here are the steps to create a second, empty text box and link it to the first one you just made.

**1. Try This: Create an Empty Text Box**
Go to **Insert ->Text Box**. From the options, select **Simple Text Box.**
**Select** the new Text Box.
**Delete** the sample type. The new Text Box has to be empty before you can link to it.

Keep going...

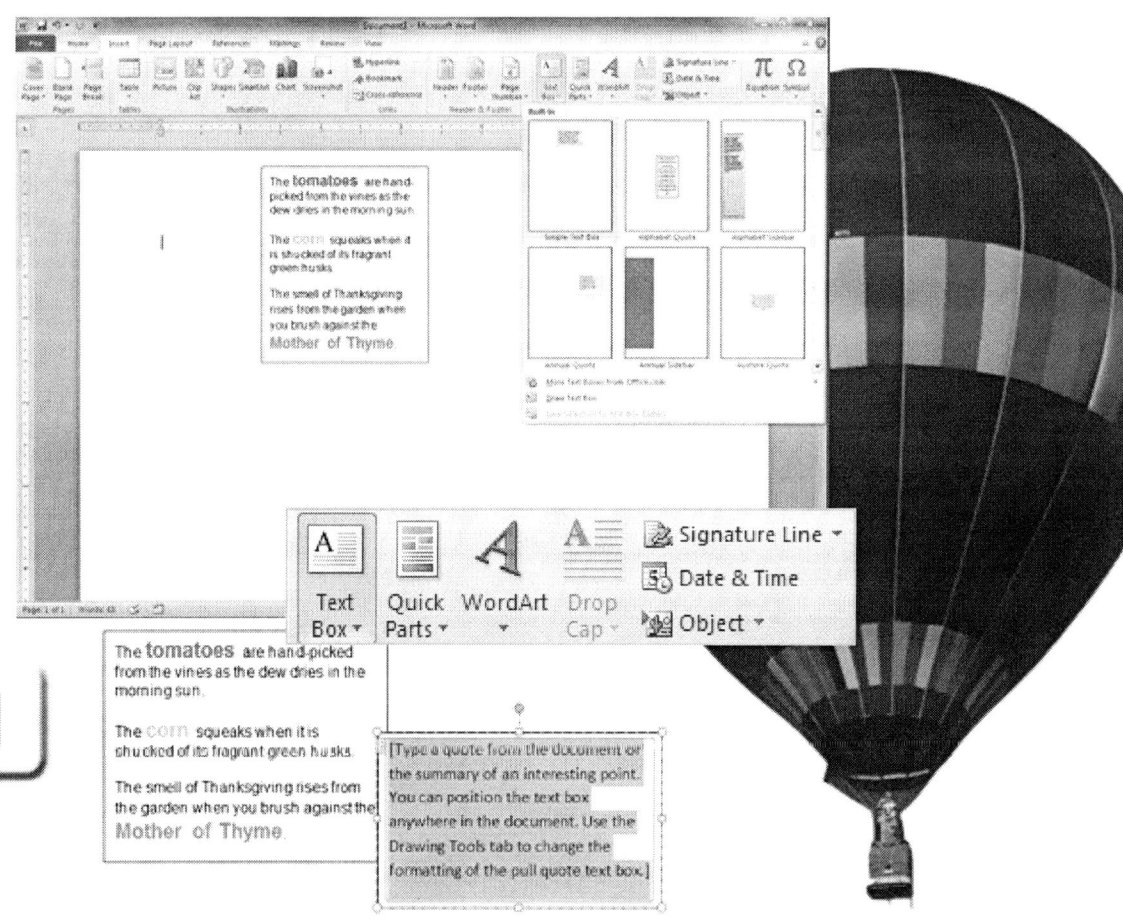

Exam 77-887: Microsoft Word Expert 2010
2. Formatting Content
2.4. Link sections: Link Text Boxes

## Use the Linked Boxes

**2. Try This, Too: Link the Text Boxes**
Click on the first Text Box.
Go to **Drawing Tools -> Format.**
Click on: **Create Link.**

**3. What Do You See?** Your should see a cup that can "pour" the text into the second Text Box.
Click on the second Text Box.

**What If It Doesn't Work?**
**Try this: Resize the Linked Text Boxes**
**Select** the first Text Box.
You should see the small handles in each corner and around the sides of the Text Box when you select it.

**Resize** the first Text Box by using the bottom handles to make it smaller. As you make the first Text Box smaller, the type shows up in the second Text Box.

**Where Have You Seen This Before?** Many desktop publishing programs, such as Microsoft Publisher, use linked Text Boxes to create a newsletter. For example, the article may begin on the first page, but the rest of the story may jump (link) to page 5.

Text Box Tools -> Format -> Create Link

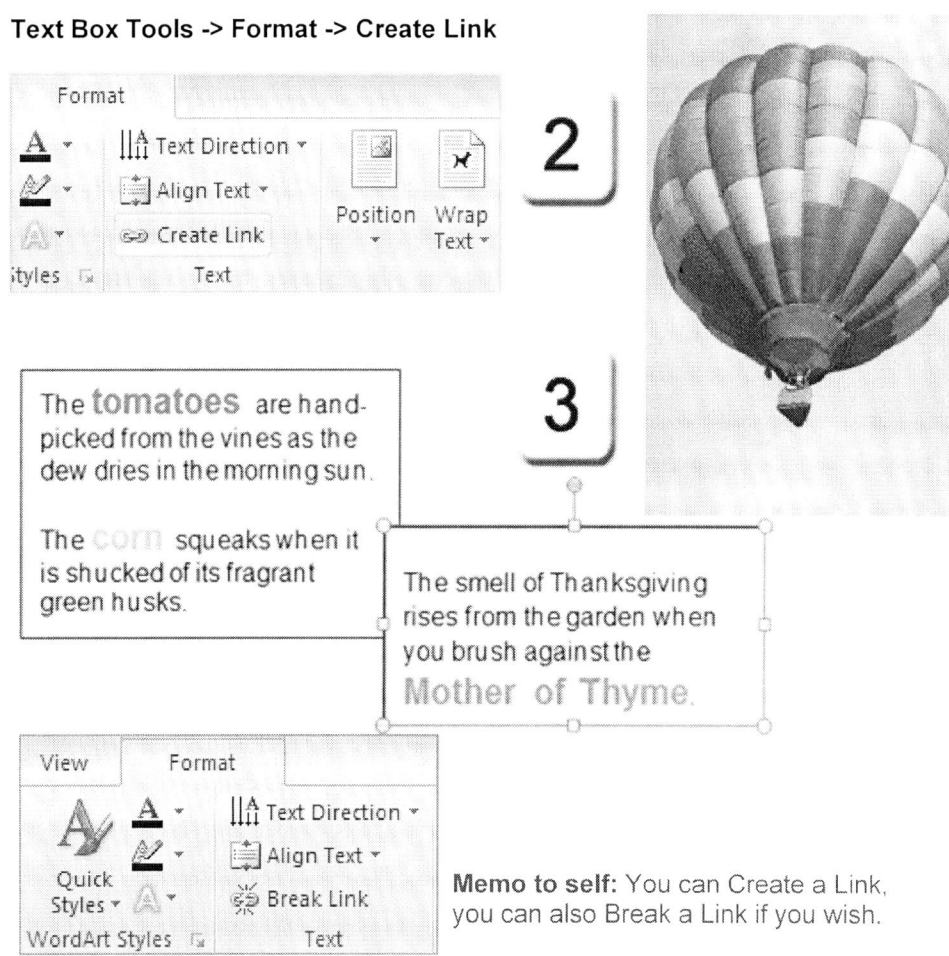

The **tomatoes** are hand-picked from the vines as the dew dries in the morning sun.

The corn squeaks when it is shucked of its fragrant green husks.

The smell of Thanksgiving rises from the garden when you brush against the Mother of Thyme.

**Memo to self:** You can Create a Link, you can also Break a Link if you wish.

Exam 77-887: Microsoft Word Expert 2010
2. Formatting Content
2.4. Link sections: Link Text Boxes

## Quick Parts

Each company or department builds a collection of documents that identifies who they are when they communicate with their clients. These documents can include letterhead, envelopes, fax cover pages, memos, blogs and newsletters. Many of these documents use the same elements that we added to this letterhead: company name, address, and a picture or graphic for the logo.

**Before You Begin**: Please open the sample letterhead you created for Charlotte's Web Site.

**1. Try This: Create a Quick Part**
**Select the text**: Charlotte's Web Site.

**2. Save Selection to Quick Part Gallery**
Go to **Insert ->Quick Parts**.
Choose **Save Selection to Quick Part Gallery**.

Keep going...

**Insert ->Quick Parts ->Document Property**

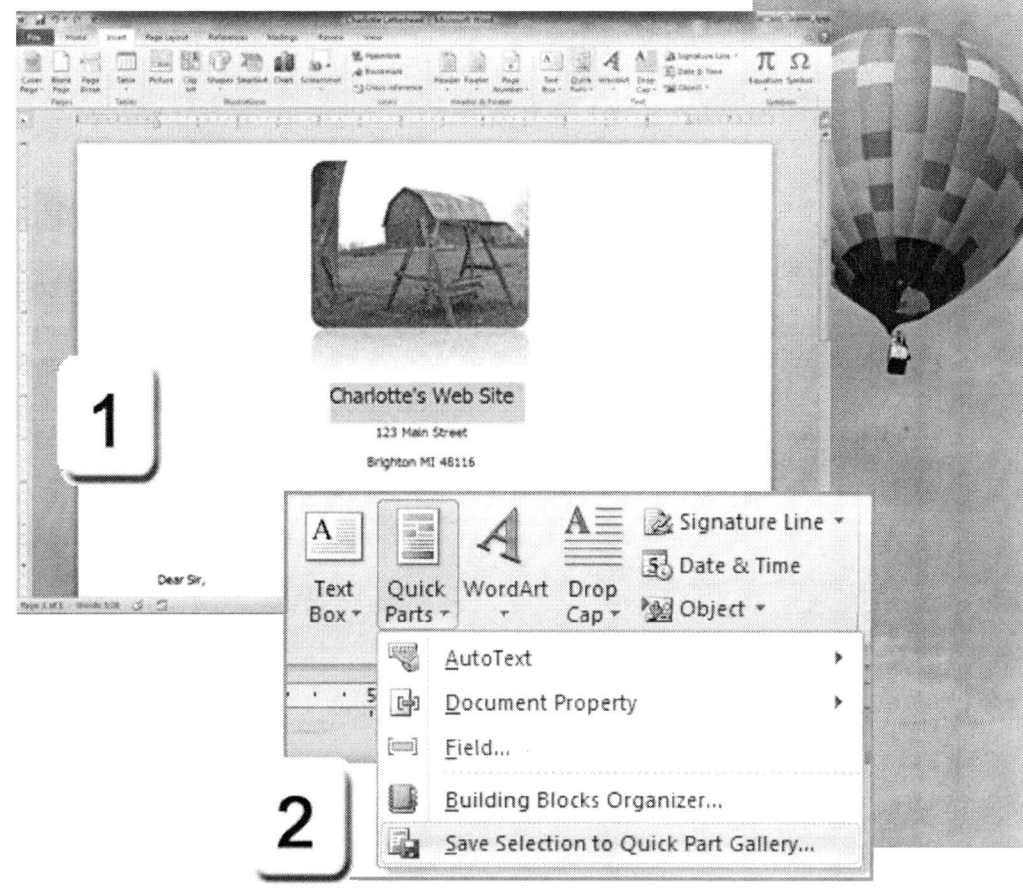

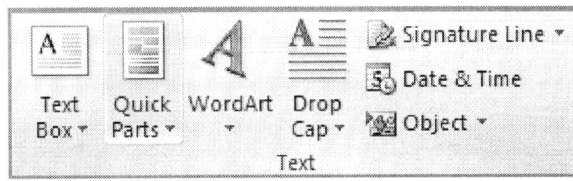

Exam 77-887: Microsoft Word Expert 2010
2. Formatting Content
2.3. Construct reusable content in a document: Create a Quick Part

Insert ->Quick Parts ->Document Property ->Company

## Edit the Building Block

**What Do You See?** When you create a new Quick Part, you should see a little **Building Block** form that you can edit. Here are the steps.

**3. Try This: Edit the Building Block**
Name: Charlotte's.
Gallery: AutoText
Category: General.
Description: (You can edit the description if you wish.)
Save in: Normal

Accept the default for the following:
Options: Insert content only.

Keep going...

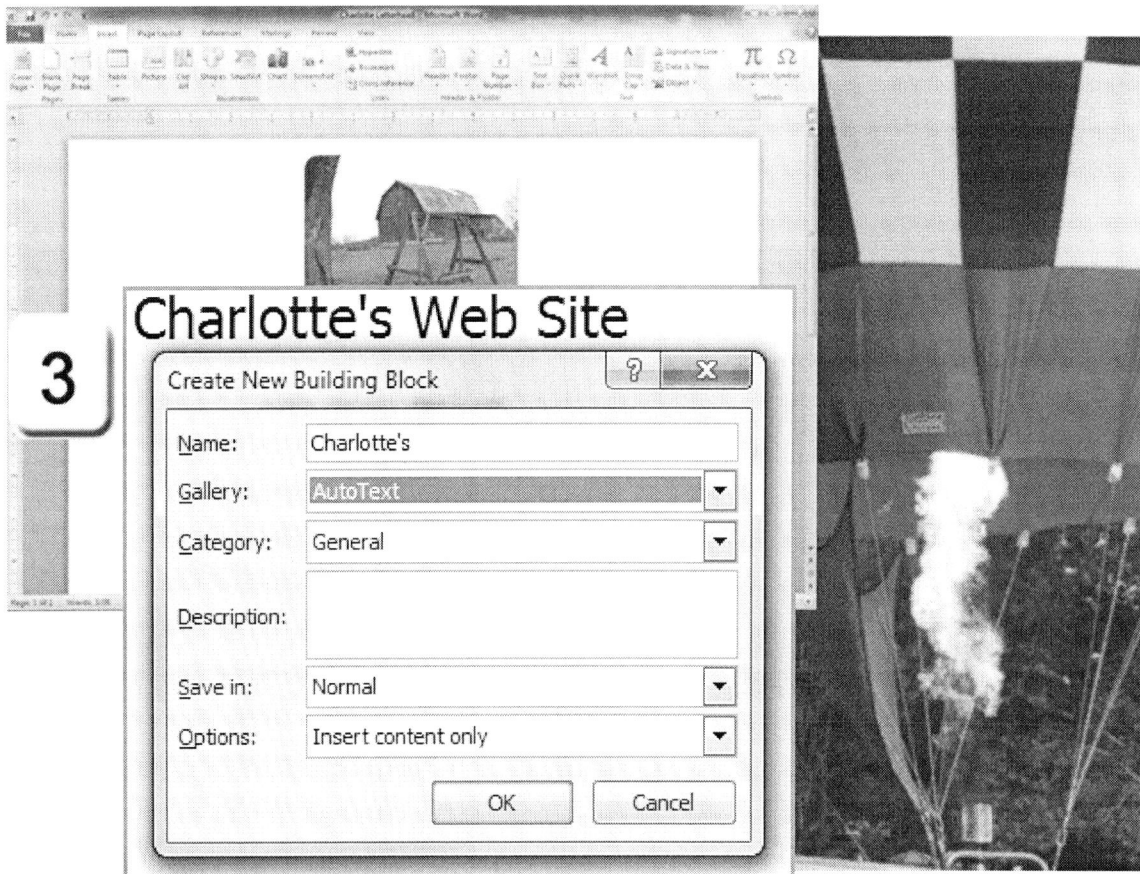

Exam 77-887: Microsoft Word Expert 2010
2. Formatting Content
2.3. Construct reusable content in a document: Edit the Building Block

## Add More Quick Parts

Say you already had a logo that you wanted to use again and again in other documents. You can save that logo to the **Quick Part Gallery.**

**1. Try This: Save Selection**
Click once on the logo to select it.
Go to **Insert ->Quick Parts**.
Choose: **Save Selection to Quick Part Gallery**
**2. Create the New Building Block**
Name: Company Logo.
Gallery: AutoText.
Category: General.
Description: Picture of barn.
Save in: Normal.

Accept the default for the following:
Options: Insert content only.

**Insert ->Quick Parts -> Save Selection to Quick Part Gallery**

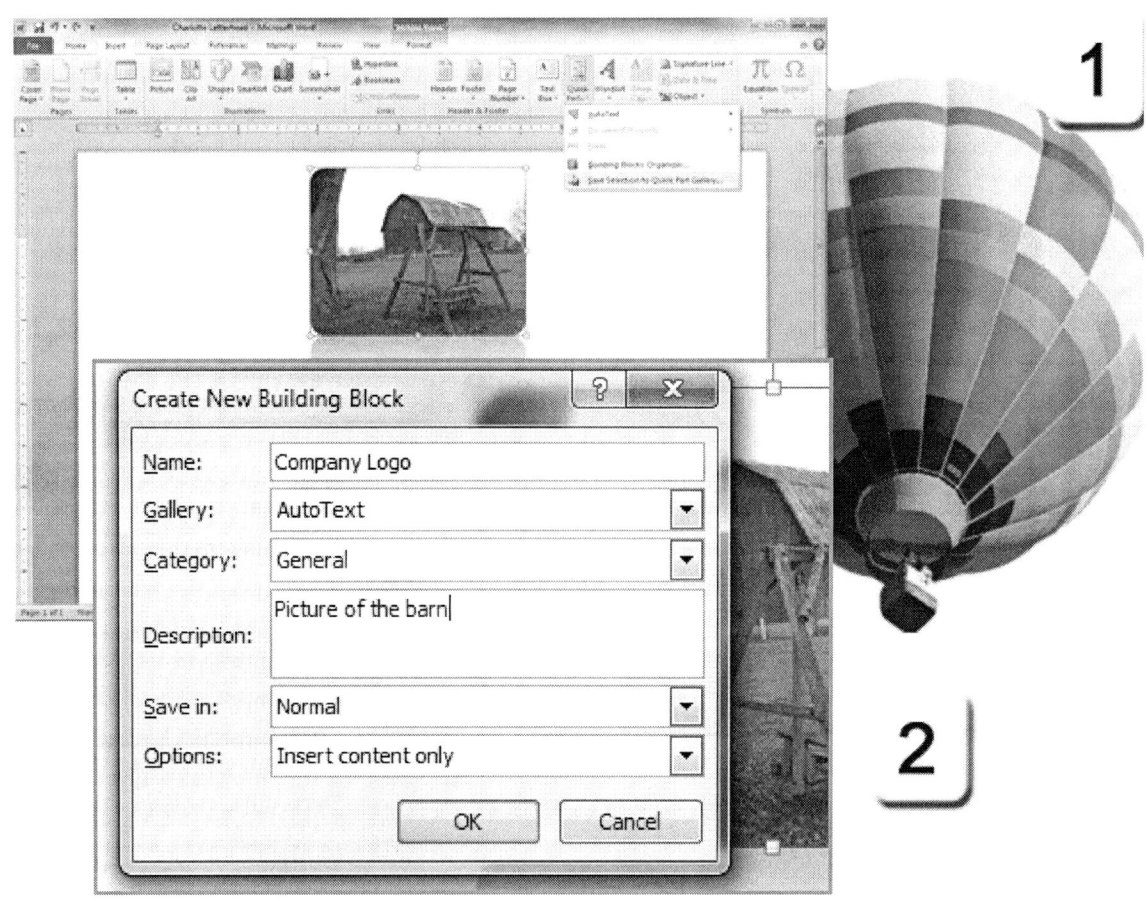

Exam 77-887: Microsoft Word Expert 2010
2. Formatting Content
2.3. Construct reusable content in a document: Create New Building Block

## Quick Parts Gallery

**What Was The Result?** When you go to Insert ->Quick Parts, you should see Charlotte's Logo in the Gallery. You can add your own Quick Parts and have them available whenever you need them.

**1. Before You Begin:** please open a new, blank document. Here are the steps.

Go to **File ->New**.
Select a Blank document.

Keep going...

**File -> New ->Blank document**

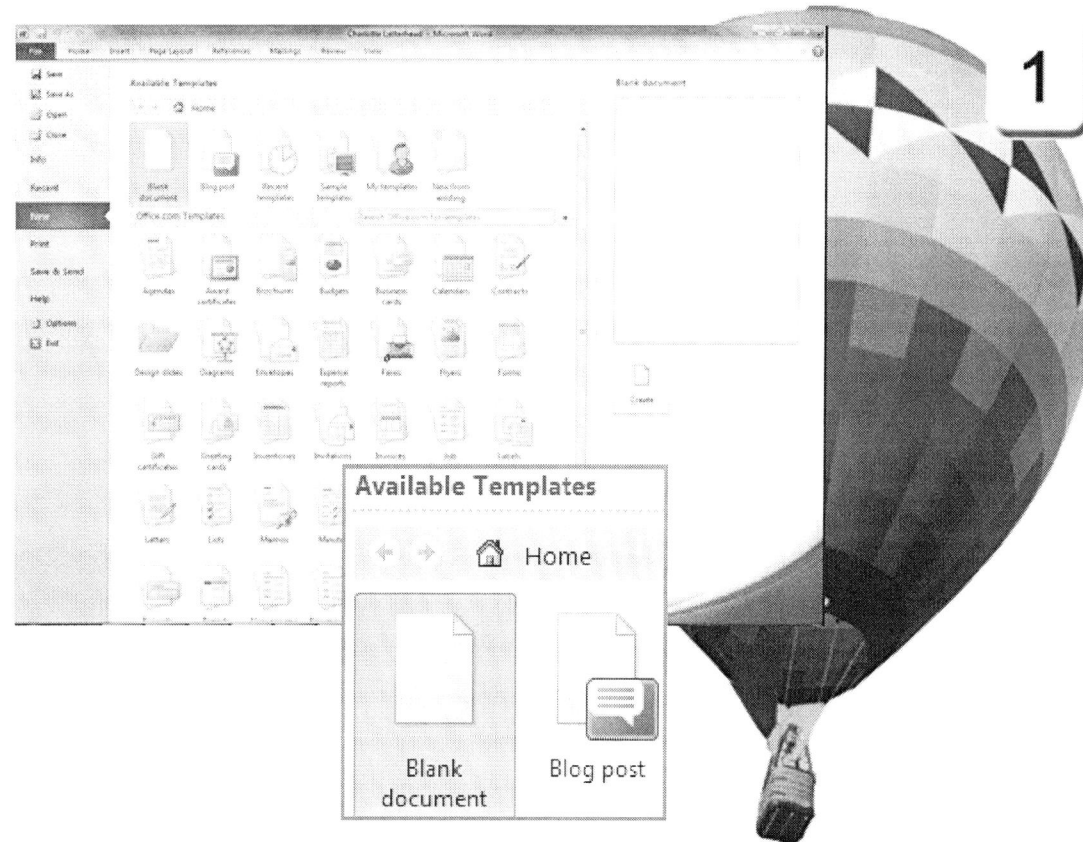

Exam 77-887: Microsoft Word Expert 2010
2. Formatting Content
2.3. Construct reusable content in a document: Quick Parts Gallery

Beginning Word 2010 Page 183 of 195

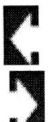

## Use Quick Parts

**2. Using the Quick Parts**
Go to **Insert ->Quick Parts**
Click on **AutoText.**

**3. What Do You See?** The AutoText Gallery should display the company name as well as the company logo.

**Did You Notice:** the text for the company name, Charlotte's Web Site, is formatted exactly as when you selected it in the letterhead we made in the previous lesson: font, size, alignment.

**What Do You Think?** Say you worked for the Livingston Regional MTEC Center. That would be one of the first phrases you might want to add to the AutoText.

**Insert ->Quick Parts->AutoText**

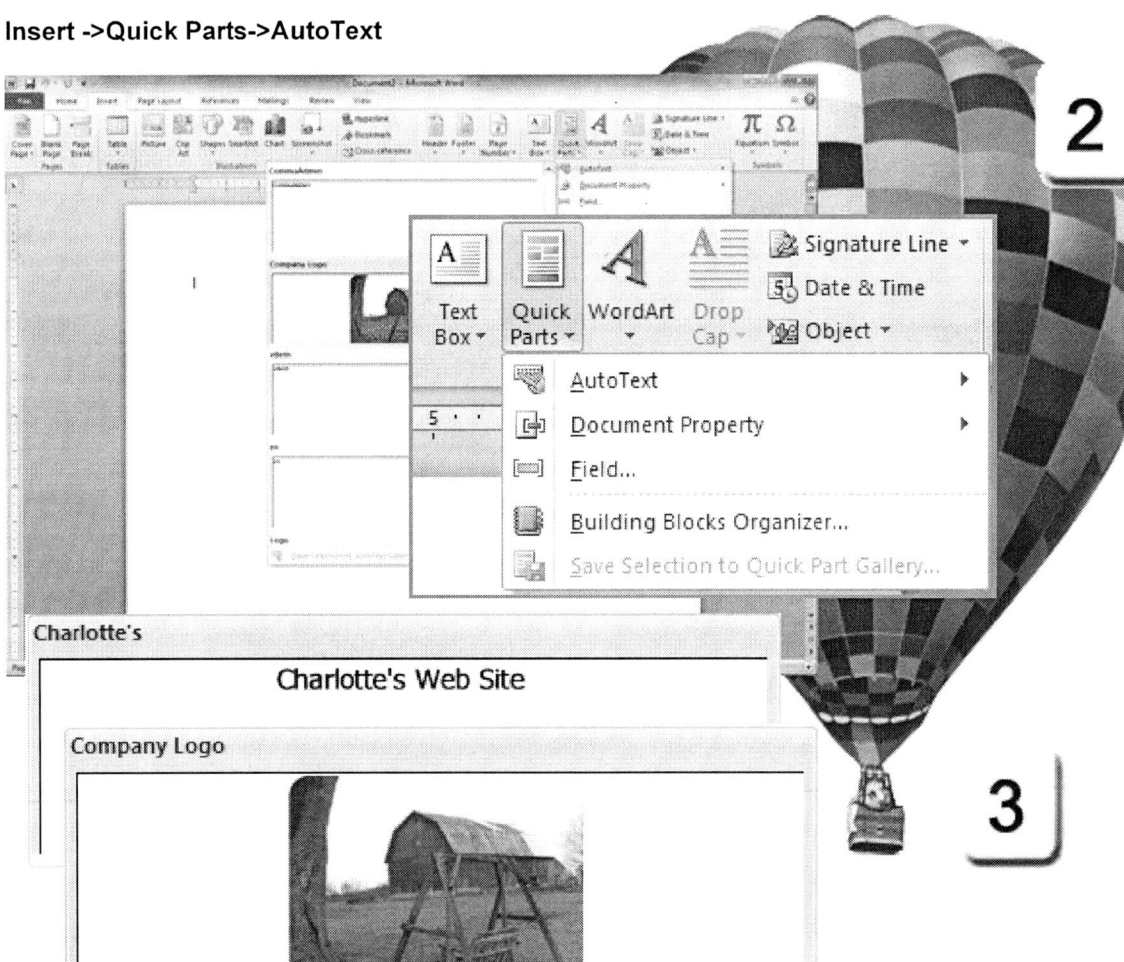

Exam 77-887: Microsoft Word Expert 2010
2. Formatting Content
2.3. Construct reusable content in a document: Quick Parts Gallery

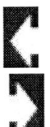

**Insert ->Footer**

## The Quick Parts Footer

Look across the **Insert** Ribbon and you will see many kinds of Quick Parts. For example, there are Quick Part Headers, Footers, and Text Boxes.

**1. Try This: Insert a Footer**
Go to **Insert ->Footer.**
Select **Building Block Organizer.**
Scroll down to Alphabet and double click the **Footers**.

**2. What Do You See?** Look at the bottom of your document. Your cursor should be in a new footer at the bottom of your page.

**Suggested Sample Type:**
Charlotte's Web Site (810) 555-1212.

The footer is formatted with the font, size, color and alignment of the Alphabet template. Can you select the type and use the tools on the **Home Ribbon** to edit the formatting?

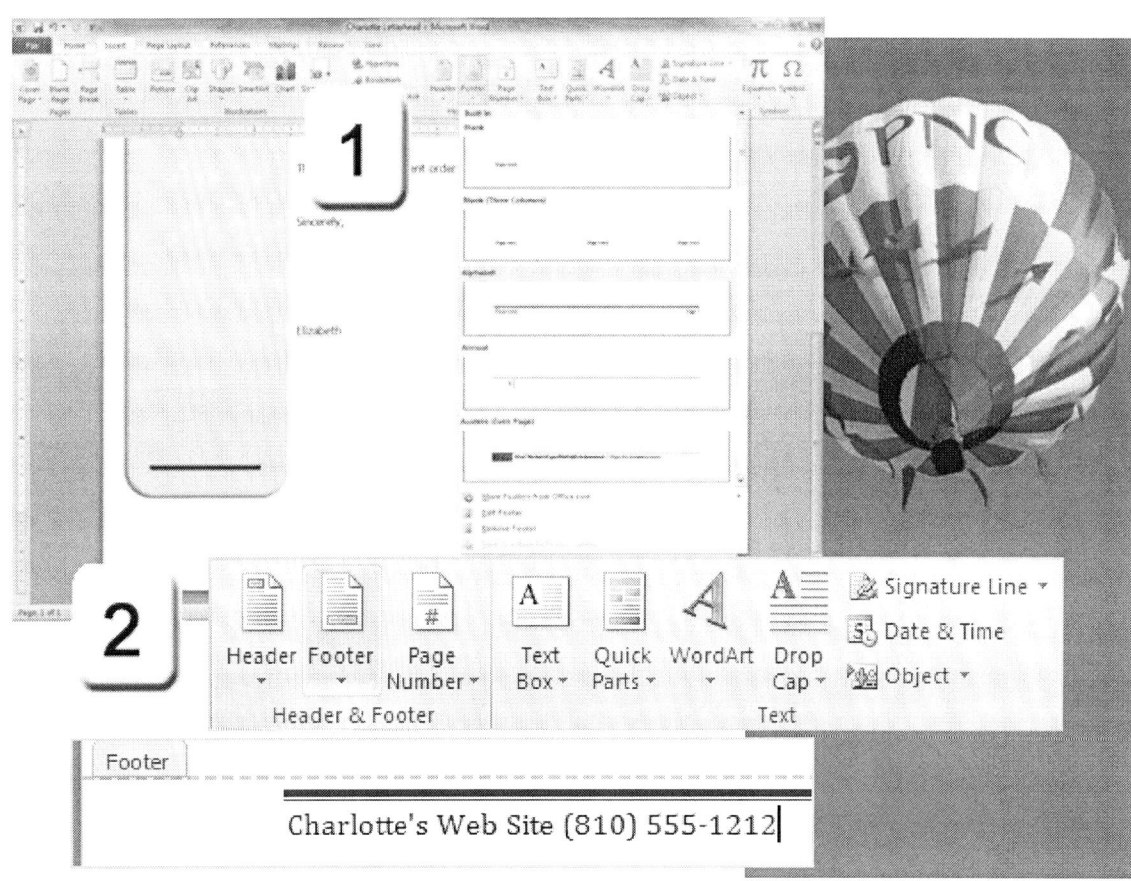

Exam 77-887: Microsoft Word Expert 2010
2. Formatting Content
2.3. Construct reusable content in a document: Quick Parts Footers

## The Building Block Organizer

The Built-In Headers, Footers, Text Boxes and AutoText are **Building Blocks**.

Microsoft Word 2010 gathers all of the Building Blocks into an an extensive table called the **Building Block Organizer**.

**Try It: Organize Building Blocks**
Go to **Insert ->Quick Parts**.
Select **Building Block Organizer**.

**What Do You See?**
Do you see the AutoText entries: words as well as pictures?

There are six properties you can edit to identify and organize your Building Blocks.

At the top of the list of Building Blocks are the column headers. Click on Name, and the list will be sorted alphabetically A-Z. You can sort the Building Blocks by Name, Gallery, or Category.

**Insert ->Quick Parts -> Building Block Organizer**

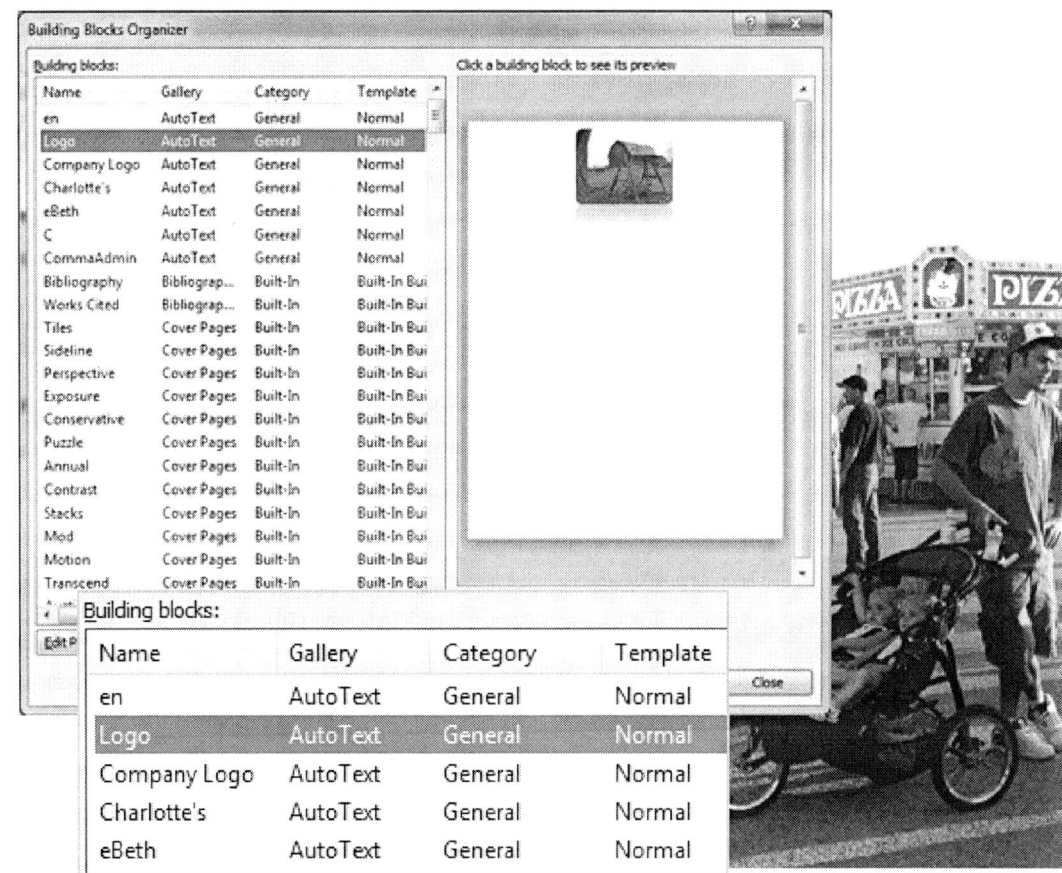

Exam 77-887: Microsoft Word Expert 2010
2. Formatting Content
2.3. Construct reusable content in a document: Building Block Organizer

## Modify Building Blocks

You can use the **Building Blocks Organizer** to manage different versions of your Building Blocks.

**Try This: Modify the Footer**
Select the Footer.
Change the Text Font and Color.
Go to **Insert ->Quick Parts**.
Select **Save Selection to Quick Part Gallery**.

**Modify the Building Block:**

Name: Alphabet Sidebar.

Gallery: Built-In.

The original Alphabet Footer is a **Built-in Quick Part**. You can add the custom Alphabet Footer and save it in the **Quick Part Gallery**.

**What Do You See?** There are two Building Blocks with the same name. However, they are organized into different Galleries.

Insert ->Quick Parts -> Save Selection to Quick Part Gallery

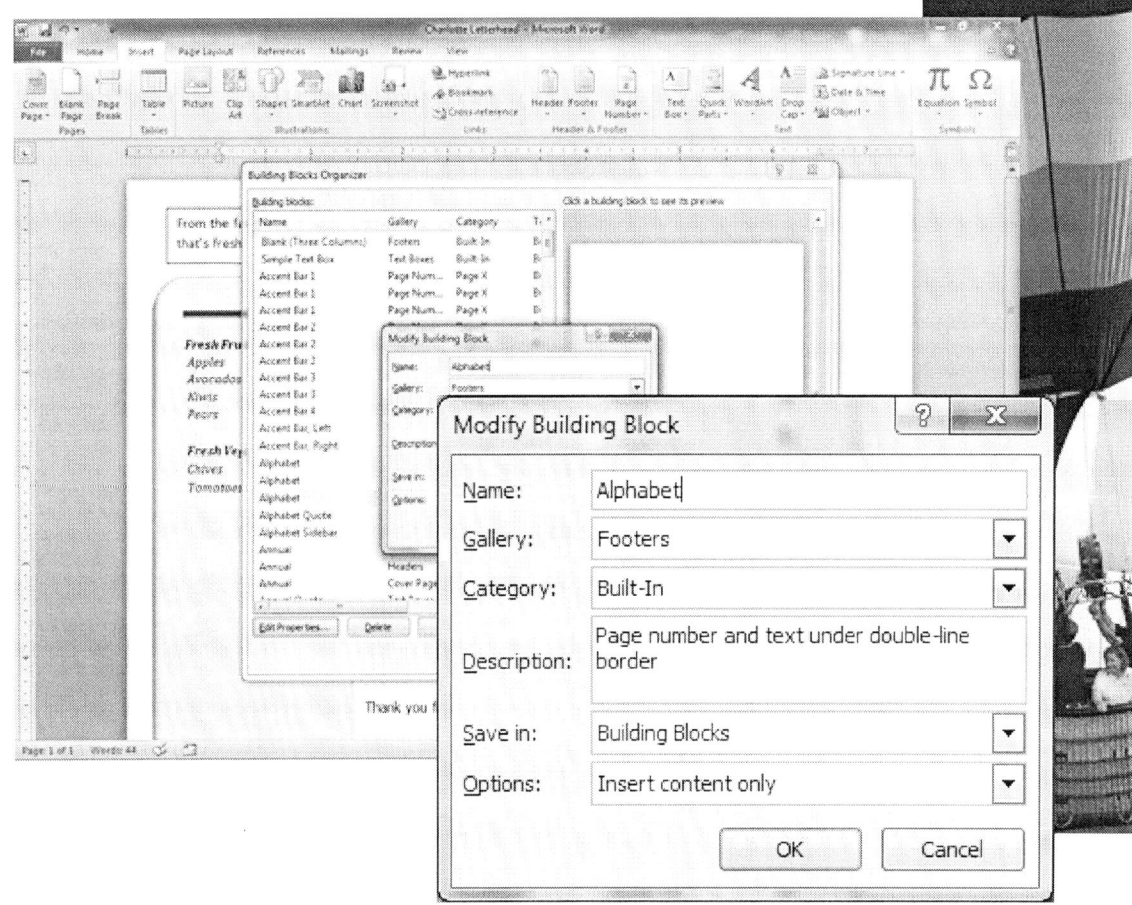

Exam 77-887: Microsoft Word Expert 2010
2. Formatting Content
2.3. Construct reusable content in a document: Building Block Organizer

## Modify Building Blocks

This lesson compared Shapes, Text Boxes and Building Blocks.

The lesson began by Inserting the Date and Time: a little Quick Part.

Well, you done good. Take an extra cookie on your way out.

**Insert ->Quick Parts -> Add Selection to Quick Part Gallery**

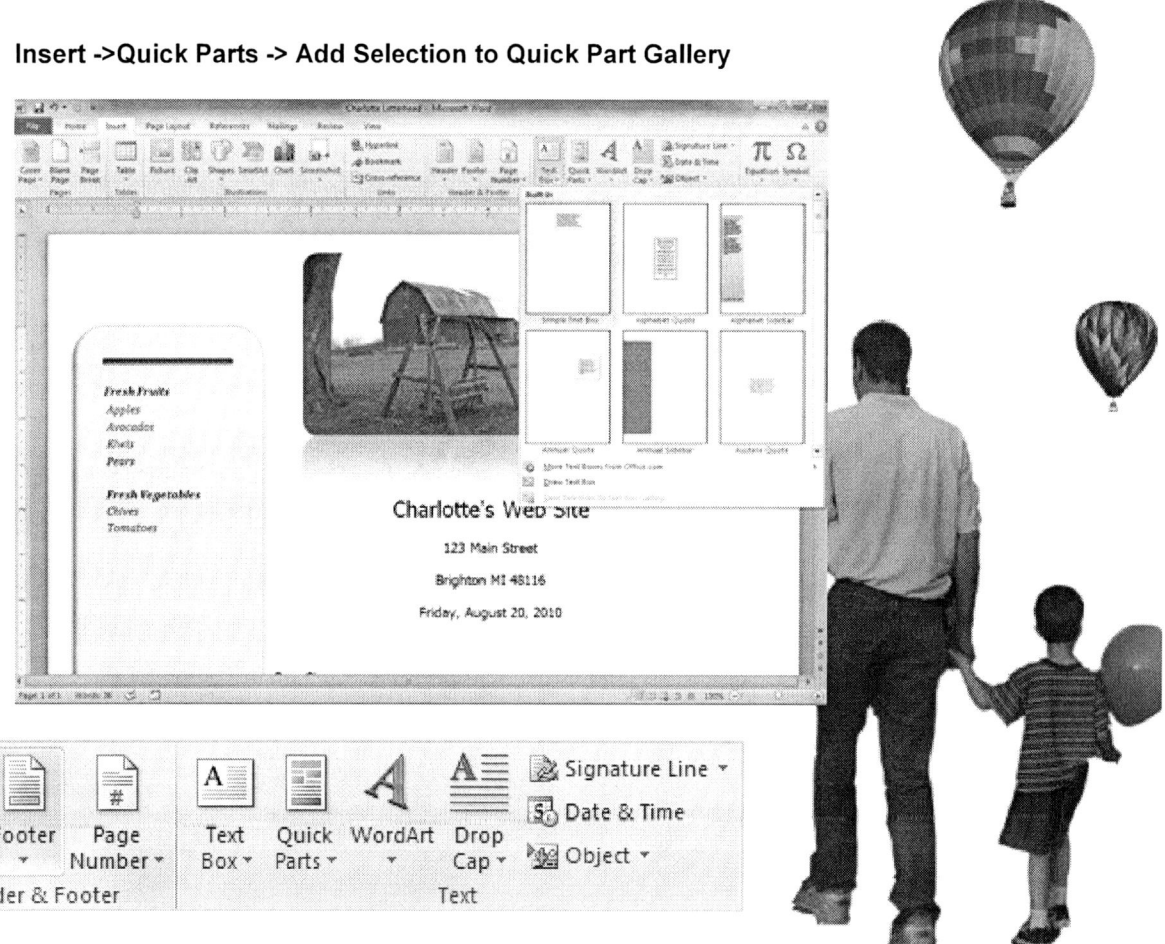

# Practice Activities

## Lesson: First Impressions

**Before You Begin:** Start Microsoft Word 2010. You should see a new, blank document.

**Try This: Do the following steps**

1. Type the Company name: Girraffin' Around
2. Insert a Giraffe picture
3. Add the Company address:
789 Safari Dr
Austin, TX
4. Format the picture with Text Wrapping: Top and Bottom
5. Align the picture and text: Centered
6. Hit the Enter key twice to leave two blank lines below the company address.
7. Insert the text: New Product Line!
8. Insert a Simple Text box.
9. Add the following text:
Shirts
Hats
Scarves
Extra-long Scarves
Sweaters
Gloves

10. Insert a second Text Box.
11. Link the first and second Text Boxes.
12. In the FIRST Text Box, add the following products:
Socks
Shoes
Boots
Sandals
Slippers
13. Resize the first Text Box so Gloves is in the first Text Box, but Socks spills into the second Text Box
14. Format the first Text Box with Shadow Style 3
15. Format the first Text Box shape to Parallelogram
16. Format the second Text Box with Text Box Style: Dashed Outline, Dark
17. Insert a new Textbox: Cubicles Sidebar
18. Format the Sidebar with Shape Outline, 3pt Weight.
19. In the Sidebar, insert the following text: We're heads above the rest with our Giraffe products!
20. Rotate the Sidebar Text direction 90 degrees.
21. Insert a Footer and add the following information: Selling Giraffe items since 2000!
22. Save this file as Your Name Practice 6.

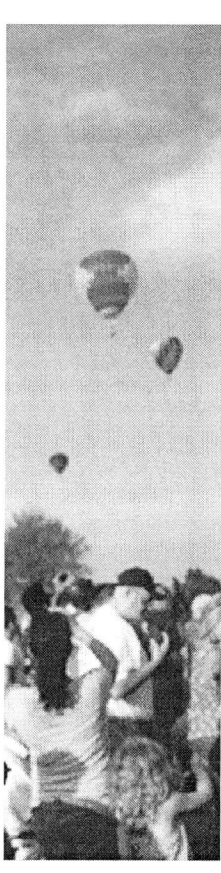

# Test Yourself

1. Which of the following can be inserted into a Word document?
(Select all correct answers)
a. Date & Time
b. Pictures
c. Quick Parts
d. Text Box
Tip: Beginning Word, page 167, 180

2. A sidebar is a type of built-in Text Box.
a. True
b. False
Tip: Beginning Word, page 169

3. Text boxes can be formatted with Quick Styles.
a. True
b. False
Tip: Beginning Word, page 171

4. Which of the following ribbons is used for formatting a Text Box?
a. Text box Tools
b. Drawing Tools
c. Shape Tools
Tip: Beginning Word, page 170

5. Which of the following formatting can be applied to a Text Box?
(Select all correct answers.)
a. Shape Styles
b. Shape Effects
c. Shape Fill
d. Shape Outline
Tip: Beginning Word, page 172

6. If two Text Boxes are linked, text from the first Text Box will continue or "spill over" into the second Text Box when the first Text Box is full.
a. True
b. False
Tip: Beginning Word, page 177

7. The Quick Part gallery does NOT include any built in headers or footers.
a. True
b. False
Tip: Beginning Word, page 185

8. Quick Parts saved to the gallery are included where?
a. In the Building Block organizer
b. In the Quick Part catalogue
c. In the ClipArt gallery
Tip: Beginning Word, page 181

9. Which of the following are in the Building Block Organizer?
(Select all correct answers)
a. Built in Headers
b. Built in Textboxes
c. AutoText
Tip: Beginning Word, page 186

10. Which is the command to insert a User-added Quick Part into a document?
a. Insert-> Quick Part-> AutoText
b. Insert-> Quick Part-> Field
c. Insert-> Quick Part-> My Quick Parts
Tip: Beginning Word, page 184

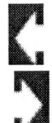

# Beginning Word Skill Test

**Before You Begin: Open a new, blank document in Microsoft Word 2010. Please do the following steps:**

1. Add the following text: Computer Training

2. Format the text: Bold, 24 pt. If you wish, you may change the font.

3. Insert a picture related to computer training.

4. Apply the picture style Bevel Perspective OR Bevel Oval.

5. Format the Text Wrapping to be Top and Bottom.

6. Move the picture above the text.

7. Insert a Simple Text Box.

8. Format the Text Box: use a Subtle Effect Accent Style

9. Change the Text Box Shape to Wave

10. Insert the following Text in the Text Box

   New Courses for Fall

11. Insert Text Box: Decorative Quote.

12. Move the Second Text Box under the First.

13. Add the following Text to the Second Text Box

   Word
   Excel
   PowerPoint
   Outlook
   Access
   Publisher
   OneNote

14. Add a Third Text Box: Simple Text Box

15. Link the Second & Third Text Boxes

16. Resize the Second Text box so Access is the last item—Publisher and OneNote will spill into the third Textbox.

17. Insert SmartArt: Vertical Chevron List

18. Add the following Text:

   Information Technology
   Human Resources
   Clerical

19. Remove any unused shapes

20. Format the SmartArt with SmartArt Style Sunset Scene and change the color to orange.

21. Add a new Shape to the SmartArt and add the following text: Management

22. Insert another image from ClipArt.

23. Apply an Artistic Effect to the image.

24. Save the file as Your Name Beginning Word Skill Test and submit to your instructor.

# Beginning Microsoft Word 2010: Index
**Microsoft Office Specialist (MOS):** Exam 77-881 Word 2010

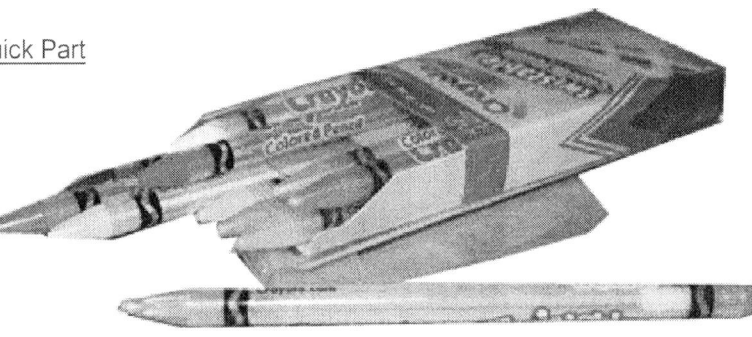

# Beginning Microsoft Word 2010: Glossary
**Microsoft Office Specialist (MOS):** Exam 77-881 Word 2010

**Alignment**-- how text is lined up on a page, relative to the edges.  Can be left, right, centered, top or bottom. *pg.36*

**Auto Correct**-- tool that automatically corrects misspellings and typos from a long list of common mistakes  *pg.72*

**Auto Text**-- this function offers to complete common words.  It also changes certain sets of characters into formatted symbols *pg.72*

**Building Blocks** (see also **Quick Parts**)-- content that can be made into Quick Parts *pg.167*

**Clip Art gallery**-- collection of image files from Microsoft, available for use in Microsoft Office programs *pg.51*

**Clip Art**-- image file from Microsoft, available for use in Microsoft Office programs *pg.50*

**Clipboard**-- a help application that stores text or pictures to be pasted. Activated with use of the cut or copy commands.  *pg.69*

**Compress (picture)** -- reduces the size of a picture's storage size, but not it's visible size *pg.109*

**Crop**-- trims the edges of the picture *pg.114*

**File format**-- refers to the type of coding used in a file, defining what program(s) will open the file and how the program treats the contents. *pg.86*

**Font case**-- refers to use of upper- and lowercase lettering *pg.34*

**Font**-- the type face, or how the text appears *pg.33*

**Footer**-- material separate from the document contents that appears at the bottom of the page *pg.185*

**Full Screen Reading View**-- document is displayed with no toolbars or ribbons and text is displayed on side-by-side pages like a book *pg.146*

**Grammar checker**-- to check for grammar and style errors in a document *pg.70*

**Groups (on Ribbons)**-- related commands arranged together and named by the relation, located on Ribbons *pg.45*

**Handles**-- small icons on the corner and sides of objects, such as pictures, shapes or text boxes,  in an Office document or file to show where the edges of the object are.  Can be used to resize an object. *pg.53*

**Header**-- material separate from the document contents that appears at the top of the page *pg.186*

**Leading** (see also line spacing)-- Amount of space between lines of text, such as double-spaced with one blank line between lines of text. *pg.37*

**Line spacing** (see also **leading**)-- amount of space between lines of text, such as double-spaced with one blank line between lines of text. *pg.37*

**Linked text boxes**-- when linked, text "spills" from the first box to continue to the subsequent linked box or boxes. *pg.177*

**Live Preview**-- allows the user to see possible changes to text, images, shapes, etc. before applying those changes *pg.32*

# Beginning Microsoft Word 2010: Glossary
**Microsoft Office Specialist (MOS):** Exam 77-881 Word 2010

**Math Auto Correct**-- tool that transforms certain text codes into math symbol *pg.73*

**Mini Toolbar**-- floating toolbar with commonly used font commands that appears when text is selected *pg.67*

**Plain text**-- text with no formatting *pg.29*

**Print Layout**-- view of a document that shows the page as it would appear printed *pg.146*

**Quick Parts** (see also **Building Blocks**)-- premade content available to add to a document *pg.180*

**Ribbon**-- commands arranged in tabs of functions that work together. The new display of menu commands for Office 2007 and 2010 *pg.45*

**Rich text**-- text with simple formatting such as font size, alignment, color and application of bold or underlined *pg.38*

**Right-click**-- using the right mouse button to access the options menu *pg.71*

**Shape**-- a text box with custom formatting. Shapes are modified with the Drawing Tools *pg.115*

**Side bar**-- Text box along the edge of the document, separate from the document contents *pg.169*

**SmartArt**-- editable graphics, charts and diagrams *pg.134*

**Spell checker**-- tool to check for misspelled words in a document *pg.70*

**Styles**--collection of preset formatting to be applied to text or objects. *pg.133*

**Symbol (Insert)**-- command to insert special characters, including math symbols, Greek letters, and other items from the Symbol collection *pg.75*

**Text box**-- A shape specifically for adding text *pg.131*

**Text wrapping**-- how text interacts with pictures or objects *pg.165*

**Title bar**-- the bar at the top of a program that includes the program name and, if applicable, the current file name *pg.44*

**WYSIWYG**- acronym for 'what you see is what you get', which applies to programs that show how the document or file will be displayed as a finished product *pg.145*